W9-ALY-622

SHIP TO SHORE, INC

STORE TO SHORE COOKBOOK

MENUS, RECIPES AND SHOPPING LISTS FROM INTERNATIONAL YACHT CHEFS

Publisher and Editor .... Capt. Jan Robinson
Associate Editor .... Fernand Dionne
Production Editor... Gracie Martin
Technical Advisor .... W. H. Robinson
Cover Artist .... Pat Anderson

SHIP TO SHORE, INC

10500 Mt. Holly Road
Charlotte, NC 28214-9219
Phone 704-394-2433 : Fax 704-392-4777
email: CapJan@aol.com

P.O. Box 10898
St. Thomas, US Virgin Islands, 00801
Phone/Fax 340-775-6295

To order additional copies call **1-800-338-6072**
or
the Ship to Shore web site
www.SHIPTOSHOREINC.com
email : **CapJan@aol.com**

STORE TO SHORE
COOKBOOK

Copyright 2000 by Ship to Shore, Inc

All Rights Reserved
No part of this book may be reproduced in any form or by any means
without the prior permission from the Publisher.

First printing: October, 2000
Library of Congress catalog card
Printed in the United States of America
ISBN 0-9612686-8-9

INTRODUCTION

When I was a charter yacht chef and captain, charter guests were constantly amazed that I could turn out gourmet meals from a galley the size of most people's closets, and they were always asking for my recipes. I found that chefs on other yachts were always being asked for their galley secrets, too, so I decided to collect our recipes and publish them in a cookbook. Not only would our guests be happy but we would be sharing with others—on land or water—dishes that are easy to prepare and taste great. Two years later, the first *Ship to Shore* was published; it is now in its twelfth printing.

Store to Shore is the eighth volume in the *Ship to Shore* cookbook series. Collecting recipes was never easy and has not become any easier. The chefs are always delighted to be asked, but getting pen to paper is another story, as most chefs keep their recipes in their heads. When we do receive the recipes, quantities are often off the top of their heads or not even given. But we ask and we test and email and we test again, and then it works. The recipes you'll find in the following pages are all easy, delicious, and fun.

Store to Shore is unique in that it contains not only full-day menus, but also the recipes and a shopping list to go with each menu. You will notice that some of the spelling is in English and some is in "American"; this is because the recipes have come from chefs from all parts of the world. We also show the ingredients in both U.S. and metric measurements.

Provisioning is important to yacht chefs whether they are chartering or cruising, we have included a section of suggested "where-to-shop" places, especially in the Caribbean, where over a thousand boats charter each year.

With *Store to Shore* in your galley or kitchen, you will always be able to **make your life easier** for every occasion, informal to elegant, on land or at sea.

Oceans of happiness and bon appetit!

Capt. Jan
October 2000

Table of Contents

Yachts — Menus — Shopping lists — Recipes

ABOUT THE AUTHOR

Capt. Jan Robinson's *Store to Shore* is the eighth volume in her popular *Ship to Shore* Cookbook Series. A native of New Zealand who shuttles between residences in the U.S. Virgin Islands and North Carolina, Robinson is an accredited member of the American Institute of Wine and Food and holds certificates from the Cordon Bleu Cooking School, the Ritz Cooking School, and the Culinary Institute of America.

Robinson's television cooking credits include "The Morning Show" with Regis Philbin and the NBC special "The Cruise of the Vanity," which featured Jan and her yacht. As 'The Galley Gourmet'™ Robinson authors *Southern Boating Magazine*'s monthly column "At Ease in the Galley". She has also been profiled in numerous national and international publications and is a much sought-after host and judge of cooking competitions.

ACKNOWLEDGMENTS

My sincerest thanks and warmest appreciation to all of the wonderful yacht chefs who, once again, were willing to share their treasured recipes and their favorite menus. The *Ship to Shore* cookbook collection has only been possible because of their continued support.

Also many thanks to my friends for proof reading, testing and tasting the recipes, and moral support; to Mimi Steadman and Margot Bachman for special editing; Michelle Dunnette for her extra help. Special thanks to Fernand Dionne and Gracie Martin for their knowledge and enthusiasm in the test kitchen and to Marina Market.

This book is dedicated with love and oceans of happiness to everyone who, like me, wants to know ***how to make your life easier*** in the galley.

www.SHIPTOSHOREINC.com
1-800-338-6072
CapJan@aol.com

MEASURING UP

In this book we are using 1 lb = 450 g.

It is not practical for us to give exact conversions so it is important that you do not switch from one set of measurements to the other within a recipe.

All spoon measures are level, flour is white, all-purpose, (plain) and sugar is white, granulated, unless otherwise stated. Can sizes vary between manufacturers and countries. Should you find the quantities in this book are slightly different from what is available — use the can size nearest to the suggested size in the recipe.

The shopping lists are made to show what you actually need for that day's menu. This way you can chose how many days you would like to provision for, and then, by adding together each day, you will be able to get an accurate total of what you need.

We realize that you cannot or would not buy 1/3 (150 g) or 1/2 lb (225 g) butter — but by giving you an accurate list you will then know what you already have on hand and what you need to buy.

The only items not included in the shopping lists are — salt and pepper.

A well organized galley is the key to success in preparing meals when time is at a premium. As long as you are well organized with the basics, you will be able to take advantage of the freshest, best quality products you can find.

Store to Shore is the tool to help you make this possible.

ANTARES SHOPPING LIST

VEGETABLES:
Garlic .... 1 clove
Shallots 3
Onion, yellow.................. 1
Green bell peppers 2
Potato 1
Tomato 1

FRUITS:
Granny Smith apples 3
Lemon 1
Oranges 2

FRUITS FROZEN:
Strawberries .... 1 bag

MEAT/FRESH:
Veal scallopine................ 2 lbs

CANS AND JARS:
Chicken broth .... 1 can
Chicken soup .... 1 can

FISH & SEAFOOD/FRESH/FROZEN:
Shrimp .... 1/2 lb

CONDIMENTS:
Orange extract .... 1 tsp
Olive oil........................... 1 Tblsp
Sun dried tomatoes .... 1/2 cup

DRY GOODS:
Baking powder .... 3/4 tsp
White chocolate .... 1 lb
Flour .... 1-1/3 cups
Confectioners' sugar .... 1/3 cup
Sugar............................... 1-2/3 cups

DRY SPICES:
Basil .... 2 tsp
Cinnamon .... 1/2 tsp
Dill .... 1/2 tsp
Nutmeg .... 1/2 tsp

BREAD/DOUGH/PASTA
Pie crust 1

DAIRY/MILK/CHEESE/BUTTER
Butter .... 3/4 lb
Cream .... 3 Tblsp
Heavy/whipping cream .. 2 cups
Half and half .... 1-1/3 cups
Eggs 16
Cheddar cheese, grated .. 1-3/4 cups
Parmesan .... 1 wedge

LIQUOR/WINE/SPIRITS
Grand Marnier .... 1-1/2 Tblsp
Sherry .... 2 tsp
Triple Sec .... 2 Tblsp

S/Y ANTARES

Chef Julie Murphy
Captain Pat Murphy

MENU
Serves 6

Breakfast

*Frittata
Orange Juice and Coffee

Lunch

*Apple Cheese Quiche
*Grand Marnier Custard Squares

Hors d'oeuvre

*Shrimp Paté
Assorted Crackers

Dinner

*Veal with Pine Nuts and Sun Dried Tomatoes
Garlic Mashed Potatoes
Carrots with Orange and Lemon Slices

*Palace White Chocolate Mousse with
*Strawberry Purée

Captain Pat Murphy and Chef Julie Murphy, on board the 60-foot Gulfstar sloop ANTARES, call their charter "a delicious adventure vacation barefoot and fancy free". They tailor the days to their guests idea of a dream holiday, be it sailing, playing with all the water toys or both. Two to 6 guests sleep in honey-teak, air conditioned staterooms with private heads. They dine in style with varied dishes culled from Julie's galley.

*Indicates recipe provided

FRITTATA

Preparation time: 10 minutes   *Chef: Julie Murphy*
Cooking time: 10 minutes   *Yacht: Antares*
Cooling time: 3 minutes
Serves: 6

1 Tblsp	Butter
1	Potato, peeled, chopped
1/3 cup	Chopped green bell pepper
1/3 cup	Sliced onion
1/2 tsp	Basil
1/2 tsp	Dill
1/8 tsp	Pepper
6	Eggs, beaten
Garnish:	Green pepper slices
1	Tomato, thinly sliced
	Parmesan cheese

Melt butter in skillet and cook potato, green pepper, onion, basil, dill, and pepper. Cover and cook about 6 minutes. Add beaten eggs, cover and cook on low heat 4-5 minutes. Lift eggs so uncooked portion flows underneath. Alternate green pepper and tomato slices on top. Remove from heat. Sprinkle with parmesan, cover and cool until set, 2-3 minutes. *Cut in wedges and serve.*

APPLE CHEESE QUICHE

Preparation time: 15 minutes
Cooking time: 35 minutes
Serves: 6

Chef: Julie Murphy
Yacht: Antares

1 - 9 inch/23 cm	Unbaked pie shell
1-3/4 cups	Shredded cheddar cheese
2 cups	Peeled, finely diced green apples
1/4 cup	Minced shallots
2 Tblsp	Butter
1-1/2 tsp	Flour
1/2 tsp	Cinnamon
1/2 tsp	Nutmeg
1 tsp	Salt
3	Eggs, beaten
1-1/3 cups	Half and half

Heat oven to 350°F/180°C. Sprinkle 1/4 cup of cheese in pie shell. Bake 10 minutes. Sauté apples and shallots in butter. Sprinkle with flour, cinnamon, nutmeg and salt. Spread apple mixture in pie shell, sprinkle with remaining cheese. Mix eggs and half and half and pour in shell. Bake approximately 35 minutes or until firm.

GRAND MARNIER CUSTARD SQUARES

Preparation time: 15 minutes
Cooking time: 40 minutes
Serves: 6

Chef: Julie Murphy
Yacht: Antares

Bottom Layer:

1/3 cup	**Powdered sugar**
1 cup	**Flour**
1/2 cup	**Butter**

Preheat oven to 350°F/180°C. Combine ingredients with mixer and press into bottom of 8 inch/20 cm square pan. Bake 20 minutes.

Top Layer:

3/4 cup	**Sugar**
3/4 tsp	**Baking powder**
3	**Eggs, beaten**
1-1/2 Tblsp	**Grand Marnier**
1-1/2 Tblsp	**Orange juice**
1 tsp	**Orange extract**

Blend all ingredients. Pour on hot crust. Return to oven and bake 20 additional minutes. Allow to cool completely.

Hint: The reason I use an 8 inch/20 cm square pan instead of a spring form pan for this dessert and for cheese cakes is that I can cut from corner to corner (X), side to side (+) and make 8 uniform wedges.

SHRIMP PATE

Preparation time: 10 minutes　　　　　　　　*Chef: Julie Murphy*
Chilling time: 30 minutes　　　　　　　　　　*Yacht: Antares*
Serves: 6

1/2 lb/225 g	**Cooked shrimp**
1 clove	**Garlic**
4 Tblsp	**Butter**
3 Tblsp	**Cream**
2 tsp	**Dry sherry**
1/2 tsp	**Dill**
	Salt and pepper to taste

Process first 5 ingredients in processor or blender. Stir in dill, salt and pepper. Spoon into small ramekin, sprinkle with additional dill. Serve chilled or at room temperature.

VEAL WITH PINE NUTS AND SUN DRIED TOMATOES

Preparation time: 15 minutes
Cooking time: 40 minutes
Serves: 6

Chef: Julie Murphy
Yacht: Antares

4 Tblsp	Chopped shallots
1 Tblsp	Olive oil
2/3 cup	Pine nuts
1 Tblsp	Butter
1 cup	Chicken broth
1 cup	Beef broth
2 lbs/900 g	Veal Scaloppine
1/4 cup	Flour
1/2 cup	Butter, divided
1/4 cup	Dry white wine
1 tsp	Basil
1/2 cup	Sun dried tomatoes
1	Orange, sliced
1	Lemon, sliced

Sauté shallots in olive oil. Brown pine nuts in butter. Reduce broths to 1/2 cup by boiling uncovered 15 minutes. Pound veal to 1/8 inch/3 cm thick, coat in flour and sauté in 1/4 cup butter over medium heat 1-2 minutes per side. Transfer to plate. Add shallots, pine nuts, reduced broth, sun dried tomatoes and simmer 8 minutes. wWhisk in additional butter and basil and spoon over veal. *Serve with garlic mashed potatoes and carrots with orange and lemon slices.*

PALACE WHITE CHOCOLATE MOUSSE
WITH STRAWBERRY PUREE**

Preparation time: 20 minutes
Chilling time: 4 hours
Serves: 8

Chef: Julie Murphy
Yacht: Antares

1/2 cup	Sugar
1/4 cup	Water
4	Large egg whites, beaten to form soft peaks
1 lb/450 g	Imported white chocolate, cut in small cubes or shaved
2 cups	Whipping cream, well chilled

Combine sugar and water in saucepan, bring to boil until sugar melts. Bring to hard ball stage (255°F/125°C.) and slowly add syrup to beaten egg whites. Beat in chocolate pieces. Whip cream until stiff and fold into mousse. Pour into a glass serving bowl. Chill at least 4 hours.

STRAWBERRY PUREE SAUCE:

1 lb/450 g	Pkg frozen unsweetened strawberries
2 Tblsp	Triple Sec or Amaretto
4 Tblsp	Sugar

Purée all ingredients together. Cover and chill at least 30 minutes. Pour over mousse and serve.

Hint: As an alternative way to serve; the mousse may be placed in individual stem glasses to chill, then spoon purée sauce over and serve.

**This recipe was a winner in the 1999 VICL culinary competition.

BELLINI II SHOPPING LIST

VEGETABLES:
Avocado 1
Carrots 2
Baby carrots .... 2 bags
Garlic cloves 9
Scallions 3
Shallots 3
Red onion 1
Yellow onions 5
Green bell peppers 2
Red bell peppers 3
Yellow bell peppers 3
Tomatoes 3
Mixed lettuce .... 8 cups

FRUITS:
Lime peel, julienned .... 1 tsp
Mixed fresh fruit, diced .... 2 cups

FRESH HERBS:
Mint leaves .... garnish
Parsley, chopped .... 1 cup

DRIED SPICES:
Paprika .... 1/2 tsp
Saffron .... pinch

CONDIMENTS:
Sesame seeds .... 1 Tblsp
Wasabi .... 1/4 cup
Vanilla extract .... 1 tsp
Mustard, Dijon .... 1 Tblsp
Olive oil............................ 3/4 cups
Sesame oil .... 2 Tblsp
Vinegar, balsamic .... 3/4 cup
Vinegar, red wine .... 1/4 cup
Hot pepper sauce .... 1 Tblsp
Soy sauce .... 3/4 cup
Tabasco .... 3 dashes

DRY GOODS:
Muesli mix .... 1 cup
Arborio rice .... 3 cups
Calrose rice .... 2 cups
Sugar .... 1 Tblsp

CANS AND JARS:
Peach halves .... 1 can
Peach nectar/juice............. 2 oz
Chicken broth .... 3 cups
Vegetable broth .... 3 cups
Black olives, sliced .... 6 oz can

DAIRY/MILK/CHEESE/BUTTER
Eggs 12
Whipping cream .... 2 cups
Yogurt .... 1 cup
Mascarpone .... 4-1/2 cups
Parmesan .... 1-1/2 lbs

MEAT/POULTRY/FISH/SEAFOOD:
Bacon .... 1/2 lb
Cornish game hens 4
Tuna .... 2-1/2 lbs

LIQUOR/WINE/SPIRITS:
Champagne....................... 12 oz
Peach Schnapps................ 1/2 cup
Port wine .... 1/4 cup
White wine .... 1 cup

FROZEN:
Cool Whip .... 3/4 cup
Peach sorbet .... 1 scoop

MISCELLANEOUS:
Nori sheets....................... 6
Caviar............................... 1/4 cup
Pita bread 6
Lady fingers .... 1 bag

S/Y BELLINI II

Chefs Lela and Walter Wegmann
Captain Walter Wegmann

MENU
Serves 6

Breakfast

*Quiche
*Muesli
Warm Baguette
Cheese Platter

Lunch

*Sushi - Sashimi

Hors d'oeuvres

*Roasted Bell Pepper Salad
Toasted Pita Bread, Olives, and
Cubes of Parmesan

Dinner

*Marinated Cornish Hens with Baby Carrots
and Risotto
*Green Salad

*Tiramasu with Lime and Peaches
or
*Bellini Dessert with a *Bellini

The 48-foot luxury dive boat catamaran, BELLINI II, carries 8 guests. Swiss-born Walter and Lela Wegmann are hosts, Walter as captain and PADI diving instructor and Lela as chef. But often Walter, a superior cook himself, loves to lend a hand in the galley. The result — guests enjoy a variety of delicious dishes. "The cockpit table sits 10" says Lela, "so we can enjoy a meal together. What is better than good food with good friends and wines at the most beautiful place on planet earth — the Caribbean!

*Indicates recipe provided

QUICHE

Preparation time: 10 minutes
Cooking time: 30 minutes
Serves: 6

Chef: Lela Wegmann
Yacht: Bellini II

6	**Eggs**
1 cup	**Whipping cream**
	Salt and pepper to taste
1 cup	**Grated parmesan**
1/4 cup	**Parsley**
1/2 lb/225 g	**Bacon**
1	**Large onion, sliced**
1	**Green pepper, sliced**
1	**Tomato, sliced**

Put eggs, cream, salt and pepper, parmesan and parsley in a blender; mix well. Fry bacon and onion in a pan, remove bacon and dry on paper towel. Add the egg mixture to pan, cover and cook at low heat for about 20 minutes. Decorate with slices of pepper, tomato and bacon.

MUESLI

Preparation time: 10 minutes
Serves: 6

Chef: Lela Wegmann
Yacht: Bellini II

1 cup	**Yogurt (different flavors)**
3/4 cup	**Cool whip, divided**
2 cups	**Fresh fruits, cut in bite size pieces**
1 cup	**Muesli mix**

In a bowl, mix yogurt, and 1/2 cup cool whip, put fruits on top and sprinkle with Muesli; top with a dollop of cool whip.

Note: We usually start the day with a big breakfast; the quiche is just one of the egg dishes we do, but every day we serve the muesli and the cheese plate.

Hint: When we buy baguettes or any other bread, we keep it in the refrigerator or freezer. Reheat them before using but sprinkle water on top first, so bread can get brown and crispy.

SUSHI — SASHIMI

Preparation time: 45 minutes
Chilling time: Rice, 1 hour
Serves: 6

Chef: Lela Wegmann
Yacht: Bellini II

2 cups	Calrose rice (short grain)
4 cups	Water
1 Tbsp	Salt
1/4 cup	Rice wine vinegar
2-1/2 lbs/1-1 kg	Fresh tuna, makaele (little tuna), fillet
1	Green bell pepper
2	Carrots
2	Shallots
2 Tblsp	Sesame oil
1 Tblsp	Hot sauce
2 Tblsp	Soy sauce
6 sheets	Nori
1/4 cup	Wasabi, powdered (reconstitute with water) or in a tube
1/4 cup	Sesame seeds
1/4 cup	Caviar

In a saucepan, boil rice with water, salt and rice vinegar until rice is soft, about 20 minutes. Refrigerate. Julienne fish, carrots, peppers, and shallots and sauté in sesame oil. Stir in hot sauce and soy sauce. On the bamboo mat, lay a sheet of nori; spoon rice thinly over nori leaving the last inch of nori free of rice. Add the julienne strips of fish, carrots, peppers over rice. Roll the nori with the bamboo mat as tight as you can, about 1-1/2 inches (3.5 cm) diameter. Brush the plain end of nori with water to seal. Cut in 1 inch (2.5 cm) pieces, dip in sesame seeds or caviar. Serve with wasabi paste, pickled ginger and soy sauce in separate small bowls.

Hint: *Wet knife in water glass every time you cut!* Great lunch. Everybody just loves it—place rest of fish on same plate, garnish with anything fresh.

ROASTED BELL PEPPER SALAD

Preparation time: 20 minutes
Cooking time: 5-10 minutes
Chilling time: 20 minutes
Serves: 6

Chef: Lela Wegmann
Yacht: Bellini II

3	**Yellow bell peppers**
3	**Red bell peppers**
3	**Scallions, chopped**
1/2 cup	**Chopprd parsley**
2	**Onions, sliced**
4 Tblsp	**Olive oil**
2 Tblsp	**Balsamic vinegar**
6	**Pita bread, toasted**
6 oz/170 g	**Can sliced black olives**
1/2 lb/454 g	**Parmesan, cubed**
	Salt and pepper

Preheat oven to 350°F/180°C. You may use a broiler. Place peppers on a baking sheet and roast in the oven until soft and blistered (5-10 minutes). Chill. Gently remove the skin, halve the peppers, discard ribs and seeds. Slice 1/2 inch/1.5 cm thick. Make a sunlike design alternating both color slices. Add scallions, parsley, onion, salt and pepper. Drizzle with olive oil and balsamic vinegar. Serve with pita bread, olives and parmesan.

CORNISH HENS WITH BABY CARROTS AND RISOTTO

Preparation time: 20 minutes
Marinating time: 24 hours
Cooking time: 40 minutes
Serves: 6

Chef: Lela Wegmann
Yacht: Bellini II

4	**Cornish hens**
3 cups	**Vegetable broth—divided**
2	**Bay leaves**
5	**Cloves**
2	**Onions, chopped—divided**
3 cloves	**Garlic**
	Salt and pepper to taste
1/2 tsp	**Paprika**
Pinch	**Saffron**
3 Tblsp	**Soy sauce**
Dash	**Green tabasco**
1 Tblsp	**Dijon mustard**
1 Tblsp	**Balsamic vinegar**
3 cups	**Arborio (risotto) rice**
1 cup	**White wine**
3 cups	**Chicken broth**
4 oz/114 g	**Mascarpone cheese (can substitute sour cream)**
1 cup	**Shredded parmesan**
2 bags	**Baby carrots**
1/4 cup	**Chopped parsley**
1 cup	**Whipping cream—divided**
1/4 cup	**Port wine**

Boil Cornish hens in vegetable broth, spice with bay leaves, cloves and 1/2 the amount of onion. Cook until tender, about 20 minutes, but not well done. Marinate for 24 hours, with garlic, salt, pepper, paprika, saffron, soy sauce, green tabasco, mustard and balsamic vinegar. Scoop the fat of the top of the marinade when cold. In a large sauce pan, fry onion with risotto rice; add white wine, warmed chicken broth, water and simmer until rice is cooked. Add more broth if necessary. *Do not let dry out.* Take pan off heat, add mascarpone and parmesan, cover and set aside. Slowly cook carrots in the remaining chicken broth, add parsley, remaining onion, 1/2 cup whipping cream, cover and set aside. Take Cornish hen out of marinade, and grill on each side. Warm up the marinade, add the remaining whipping cream and stir until thick. *Serve the carrots and the Cornish hens over a bed of rice.*

SALAD

Preparation time: 10 minutes   *Chef: Lela Wegmann*
Chilling time: 30 minutes   *Yacht: Bellini II*
Serves: 6 - 8

Salad:

6 cups	**Mixed lettuce— iceberg, chiccorino red, mesclun, romaine etc.**

Vegetables:

2	**Tomatoes, sliced**
1	**Cucumber, peeled and sliced**
1	**Avocado, cubed**
1	**Red onion, chopped**

Dressing:

1/2 cup	**Olive oil**
1/2 cup	**Balsamic vinegar**
1/2 cup	**Soy sauce**
1 clove	**Garlic**
2 dashes	**Green tabasco**

Place the vegetables in the dressing and chill for 30 minutes. Add lettuce, toss and serve.

Note: The longer you chill the vegetables in the dressing, the better.

BELLINI DESSERT

Preparation time: 2 minutes   *Chef: Lela Wegmann*
                                                            Yacht: Bellini II

1 scoop	**Peach Sorbet**
	Mint leaves
1 oz/30 ml	**Peach Schnapps**
2 oz/60 ml	**Champagne**

In a martini glass, put a scoop of sorbet, top with a mint leaf; add peach schnapps and champagne.

TIRAMASU WITH LIME AND PEACHES

Preparation time: 20 minutes
Chilling time: 72 hours
Serves: 6 - 10

Chef: Lela Wegmann
Yacht: Bellini II

4 cups	Mascarpone*
1 Tblsp	Sugar
1 tsp	Vanilla essence
1 tsp	Lime peel
6	Egg yolks
6	Egg whites
1 can	Peach halves, thinly sliced
1 bag	Lady fingers
1/4 cup	Peach Schnapps

In a bowl, soften mascarpone; add sugar, vanilla essence, 1/2 tsp lime peel, egg yolks and mix until creamy. Fold in beaten egg whites. In a 2 inch (5 cm) deep dish, place a layer of lady fingers and soak with peach schnapps, a layer of cream mixture and a layer of peaches; repeat. Make sure the top layer is cream. Top with peaches and 1/2 tsp lime peel. Refrigerate for 72 hours before serving.

Note: Dessert will keep for a week.

*You may substitute sour cream and cream cheese.

BELLINI

Preparation time: 2 minutes

Chef: Walter Wegmann
Yacht: Bellini II

1 oz/30 ml	Peach Schnapps
2 oz/60 ml	Peach nectar/juice
2 oz/60 ml	Champagne

In a champagne glass, pour peach schnapps, peach juice and champagne— *serve immediately.*

BLU MOON SHOPPING LIST

VEGETABLES:
Broccoli .... 1 lb
Celery .... 3/4 cup
Garlic cloves 7
Romaine lettuce .... 1 head
Mushrooms, large 12
Green onions 2
Onion 1
Red bell pepper 1
Tomato 1

FRUITS:
Banana 1
Lemons 2
Oranges 3
Pineapple chunks .... 1 cup

FRESH HERBS:
Cilantro/coriander .... 4-5 Tblsp
Parsley, chopped .... 1/3 cup
Rosemary, chopped .... 1 Tblsp
Tarragon .... 1 bunch

MEAT/FRESH:
Bacon .... 1/2 lb
Chicken breasts .... 2 whole
Italian sweet sausages 2
Salmon filets .... 3/4 lb

CONDIMENTS:
Maple syrup .... 1 bottle
Olive oil........................... 2 Tblsp
Vanilla extract .... 1 tsp

DRY GOODS:
Almonds, unsalted,
   chopped for .... garnish
Walnuts .... 1/2 cup
Baking powder .... 2-1/2 tsp
Cornstarch .... 1 Tblsp
Coconut .... 2 cups
Cornmeal .... 1 cup

Confectioners' sugar .... Garnish
Flour .... 1 cup

DRY SPICES:
Cinnamon .... 1 tsp
Fennel seeds .... 1/4 tsp
Lemon pepper .... 1/8 tsp
Mustard .... 1/2 tsp
Nutmeg .... 1/2 tsp
Oregano .... 1-1/2 tsp
Red pepper flakes .... 1/2 tsp
Thyme .... 1/2 tsp

BREAD/DOUGH/PASTA:
Cinnamon Raisin bread . 8 slices

CANS AND JARS:
Black olives, pitted .... 1 can
Black olives, chopped ..... 1/4 cup
Capers .... 4 Tblsp
Corn, kernels .... 1 cup
Cream of coconut .... 1/3 cup
Jalapeños 3
Maraschino cherries 4
Mayonnaise .... 1/2 cup
Pineapple, crushed .... 8 oz can
Tomatoes, diced .... 1/4 cup

DAIRY/MILK/CHEESE/BUTTER
Butter .... 1/2 lb
Buttermilk .... 1 cup
Cream cheese .... 8 oz
Goat cheese..................... 6 oz
Parmesan, grated .... 1/2 cup
Eggs 3
Milk.................................. 1/4 cup
Yogurt .... 1/4 cup

LIQUOR/WINE/SPIRITS
Pernod .... 2 Tblsp
Dark rum .... 2 Tblsp
Rum .... 2 Tblsp
Wine, red .... 1/2 cup

S/Y BLU MOON

Chef Julie Bennett
Captain Chris Bennett

MENU
Serves 4

Breakfast

Assorted Juices
*Cinnamon French Toast Casserole

Lunch

*Chicken Salad with Tarragon
*Crackling Cornbread

Hors d'oeuvre

*Mushrooms stuffed with Italian Sausage

Dinner

*Fillet of Salmon with Goat Cheese and Olives
Jasmine Rice
*Broccoli with Orange Sauce

*Piña Colada Mousse

Tailor-made for chartering, BLU MOON, a 51-foot Beneteau sloop, is all about performance, speed, comfort, style, adventure — and imaginative menus. Chris Bennett is captain and his wife, Julie, first mate and chef. Chris studied mechanical engineering at the London Institute of Technology. Julie has degrees in fine arts and business. Both are NAUI divers, both love sailing and Chef Julie loves mixing exotic dishes with down-home cooking. Each night guarantees a gourmet dinner under the stars.

*Indicates recipe provided

CINNAMON FRENCH TOAST CASSEROLE

Preparation time: 20 minutes
Cooking time: 25 minutes
Serves: 4

Chef: Julie Bennett
Yacht: Blu Moon

8 slices	Cinnamon raisin bread
4 Tblsp	Unsalted butter, softened
1	Banana
1/4 cup	Milk, room temperature
1/4 cup	Orange juice
1 tsp	Orange zest
2	Large eggs, separated
1/2 cup	Pure maple syrup
1 tsp	Vanilla extract
1 tsp	Cinnamon
1/8 tsp	Nutmeg
Garnish:	Powdered sugar
	Maple syrup
	Dark rum

Preheat oven to 325°F/160°C. Spread both sides of bread with butter. Cut bread diagonally in half. Arrange bread pieces on cookie sheet and bake 10 minutes. Remove bread from oven. Increase temperature to 350°F/180°C.

Grease a 9 x 12 inch (23 x 30 cm) pan with 2 inch (5 cm) sides. Arrange bread in 2 rows, overlapping slices slightly. Slice banana in long pieces and tuck in between bread slices. Whisk milk, orange juice, orange zest, egg yolks, maple syrup, vanilla, cinnamon and nutmeg in medium bowl until well blended. Beat egg whites in another bowl until soft peaks form. Fold into egg mixture. Pour batter over bread. Bake until top is brown, about 25 minutes. Sprinkle with powdered sugar. Cut into portions. *Warm maple syrup and rum together and serve.*

CHICKEN SALAD WITH TARRAGON

Preparation time: 15 minutes　　　　　　　*Chef: Julie Bennett*
Cooking time: 15 minutes　　　　　　　　*Yacht: Blu Moon*
Chilling time: 2 - 3 hours
Serves: 4

2	**Whole chicken breasts**
1/4 cup	**Plain yogurt**
1/4 cup	**Sour cream**
1/2 cup	**Mayonnaise**
1	**Large lemon, juiced**
1 tsp	**Lemon zest**
3/4 cup	**Chopped celery**
1/3 cup	**Chopped walnuts, or pecans**
2 Tblsp	**Chopped fresh tarragon**
	Salt and pepper
1 cup	**Fresh pineapple chunks, or canned**
1 head	**Romaine lettuce, torn**
1/2	**Red bell pepper sliced**
	Walnut pieces
2	**Green onions, chopped**
	Fresh tarragon sprigs

Boil chicken until just cooked about 15 minutes. Remove meat from bone and shred. In a bowl whisk together yogurt, sour cream and mayonnaise; add chicken and stir. Add lemon juice, zest, celery, walnuts, tarragon, salt and pepper; toss well. Chill for 2 to 3 hours. Fold pineapple chunks into chicken salad shortly before serving.

Arrange lettuce on each plate. Spoon chicken salad on top of lettuce. Top with bell pepper slices, walnuts and green onions. *Garnish with tarragon sprigs and serve with warm pita breads.*

CRACKLING CORNBREAD

Preparation time: 10 minutes
Cooking time: 20 - 25 minutes
Makes: 9 squares

Chef: Julie Bennett
Yacht: Blu Moon

1 cup	Stone ground cornmeal
1 cup	Flour
1/3 cup	Sugar
2-1/2 tsp	Baking powder
1/4 tsp	Salt
1 cup	Buttermilk
1 cup	Diced crisp-cooked bacon
1 cup	Canned corn kernels, drained
6	Sliced jalapeños
6 Tblsp	Melted butter
1	Egg, slightly beaten

Preheat oven to 400°F/200°C. Mix all ingredients thoroughly. Spread in a greased 9 x 9 inch (23 x 23 cm) baking dish and bake for approximately 20 minutes, or until edges are light brown and a knife inserted in the center comes out clean. Cut into 3 inch (7.5 cm) squares and serve warm.

Hint: *May also be made in greased muffin cups.*

MUSHROOMS STUFFED WITH ITALIAN SAUSAGE

Preparation time: 15 minutes   Chef: Julie Bennett
Cooking time: 30 minutes   Yacht: Blu Moon
Serves: 4

2	**Italian sweet sausages**
1/4 tsp	**Fennel seeds**
1/4 tsp	**Red pepper flakes, or to taste**
1/3 cup	**Finely chopped onion**
2 cloves	**Garlic, minced**
1/4 cup	**Chopped black olives**
1/3 cup	**Bechamel sauce (see recipe below)**
	Salt and pepper
1/4 cup	**Chopped parsley**
12	**Large mushroom caps**
1/2 cup	**Grated parmesan cheese**

Preheat oven to 450°F/230°C. Remove sausage meat from casing and crumble. In a skillet gently sauté the sausage until cooked. Season with fennel and red pepper flakes. Remove sausage and drain; set aside in a bowl. Sauté onion and garlic in skillet, until tender. Add to sausage. Stir olives and Bechamel sauce into sausage, mix thoroughly. Season to taste with salt and pepper. Mix in chopped parsley. Stuff mushroom caps with mixture. Sprinkle with parmesan cheese. Bake for 15 minutes, or until bubbly and brown. Let sit for 5 minutes before serving.

Bechamel Sauce:

2 tsp	**Butter**
2 tsp	**Flour**
1/3 cup	**Milk**
	Nutmeg
	Salt and pepper

Melt the butter in a small saucepan. Add the flour and stir until the butter completely absorbes the flour, about 1 minute. Remove from heat and gradually pour in milk. Return to heat and bring slowly to a boil; cook gently for a few minutes. Add nutmeg, salt and pepper to taste.

FILET OF SALMON WITH GOAT CHEESE AND OLIVES

Preparation time: 15 minutes   *Chef: Julie Bennett*
Cooking time: 30 minutes   *Yacht: Blu Moon*
Serves: 4

2 Tblsp	Olive oil
1/2 cup	Chopped onion
4 cloves	Garlic, minced
1/2 cup	Dry red wine
16	Medium sized pitted black olives
4 Tblsp	Capers
1 Tblsp	Chopped fresh rosemary or 1 tsp dry
1 tsp	Dried oregano
1/8 tsp	Red pepper flakes
1/2 cup	Diced tomatoes
	Salt and pepper, to taste
4 - 7 oz/200 g	Salmon filets
6 oz/170 g	Goat cheese
2 Tblsp	Pernod or other anise liqueur
Garnish:	
4 Tblsp	Fresh chopped coriander

Preheat oven to 450°F/230°C. In a skillet heat olive oil and sauté onion and garlic until just tender. Add wine, olives, capers, rosemary, oregano, red pepper flakes, tomatoes, salt and pepper. Bring to a boil and simmer about 5 minutes. Pour wine mixture into baking dish and place salmon filets on top. Spoon goat cheese on top of salmon and bake for 15 minutes. Turn oven to broiler. Sprinkle liqueur over goat cheese and broil 2 minutes. Garnish. *Serve over rice.*

Note: *This is also excellent with other fish e.g. Halibut.*

BROCCOLI WITH ORANGE SAUCE

Preparation time: 10 minutes   *Chef: Julie Bennett*
Cooking time: 15 minutes   *Yacht: Blu Moon*
Serves: 4

1 lb/450 g	**Fresh broccoli**
2 Tblsp	**Butter**
1 clove	**Garlic**
1 Tblsp	**Cornstarch**
1 cup	**Fresh orange juice**
1 tsp	**Freshly grated orange peel**
1/2 tsp	**Thyme**
1/2 tsp	**Oregano**
1/2 tsp	**Dry mustard**
1/8 tsp	**Lemon pepper**
1 Tblsp	**Finely chopped parsley**
Garnish:	**Chopped unsalted almonds or cashews**

Steam broccoli while making orange sauce. Melt butter in a saucepan, add garlic, cover and cook over medium heat for 1 minute. Stir in cornstarch and slowly add orange juice, orange peel, thyme, mustard and lemon pepper, stirring constantly for 2-3 minutes. Add parsley and cook another 1-2 minutes until sauce boils and thickens. Pour over broccoli and serve. Garnish. *The sauce may be made ahead of time, then quickly reheated before serving.*

PINA COLADA MOUSSE

Preparation time: 15 minutes   *Chef: Julie Bennett*
Chilling time: 1 hour   *Yacht: Blu Moon*
Serves: 4

8 oz/225 g	**Softened cream cheese**
1/3 cup	**Cream of coconut**
2 Tblsp	**Rum or 1/2 tsp. rum extract**
2 cups	**Cool Whip or other whipped topping**
8-1/4 oz/230 g	**Can crushed pineapple in syrup**
2 cups	**Flaked coconut**
	Nutmeg, freshly grated
4	**Maraschino cherries**

In a bowl beat cream cheese, cream of coconut and rum until smooth. Fold in Cool Whip, pineapple with syrup and coconut. Chill well. Spoon mousse into tall goblets. *Sprinkle with a generous portion of freshly grated nutmeg and top with cherry.*o

BONJEZ SHOPPING LIST

VEGETABLES:
Garlic cloves 4
Mushrooms, large 12
Spring onions 4
Onions 2
Green bell pepper 1
Red bell pepper 1
Spinach .... 1 lb
Tomato 1
Zucchini 1

FRUITS:
Lemon juice .... 6 Tblsp

FRESH HERBS:
Basil, chopped .... 2 Tblsp
Chives, chopped .... 1 Tblsp
Coriander .... 1 bunch
Mint, chopped .... 1/3 cup
Oregano, chopped .... 1 Tblsp
Parsley .... 1 bunch
Rosemary .... 1 pkt

FISH/FRESH:
Salmon filets .... 1-1/2 lbs
Scallops .... 8 oz
Shrimp, small .... 1/2 lb
White fish .... 1 lb

CONDIMENTS:
Olive oil .... 1/3 cup
Sweet chili sauce .... 2 tsp
Fish sauce .... 2 Tblsp
Sun dried tomatoes .... 1/4 cup
Rice wine vinegar .... 1/2 cup

DRY GOODS:
Baking powder .... 1-1/4 tsp
Baking soda .... 1/4 tsp
Flour .... 3-1/4 cups
Flour, whole wheat .... 1/2 cup
Flour, self rising .... 3 cups
Sugar .... 2 cups
Sugar, brown .... 1/4 cup

NUTS:
Almonds .... 1/4 cup
Cashews, chopped .... 1/2 cup
Pecans, chopped .... 1/2 cup

DRIED SPICES:
Cinnamon .... 1 tsp
Oregano .... 1/2 tsp

BREAD/DOUGH/PASTA:
Vermicelli .... 9 oz

CANS AND JARS:
Chicken broth .... 1 cup
Pineapple, crushed .... 20 oz can

DAIRY/MILK/CHEESE/BUTTER
Butter .... 3/4 lb
Eggs 8
Parmesan, grated .... 1/2 cup

LIQUOR/WINE/SPIRITS
Beer .... 1-1/2 cups
White wine .... 1/2 cup

S/Y BONJEZ

Chef Andrea Logie
Captain Ivan van Heerden

MENU
Serves 6

Breakfast

*Tropical Muffins
*Spring Vegetable Frittata

Lunch

*Warm Seafood and Noodle Salad
*Beer Bread with Sun Dried Tomatoes and Herbs

Hors d'oeuvre

*Mushrooms with Herb Nut Butter

Dinner

*Salmon with Herb Shrimp Sauce
Mango Salsa Couscous
Steamed Fresh Vegetables

*Pineapple Crumble

BONJEZ, a 56-foot custom-built wooden ketch, draws attention wherever she goes. Captain Ivan van Heerden and First Mate/Chef Andrea Logie call their charters "the Bonjez experience". Ivan, a qualified dive master, has a degree in marine biology which makes viewing the underwater world with him a unique experience. Andrea designs her menus to suit her guests, always keeping in mind that she wants them to enjoy and remember what she serves in the elegant cockpit of this graceful craft.

*Indicates recipe provided

SPRING VEGETABLE FRITTATA

Preparation time: 10 *minutes*
Cooking time: 10 - 15 *minutes*
Serves: 6

Chef: Andrea Logie
Yacht: Bonjez

2 Tblsp	**Butter**
4	**Spring onions, chopped**
1 clove	**Garlic, crushed**
	Salt and pepper
1	**Green bell pepper, chopped**
1	**Small tomato, chopped**
1	**Zucchini, chopped**
6	**Eggs, beaten**

Garnish:

1/4 cup	**Parmesan**
	Parsley

Preheat oven to 375°F/190°C. Heat butter in a skillet and cook onion and garlic. Season with salt and pepper. Add bell pepper, tomato, and zucchini. Cook stirring occasionally until vegetables are crisp and tender. Add eggs and bake in oven until set, about 5 minutes. Sprinkle with parmesan cheese and garnish with parsley. *Serve with English muffins or toast.*

WARM SEAFOOD AND NOODLE SALAD

Preparation time: 20 minutes
Cooking time: 15 minutes
Serves: 6

Chef: Andrea Logie
Yacht: Bonjez

9 oz/250 g	Vermicelli
1/4 cup	Olive oil
1	Large onion, sliced
1	Large red bell pepper, sliced
1 lb/450 g	White fish, cubed
8 oz/225 g	Scallops
1 lb/450 g	Large shrimp, cooked
1 lb/450 g	Fresh spinach, shredded

Garnish:

1/3 cup	Chopped fresh mint
1/3 cup	Coriander
1/2 cup	Chopped cashews

Dressing:

1/2 cup	Rice wine vinegar
2 Tblsp	Lemon juice
2 Tblsp	Fish sauce
1 Tblsp	Sugar
2 tsp	Sweet chili sauce

Cook and drain vermicelli. Heat 2 Tblsp oil in a large skillet, add onion and bell pepper, stir fry and remove. Heat remaining oil and cook fish and scallops until tender. Combine all dressing ingredients, add to skillet and stir. Add shrimp, vegetables and vermicelli; serve over spinach. Sprinkle with mint, coriander and cashews.

Hint: *A loaf of onion, dill or other fresh bread completes this delicious meal.*

BEER BREAD WITH SUN DRIED TOMATOES AND HERBS

Preparation time: 20 minutes
Cooking time: 45 minutes
Serves: 6

Chef: Andrea Logie
Yacht: Bonjez

1/4 cup	Chopped fresh parsley
2 Tblsp	Chopped basil
1/2 tsp	Oregano
1/4 cup	Chopped sun dried tomatoes
1 tsp	Black pepper
1/4 cup	Grated parmesan
2 cloves	Garlic, chopped
3 cups	Self rising flour
1 tsp	Salt
2 tsp	Sugar
1-1/2 cups	Beer
2 tsp	Olive oil

Preheat oven to 450°/230°C. Grease loaf tin. Combine herbs, tomatoes, cheese and garlic. Sift flour, salt and sugar together. Add herb mixture and beer. Stir for 1 minute, then spoon into tin. Bake for 10 minutes, reduce heat to 350°/180°C. Bake for 30 minutes more. Brush with oil and bake until brown, another 5 to 10 minutes. Turn onto wire rack to cool.

MUSHROOMS WITH HERB NUT BUTTER

Preparation time: 20 minutes
Cooking time: 20 minutes
Serves: 6

Chef: Andrea Logie
Yacht: Bonjez

12	**Large mushrooms**
1 Tblsp	**Olive oil**
1	**Onion, finely chopped**
1/4 cup	**Blanched almonds**
1 clove	**Garlic, chopped**
1 Tblsp	**Lemon juice**
1/4 cup	**Chopped parsley**
3 Tblsp	**Fresh thyme or 1 tsp dried**
3 Tblsp	**Fresh rosemary or 1 tsp dried**
1 Tblsp	**Chopped fresh chives**
1/2 tsp	**Salt**
1/2 tsp	**Pepper**
6 Tblsp	**Butter**

Preheat oven to 350°/180°C. Remove stems from mushrooms and set caps aside. Chop stems and sauté with onions. Place almonds, garlic, lemon juice, herbs, salt, pepper and butter in food processor. Process until smooth. Place mushrooms in a baking dish, spoon onion mixture into each cap. Top with almonds and herb mixture. Bake for 10 to 15 minutes.

Hint: *Best cooked just before serving, but can be assembled up to 2 hours ahead and stored in the refrigerator.*

SALMON WITH HERB SHRIMP SAUCE

Preparation time: 5 minutes   *Chef: Andrea Logie*
Cooking time: 15 - 20 minutes   *Yacht: Bonjez*
Serves: 6

1-1/2 lbs/675 g	**Salmon fillet**
1/2 cup	**Dry white wine**
1 Tblsp	**Butter**
2 Tblsp	**Flour**
1 cup	**Chicken broth**
3 Tblsp	**Lemon juice**
1/2 lb/225 g	**Shrimp, small and cooked**
1 Tblsp	**Fresh oregano or 1/2 tsp dried**
1 Tblsp	**Fresh rosemary or 1/2 tsp dried**
1/2 tsp	**Black pepper**
Garnish:	**Sprigs of fresh rosemary**

Preheat oven to 350°F/180°C. Place salmon in 9 x 12 inch (23 x 30 cm) baking dish; add wine. Bake until opaque and salmon flakes easily, about 10 minutes. In a small saucepan, melt butter, add flour stirring constantly. Gradually stir in broth and lemon juice. Cook, simmering constantly until mixture boils and thickens, about 2 minutes. Add shrimp, oregano, rosemary and pepper. Heat for 2 minutes. Place salmon on warmed platter. Pour salmon juices into sauce and stir. *Spoon sauce over salmon and garnish with rosemary. Serve with* **Mango Salsa** *and couscous.*

PINEAPPLE CRUMBLE

Preparation time: 10 minutes   *Chef: Andrea Logie*
Cooking time: 45 minutes   *Yacht: Bonjez*
Serves: 6

1 cup	**Butter**
2-1/2 cups	**Flour**
1 cup	**Sugar**
20 oz/560 g	**Can crushed pineapple, drained**
1/4 cup	**Brown sugar**

Preheat oven to 400°F/200°C. Cut butter into flour and sugar until crumbly. Press half into a greased pie dish. Fill with pineapple and sprinkle with brown sugar. Cover with remaining crumbly mixture and bake until it starts to turn brown. *Delicious served with fresh whipped cream or ice cream.*

TROPICAL MUFFINS

Preparation time: 10 minutes
Cooking time: 20-30 minutes
Makes: 12 muffins

Chef: Andrea Logie
Yacht: Bonjez

2/3 cup	**All purpose flour**
1-1/4 tsp	**Baking powder**
1/2 tsp	**Salt**
1/2 cup	**Whole wheat flour**
1/4 tsp	**Baking soda**
3/4 cup	**Sugar**
1 tsp	**Cinnamon**
2	**Eggs**
1/2 cup	**Pecans, chopped**

Preheat oven to 350°F/180°C. Mix all ingredients well. Fill muffin tins 3/4 full. Bake 20 to 30 minutes.

CAP II SHOPPING LIST

VEGETABLES:
Avocados 2
Garlic .... 1 bulb
Green onion 1
Red onion 1
Tomatoes, roma 8-10

FRUITS:
Apple skins .... garnish
Lemons 2
Pears 6
Blackberries .... 1/4 cup
Blueberries .... 1/2 cup
Boysenberries .... 1/2 cup
Raspberries........................ 1/2 cup
Strawberries, sliced .... 1/2 cup

FRESH HERBS:
Basil .... 1 bunch
Mint .... 1 bunch

DRIED SPICES:
Cinnamon stick 1
Ginger, ground .... 1/2 tsp

CONDIMENTS:
Vanilla bean .... 1 *or*
   Vanilla extract .... 2 Tblsp
Pesto .... 2 Tblsp
Olive oil .... 3 Tblsp
Vinegar, balsamic .... 2 Tblsp
Mayonnaise .... 1 cup

DRY GOODS:
Flour .... coating
Italian bread crumbs .... 3/4 cup
Sugar, brown .... 1/4 cup
Sugar .... 5 Tblsp

CANS AND JARS:
Teriyaki sauce .... 10 oz
Caramel sauce .... 1/2 cup
Cherry pie filling .... 21 oz can
Sundried tomatoes .... 1/2 cup
Chicken broth .... 3 cups

DAIRY/MILK/CHEESE/BUTTER
Butter .... 2 Tblsp
Eggs 4
Whipping cream .... 1/2 cup
Yogurt .... 2 cups

MEAT/POULTRY/FISH/SEAFOOD:
Duck breast .... 2-1/2 lbs
Salmon, cooked .... 1-1/2 lbs

LIQUOR/WINE/SPIRITS:
Amaretto .... 2 Tblsp
Pinot Noir .... 1 cup

MISCELLANEOUS:
Crêpes 12
Baguette 1

S/Y CAP II

Chef Michelle Dunnette
Captain Mike Murdoch

MENU
Serves 6

Breakfast

*Fruit Crêpes

Lunch

*Salmon Cakes with Pesto Mayonnaise

Hors d'oeuvre

*Double Tomato Italian Bruschetta

Dinner

*Chilled Avocado Mint Soup
*Duck Breast with
*Blackberry Pinot Noir Sauce

*Poached Pears with Amaretto Sabayon

The French-built, sleek sailing yacht CAP II, a 76-foot Bordeaux, turns heads wherever she sails. She carries 6 to 8 guests and is fully air conditioned below. Captain Mike Murdoch was brought up on the water in Vancouver. Chef Michelle Dunnette escaped Minnesota winters to travel and eventually crew on yachts in the Mediterranean where she learned her culinary skills from four different professional chefs. One guest's single complaint: "The only difficulty will be returning to shore".

*Indicates recipe provided

FRUIT CREPES

Preparation time: 15 minutes　　　　　　*Chef: MichelleDunnette*
Cooking time: 5 minutes　　　　　　　　　*Yacht: Cap II*
Serves: 6

12	**Crêpes (already made)**
1/2 cup	**Raspberries**
1/2 cup	**Blueberries**
1/2 cup	**Strawberries, sliced**
1/2 cup	**Boysenberries**
4 Tblsp	**Lemon balm, julienned**
1/2 cup	**Heavy cream**
1 Tblsp	**Sugar**

Place berries and 1/4 cup water in a medium sauté pan and cook over medium heat 3 - 4 minutes until warmed. Toss in 3 Tblsp lemon balm. In a separate bowl whisk heavy cream and sugar until soft peaks form. Fill each crêpe with warm berries and fold into quarters, top with whipped cream.

Hint: *A few tablespoons of Grand Marnier may be added to berries instead of lemon balm.*

SALMON CAKES WITH PESTO MAYONNAISE

Preparation time: 10 minutes   *Chef: Michelle Dunnette*
Cooking time: 10 minutes   *Yacht: Cap II*
Serves: 4 - 6

1-1/2 lbs/680 g	**Salmon, cooked***
1/3 cup	**Finely chopped red pepper**
3 Tblsp	**Finely chopped green onion or chives**
3/4 cup	**Italian flavored bread crumbs**
1/2 cup	**Mayonnaise**
	Flour
	Butter

Pesto Mayonnaise:

1/2 cup	**Mayonnaise**
2 Tblsp	**Prepared pesto**
	Juice of 1/2 lemon

Combine salmon, pepper, chives, bread crumbs, and mayonnaise. Shape into cakes approximately 1-1/2 inches (3.5 cm) in diameter by 1 inch (2.5 cm) high. Heat butter in skillet, dip cakes in flour and (shake off excess) put into the pan. (Flour may be eliminated if using nonstick pan). Cook on medium-high heat until the cakes are nicely browned . Whisk mayonnaise pesto and lemon juice together. Serve a dollop on top of each cake.

*You can use canned salmon

Hint: *These can easily be baked on a cookie sheet; turn once during baking—skip flour. Bake at 375°F/190°C.*

DOUBLE TOMATO ITALIAN BRUSCHETTA

Preparation time: 25 minutes   *Chef: Michelle Dunnette*
Cooking time: 5 minutes   *Yacht: Cap II*
Makes: 2 cups

8 - 10	**Roma tomatoes, cored and chopped**
1/2 cup	**Sundried tomatoes, softened and cut in thin strips**
1 Tblsp	**Minced garlic**
3 Tblsp	**Olive oil**
2 Tblsp	**Balsamic vinegar**
	Salt and pepper
1 bunch	**Fresh basil leaves, chopped**
1	**Baguette, sliced and toasted**

Combine tomatoes, sundried tomatoes and garlic. Stir together olive oil and vinegar. Drizzle olive oil, vinegar over tomato mixture and blend. Season with salt and pepper. Add basil just before serving. Serve with toasted baguette slices.

Tip: Can store 2 days or more.

Hint: *Very important **not** to use pulp of tomatoes–it may seem like a waste but the bruschetta will be watery with the tomato cores. This can also be used over fish or chicken.*

CHILLED AVOCADO MINT SOUP

Preparation time: 15 minutes   *Chef: Michelle Dunnette*
Cooking ime: 5 minutes   *Yacht: Cap II*
Chilling time: 1 hour
Serves: 6

2	**Avocados**
1 cup	**Plain yogurt**
3 cups	**Chicken broth, cooled**
1/4 cup	**Chopped fresh mint**
1	**Lemon, juiced**
	Salt and pepper to taste
Garnish:	**Mint leaves and yogurt**

Purée all ingredients together. (May want to alter the amounts a little to achieve desired consistency). Garnish with mint leaf and swirl of plain yogurt.

Hint: *Serve in martini glasses.*

DUCK BREAST WITH
BLACKBERRY PINOT NOIR SAUCE

Preparation time: 20 minutes   *Chef: Michelle Dunnette*
Cooking time: 20 minutes   *Yacht: Cap II*
Serves: 6

2-1/2 lbs/1.1 kg   Duck breast, cut in 6 equal portions

BLACKBERRY PINOT NOIR SAUCE:

2 oz/60 g	**Blackberries***
1 Tblsp	**Butter**
1 Tblsp	**All purpose flour**
1 cup	**Pinot noir wine**
1/2 tsp	**Ground ginger**
	Salt
	Freshly ground black pepper

Preheat oven to 350°F/180°C. Sear duck breasts on both sides in a dry pan over medium heat. Put seared breasts in baking dish and cook in oven until juices run clear, 10 to 15 minutes depending on thickness of breasts. Duck is best served medium rare to medium.

Sauce: Purée blackberries and pass through sieve to remove seeds. Mix wine into blackberries. Melt butter in a saucepan and stir in flour; cook 1 to 2 minutes, stirring continuously. Add blackberries and wine mixture to saucepan, stirring until well blended. Add ginger and continue to cook over low heat, stirring occasionally until thickened, about 5 minutes.

Place duck breasts on 6 warmed plates and serve with sauce.

*Fresh, frozen or canned blackberries may be used, but make sure they are well drained.

POACHED PEARS WITH AMARETTO SABAYON

Preparation time: 15 minutes
Cooking time: 1 hour
Serves: 6

Chef: Michelle Dunnette
Yacht: Cap II

6	**Pears, peeled, stems left on. Cut bottom so pear will sit flat**
1/4 cup	**Brown sugar**
1	**Vanilla bean or**
2 Tblsp	**Vanilla**
1	**Cinnamon stick**
4	**Egg yolks**
2 Tblsp	**Cold water**
1/4 cup	**Sugar**
2 Tblsp	**Amaretto**
	Skin of green apple or pineapple leaves

Poach pears: Fill deep pot with 2 inches of water. Add brown sugar, vanilla and cinnamon. Set pears in and bring to a boil, then cover and simmer at least 20 minutes, up to 1 hour. Let cool in liquid. Remove pears and set on paper towels to dry. Just before serving, prepare...

Sabayon: Put egg yolks, cold water and sugar in top of double boiler whisk until foamy and until tripled in volume, about 8 minutes. Keep heat low. Mixture should be pale in color. Add Amaretto. Pour sabayon on plates, place pears on top. Serve.

Note: Use apple skin or pineapple leaf and cut a leaf for each pear.

Hint: *To make a more attractive presentation, use a few drops of chocolate sauce in sabayon and pull a knife through.*

CATBALU SHOPPING LIST

VEGETABLES:
Asparagus .... 1 bunch
Garlic .... 2 bulbs
Leeks 2
Onions, large 3

FRUITS:
Limes 2

FRESH HERBS:
Parsley .... 1 bunch

CONDIMENTS:
Olive oil .... 1-3/4 cups

DRY GOODS:
Flour .... 5 Tblsp

NUTS:
Walnuts, broken .... 1-1/2 cups

DRIED SPICES:
Bay leaf 1
Cinnamon .... pinch
Mustard .... 1 tsp
White pepper .... 1/4 tsp
Red pepper flakes .... 1/2 tsp

BREAD/DOUGH/PASTA:
Penne .... 1 lb

CANS AND JARS:
Tahini .... 2 Tblsp
Hot chili sauce .... 1/2 tsp
Soy sauce .... 1 tsp
Garbanzo beans .... 14 oz can
Black olives, chopped ..... 3 oz
Vegetable broth .... 1 cup

DAIRY/MILK/CHEESE/BUTTER
Butter .... 1/4 lb
Eggs 3
Milk .... 1-3/4 cups
Yogurt .... 3-4 Tblsp
Gruyère, grated .... 1-1/4 cups
Mozzarella, cubed .... 3-1/2 oz
Parmesan, grated .... 3/4 cup

LIQUOR/WINE/SPIRITS
Sherry, dry .... 1 Tblsp
White wine .... 1/2 cup

S/Y CATBALU

Chef Jennifer Solomon
Captain Mark Solomon

A VEGETARIAN MENU
Serves 6

Breakfast

Continental Breakfast
Coffee, Tea, or Milk

Lunch

*Penne with Walnuts, Pumpkin, and
*Parsley Pesto

Hors d'oeuvre

*Hummus with Black Olives

Dinner

*Gruyère Cheese and Onion Soup
Crusty Bread
*Stuffed Asparagus Pancakes
Mixed Green Salad

Captain Mark Solomon on CATBALU describes his high performance 60-foot wooden catamaran as luxury and pleasure in paradise — and the perfect family yacht. She accommodates up to 8 guests in comfort and style and is well equipped with a supply of water toys and activities for both young and older. Chef Jennifer Solomon selects her menus to suit her guests with, always, tempting offerings. CATBALU charters in the British Virgin Islands during the winter and the Grenadines in the summertime.

*Indicates recipe provided

PENNE WITH WALNUTS, LEEKS, AND PARSLEY PESTO

Preparation time: 35 minutes   *Chef: Jennifer Solomon*
Cooking time: 15 minutes   *Catbalu*
Serves: 6

1 lb/450 g	Penne pasta
1/3 cup	Olive oil
1-1/2 cups	Broken walnuts
1 Tblsp	Butter
2 tsp	Crushed garlic
2	Leeks, finely chopped
1/2 tsp	Red pepper flakes
1/2 cup	White wine
	Salt and freshly ground pepper
1/3 cup	Parsley pesto (see recipe below)
1/4 cup	Grated parmesan or
3-1/2 oz/100 g	Fresh mozzarella, cut in cubes

Cook pasta according to directions. Heat the oil and gently fry the walnuts until they turn pale gold. Lift from pan and reserve, saving oil in pan. In another pan melt butter, stir in garlic and cook for 30 seconds; add leeks, red pepper flakes, and wine, cover and cook gently until tender and wine reduced. Season with a little salt and plenty of pepper. Drain the pasta, toss with saved oil. Mix in walnuts, pesto, garlic and leeks. *Top with grated parmesan or mozzarella cubes.*

PARSLEY PESTO:
Makes 3/4 cup

1 bunch	Parsley, remove stalks
3 cloves	Garlic
1/4 cup	Fresh grated parmesan cheese
1/2 cup	Olive oil
Pinch	Salt
1/4 tsp	White pepper

Place all ingredients in a food processor and purée to a smooth soft paste.

HUMMUS WITH BLACK OLIVES

Preparation time: 5 minutes   *Chef: Jennifer Solomon*
Chilling time: 2 hours   *Yacht: Catbalu*
Serves: 6

14 oz/390 g	Can garbanzo beans (chick peas)
2	Garlic cloves
2 Tblsp	Tahini*
2 Tblsp	Olive oil
3 Tblsp	Lime juice
2 Tblsp	Water
3-4 Tblsp	Yoghurt, plain
3 oz/85 g	Black olives, roughly chopped

Blend garbanzo beans in food processor with remaining ingredients except black olives. Blend until smooth, adjust seasoning and mix in black olives. Spoon into serving dish, cover and chill for at least 30 minutes, the longer the better to let flavors develop. This is very easy and looks good.

Hint: Traditionally the Hummus is made with 1/2 pint of olive oil; this recipe is a much lighter. Hummus is a Middle Eastern dish and goes well with couscous. Also serve as a dip with crudités.

*Tahini is a paste made from sesame seeds. If difficult to find use peanut butter. Adjust garlic to your taste.

Note: If using dried beans, cook according to instructions.

Tip: Michael from M/Y Marge's Barge adds yogurt cheese to the hummus.

GRUYERE CHEESE AND ONION SOUP

Preparation time: 15 minutes
Cooking time: 20 minutes
Serves: 6

Chef: Jennifer Solomon
Yacht: Catbalu

2 Tblsp	Butter
3	Large onions, sliced
4 cloves	Garlic, chopped
1 tsp	Mustard powder
1 tsp	Salt
1 tsp	Freshly ground black pepper
1 cup	Vegetable stock
2 cups	Water
3 Tblsp	Butter
3 Tblsp	Flour
1-1/2 cups	Milk
1 -1/4 cups	Grated Gruyère cheese
1 Tblsp	Sherry
1 tsp	Soy sauce
1/2 tsp	Hot chili sauce

Melt butter in a large saucepan, then sauté onions with the garlic, mustard, salt, and pepper until soft, without letting them brown. Add the water, bring to a boil, then cover and simmer over a low heat until the onions are tender. In another saucepan melt the butter then stir in flour. Continue stirring while the mixture cooks, about 1 minute. Add milk and keep stirring until sauce boils and thickens; boil for a minute or so, then remove from heat and stir in grated cheese. Add cheese sauce to onion mixture then stir in sherry, soy, and chili sauce. Cook over a very low heat for a further 10 minutes. Do NOT boil. Serve with a crusty bread. *Serve immediately, or make ahead and reheat when needed.*

Note: *This soup is very rich and filling.*

STUFFED ASPARAGUS CREPES

Preparation time: 25 minutes
Cooking time: 15 - 20 minutes
Serves: 6

Chef: Jennifer Solomon
Yacht: Catbalu

4 Tblsp	Milk
4	Peppercorns
1	Bay leaf
1	Bunch asparagus
	Pinch Salt and pepper
1 Tblsp	Butter
2 Tblsp	Plain flour
3	Eggs, separated
Pinch	Cinnamon
2 Tblsp	Parmesan cheese
6	Thin pancakes

Preheat oven to 400°F/200°C. Steam asparagus until tender, season with salt and pepper. Pour milk in a pan with peppercorns and bay leaf, bring to boil and leave to infuse, about 10 minutes; strain and discard flavorings. Melt butter, add flour and gradually stir in milk to make white sauce; it should be thick. Allow to cool and add egg yolks.

Blend asparagus and sauce in food processor. Add cinnamon and 1 Tblsp parmesan cheese. Whisk egg whites until stiff. Fold mixture into egg whites. Spoon generous amount in center of each pancake*, fold two sides loosely at top. Arrange in dish, sprinkle with remaining parmesan cheese. Bake for 15 - 20 minutes until souffle has risen and pancakes are crisp.

*Pancakes can be made ahead of time and kept in the refrigerator with cling film (plastic wrap) separating them.

Hint: *Can be made with broccoli, carrots and a number of other fillings. Much better 'behaved' than traditional soufflés!*

CHRISTMAS WINDS SHOPPING LIST

VEGETABLES:
Garlic cloves 4
Iceberg lettuce .... 1 head
Romaine lettuce .... 1 head
Onion, small 1
Green bell pepper 1
Pimento .... garnish
Spinach .... 10 oz pkg
Tomato 1

FRUITS:
Cantaloupe .... 1 cup
Limes 2
Mangos 4
Orange juice .... 1-1/2 cups
Strawberries .... 1 pint

FRESH HERBS:
Alfalfa sprouts .... 1/2 cup
Dill .... 1 tsp
Ginger .... 2 inch pc
Mint leaves .... garnish
Parsley .... garnish
Tarragon .... 1 tsp

DRIED SPICES:
Bay leaf 1
Cayenne .... 1 tsp
Cinnamon .... 1 tsp
Ginger, ground .... 1/4 tsp
Garlic salt........................ 1/4 tsp
Mustard .... 1 tsp
Nutmeg .... 1/2 tsp
Onion salt .... 1/4 tsp
Paprika .... garnish
White pepper .... 1/8 tsp

CONDIMENTS:
Catsup .... 1-1/4 cups
Coconut, flakes .... 1/4 cup
Mayonnaise .... 1-1/4 cups

Oil .... 1/2 cup
Vinegar, red wine .... 1/4 cup
DRY GOODS:
Flour .... 1/4 cup
Oatmeal .... 1/2 cup
Sugar .... 1/4 cup
Sugar, brown .... 1/2 cup

NUTS:
Sunflower seeds.............. 1/4 cup

BREAD/DOUGH/PASTA:
Bread crumbs .... 1/3 cup
Pita bread 2
Graham cracker crust 1

CANS AND JARS:
Honey .... 3 Tblsp
Horseradish .... 1/2 tsp
Hot mustard .... 1 tsp
Maple syrup .... 1 bottle
Artichokes, non oil .... 14 oz can
Pimento .... 1 jar/can

DAIRY/MILK/CHEESE/BUTTER
Butter.............................. 6 Tblsp
Eggs 8
Yogurt .... 8 oz
Cream cheese.................. 3 oz
Parmesan, grated .... 3/4 cup

SEAFOOD:
Crab meat .... 6 oz can

MEAT:
Ham slices 12
Leg of lamb, bone in .... 4 lbs

FROZEN:
Asparagus .... 10 oz pkg

More Store to Shore Shopping Lists available…1-800-338-6073 –CapJan@aol.com
www.shiptoshoreinc.com

S/Y CHRISTMAS WINDS

Chef Helen Hoyt
Captain Peter Hoyt

MENU
Serves 4

Breakfast

Juice
*Scrambled Egg Pockets

Lunch

*Crab Artichoke Supreme
*Strawberries and Spinach Salad
Hot Fresh Bread or Focaccia

Hors d'oeuvre

*Ham Asparagus Roll Up

Dinner

*Citrus Cantaloupe Soup
*Gingered Leg of Lamb
Couscous
Pea Pods
Hot Rolls

*Mango Crisp

CHRISTMAS WINDS, a spacious 40-foot modern catamaran, carries 4 double staterooms, each with its own bathroom. Peter Hoyt is captain and Helen, his wife, crew and chef. They have been chartering in the Caribbean for fifteen years, and love it. Their lifestyle — free, easy, adventuresome and fun — has been more than they hoped for when they began chartering. They enjoy sharing their carefree world of exploring and relaxing along with Helen's culinary delights from her well-stocked galley.

*Indicates recipe provided

SCRAMBLED EGG POCKETS

Preparation time: 20 minutes　　　　　　　　*Chef: Helen Hoyt*
Cooking time: 10 minutes　　　　　*Yacht: Christmas Winds*
Serves: 4

1	**Small tomato, seeded and chopped**
2 Tblsp	**Chopped onion**
2 Tblsp	**Chopped green bell pepper**
8	**Eggs, beaten**
1 tsp	**Chopped fresh tarragon leaves or**
	1/2 tsp dried
1/4 tsp	**Salt**
2	**Pita breads, 6inches (15 cm) diameter**
1/2 cup	**Alfalfa sprouts**

Spray 10 inch (25 cm) nonstick skillet with cooking oil. Over medium-high heat, cook tomato, onion and pepper, about 3 minutes, stirring occasionally, until tender. Mix eggs, tarragon and salt, pour into skillet. As mixture begins to set at bottom and side, gently lift cooked eggs with spatula so that uncooked portion can flow to the bottom. Cook 3 to 5 minutes or until eggs are thickened throughout but still moist. Cut pita bread in half and open to form pockets. Spoon mixture into pita bread and top with sprouts.

Hint: *This is a good quick recipe for those mornings when you have to have breakfast under sail or when trying to get your guests to an early flight.*

CRAB ARTICHOKE SUPREME

Preparation time: 20 minutes   *Chef: Helen Hoyt*
Cooking time: 15-20 minutes   *Yacht: Christmas Winds*
Serves: 4

4	**Scallop shells**
6 oz/170 g	**Can crabmeat**
14oz/390 g	**Can of artichoke hearts, non marinated, diced**
3/4 cup	**Grated parmesan cheese**
1 cup	**Mayonnaise**
1/3 cup	**Bread crumbs to thicken, can use less**
Garnish:	**Paprika, pimento, and parsley**

Preheat oven to 350°F/180°C. Grease scallop shells with cooking spray. Mix together crabmeat, artichoke hearts, parmesan cheese, mayonnaise, and bread crumbs. Fill each scallop shell with mixture. Sprinkle extra bread crumbs and paprika on top. Place shells on cookie sheet and bake 15 to 20 minutes or until hot and lightly browned. *Garnish.*

Serve with a side salad and hot fresh bread or Fococcia. So easy and elegant served in the scallop shell.

STRAWBERRIES AND SPINACH SALAD

Preparation time: 10 minutes   *Chef: Helen Hoyt*
Chilling time: 8 hours   *Yacht: Christmas Winds*
Serves: 4

1 pint	**Fresh strawberries**
10 oz/284 g	**Pkg baby spinach**
1 tsp	**Dill week**
1/4 cup	**Sunflower seeds**

Vinaigrette:

1/2 cup	**Oil**
1/4 cup	**Red wine vinegar**
1/4 cup	**Sugar**
1/4 tsp	**Garlic salt**
1/4 tsp	**Onion salt**
1/4 tsp	**Pepper**
1 tsp	**Dry mustard**

Wash and slice the strawberries. Mix spinach, dill, strawberries and seeds. Add vinaigrette just before serving.

Mix the vinaigrette ingredients in a jar and refrigerate. Each time you open the refrigerator, give it a shake.

Hint: It is such an easy salad. Looks very pretty and tastes delicious. Serves four for lunch, and six to eight as a side salad or appetizer.

Note: *This recipe was given to me by one of my charter guests, Diana Bos, from Holland, Michigan.*

HAM ASPARAGUS ROLL UP

Preparation time: 15 minutes   *Chef: Helen Hoyt*
Chilling time: 1 hour   *Yacht: Christmas Winds*
Serves: 6 - 8

10 oz/285 g	**Pkg frozen asparagus spears**
3 oz/85 g	**Cream cheese**
1/2 tsp	**Horseradish**
2 Tblsp	**Mayonnaise**
12	**Slices of ham**

Cook and drain the asparagus spears. Blend together cream cheese, horseradish and mayonnaise. Spread on each slice of ham. Place 1 or 2 asparagus spears along edge of ham slice. Roll and chill. Slice into bite size pieces.

Hint: *These can also be used for lunch with Hollandaise sauce.*

CITRUS CANTALOUPE SOUP

Preparation time: 10 minutes   *Chef: Helen Hoyt*
Chilling time: 2 hours   *Yacht: Christmas Winds*
Serves: 6

4 cups	**Cubed cantaloupe**
1-1/2 cups	**Orange juice**
1/3 cup	**Vanilla yogurt**
2 tsp	**Honey**
1/4 tsp	**Ground ginger**
1/4 tsp	**Ground nutmeg**
Garnish:	**Yogurt and mint leaves**

Process all ingredients in a blender and chill. Before serving top each bowl with a dollop of yogurt and a mint leaf.

Hint: *Can be made a day or two ahead and stored in refrigerator. You can use half honeydew and half cantaloupe.*

GINGERED LEG OF LAMB

Preparation time: 15 minutes   *Chef: Helen Hoyt*
Cooking time: 1-1/2 hours   *Yacht: Christmas Winds*
Serves: 6

4 lbs/1.8 kg	Leg of lamb
4 cloves	Garlic, thinly sliced
2 inch/5 cm	Piece of ginger, peeled and thinly sliced

Marinade:

1-1/4 cups	Ketchup
2 Tblsp	Honey
3 Tblsp	Worchestershire sauce
1 tsp	Hot mustard
1	Lime, juiced
1 tsp	Cayenne pepper
1/2 tsp	Salt
	White pepper to taste

Preheat oven to 375°F/190°C. Put all ingredients for marinade in small saucepan and bring to boil, stir continually. Remove from heat and allow to cool. Make small incisions in leg of lamb and push slivers of garlic and ginger into them. Place lamb in large dish and pour marinade over. Place in refrigerator for at least 2 hours. Turn lamb once or twice. Bake in marinade about 1-1/2 hours for medium. Thin with water if sauce gets too thick. Allow to rest before serving. Reheat sauce and serve over lamb, or serve separately.

Hint: Lamb is best eaten medium to medium—rare.

Serve with coucous, green pea pods, hot rolls, followed by **Mango Crisp** *for dessert.*

Note: As an alternative meal suggestion — after lamb has been cooking 30 minutes; add potatoes, cut in quarters, thick slices of onions, red peppers, and some carrots. Serve with a green vegetable and mint sauce (Crosse & Blackwell), not mint jelly.

MANGO CRISP

Preparation time: 10 minutes　　　　　　　　*Chef: Helen Hoyt*
Cooking time: 30 minutes　　　　　　　*Yacht: Christmas Winds*
Serves: 4 - 6

1 tsp	Butter
3 cups	Mango chunks
1/2	Lime, juiced
1/2 cup	Oatmeal
1/4 cup	Flour
1/2 cup	Brown sugar
1/4 cup	Flaked coconut
1 tsp	Cinnamon
1/2 tsp	Salt
1/4 tsp	Grated nutmeg
5 Tblsp	Butter, softened

Preheat oven to 375°F/190°C. Butter an 8 inch (20 cm) baking dish. Arrange mango chunks in single layer.Squeeze lime juice over. In mixing bowl, combine oatmeal, flour, brown sugar, coconut, cinnamon, salt and nutmeg. Cut butter into pieces and work into dry mixture until crumbly. Sprinkle evenly over mango. Bake 30 minutes or until brown and bubbly. *Serve hot or room temperature with heavy cream, yogurt or ice cream.*

Hint: *You can use frozen or canned mango if fresh is not available.*

CONQUEST II SHOPPING LIST

VEGETABLES:
English cucumber 1
Garlic cloves 7
Ginger .... 1 inch pc
Lettuce leaves 4
Iceberg lettuce, small ..... 1 head
Red onions 2
Potatoes, new 12
Tomato, large 1

FRUITS:
Bananas 4
Limes 2
Lemons 3
Mango 1
Orange 1
Strawberries 12

FRESH HERBS:
Ginger .... 1 inch pc
Thyme sprigs 6-7
Rosemary sprigs 2

DRIED SPICES:
Bay leaf 1
Cinnamon .... 1 tsp
Nutmeg, freshly ground . 1 tsp
White pepper .... 1/8 tsp
Peppercorns, black 6

CONDIMENTS:
Baking soda .... 1/2 tsp
Semi-sweet chocolate ..... 8 oz
Vanilla extract .... 1-1/2 tsp
Olive oil .... 4-1/2 cups
Peanut oil .... 2 Tblsp
Vinegar, champagne .... 1 Tblsp
Vinegar, red wine .... 1/4 cup
Mayonnaise .... 2 Tblsp

DRY GOODS:
Flour .... 1-1/4 cups
Sugar .... 1/2 cup
Sugar, brown .... 1 cup
Sugar, confectioners' ...... dusting

BREAD/DOUGH/PASTA:
Bahamian .... 4 slices
Panko .... 2 cups
Graham cracker crust 1
Tortillas, large 4

CANS AND JARS:
Caramel sauce .... 1 jar
Maple syrup .... 1 cup
Soy sauce .... 1/4 cup
Butter pickles, diced .... 3 Tblsp
Scotch Peppers, pickled . 1 jar

DAIRY/MILK/CHEESE/BUTTER
Butter 1/4lb
Unsalted .... 1/4 lb
Eggs 11
Feta .... 6 oz

SEAFOOD/FISH:
Conchs 4
Mahi Mahi .... 2 lbs

MEAT:
Turkey, sliced .... 3/4 lb

FROZEN:
Vanilla ice cream .... 1 quart

LIQUORS/WINE/SPIRITS:
Dark rum .... 3 Tblsp

M/Y CONQUEST II

Chef Pamela Carter
Captain Richard Ackerman

A DAY IN THE BAHAMAS

MENU
Serves 4

Breakfast

Fresh Squeezed Orange Juice
*Down Island French Toast Served with
Fresh Strawberries, Pineapple and Mango
Hot Maple Syrup

Picnic Lunch

*Turkey Tortilla Wraps
Tara Chips
*Chocolate Chip Cookies
Fresh Fruit and Cooler with assorted drinks

Hors d'oeuvre

*Cracked Conch Served with Fresh Tartar Sauce
Kalik Beer (Bahamian Beer) served in frosty glasses

Dinner

*Conquest Salad
*Grilled Dolphin with Caramelized Onions
*Oven Roasted New Potatoes
Assorted Breads

*Bananas Foster, Ice Cream with Caramel Sauce

Cruising aboard CONQUEST II, a 107-foot Denison motor yacht, begins
in the crystal-clear waters of the Bahamas. Captain Richard Ackerman
carries a full inventory of water toys including twin wave runners and a
28-foot Mako rigged for fishing and skiing. A 14-foot runabout and a
kayak can be used for exploration. Three extravaganza meals are served
each day created by Chef Pamela Carter who runs the galley like a 5-star
restaurant, even when it's a picnic lunch on shore.

*Indicates recipe provided

DOWN ISLAND FRENCH TOAST

Preparation time: 20 minutes *Chef: Pamela Carter*
Cooking time: 10 minutes *Yacht: Conquest II*
Serves: 4

4	**Eggs**
1 cup	**Half and half**
1 tsp	**Vanilla**
1 tsp	**Cinnamon**
1 tsp	**Freshly ground nutmeg**
1 Tblsp	**Dark rum**
4 Tblsp	**Butter**
4 slices	**Bahamian bread, 1-inch (2.5 cm) thick**
1/4	**Pineapple, diced**
1	**Mango, diced**
8	**Strawberries, sliced**
	Confectioners' sugar, dusting
1 cup	**Maple syrup**
Garnish:	
4	**Strawberries made into a rose***

Whisk together the eggs, half and half, vanilla, cinnamon, nutmeg and rum. Place bread slices in a baking dish just large enough to hold all slices in one layer. Pour egg mixture over them. Soak slices, turning them over once or twice to allow bread to absorb liquid, about 10 minutes. Mix pineapple, mango and strawberries together. In a 12 inch (30 cm) non stick skillet, melt butter over low heat until foam subsides, and cook bread slices until golden, about 5 minutes on each side. Dust French toast with confectioners' sugar and serve with maple syrup.

Presentation: Cut French toast at an angle and arrange it standing side by side. Place fruits around the plate and add the strawberry.

*Select a strawberry that will sit up nicely on it's stem. Holding the stem carefully feather three slices from the top to the stem cutting in to make a petal. On the tip cut a small triangle and remove. The green part should be fresh looking. When finished the strawberry should sit on the green part and it's petals slightly pulled out to resemble a rose.

Hint: I make the egg mixture the day before.

Tip: *When in the Bahamas use Bimini Bread or Mrs. Smith's from Staniel Cay, Exumas. If you find yourself at Staniel you can call on VHF 16 for Berke and order your bread. Or if you are on land, use day old brioche or challah (a traditional Jewish yeast bread. It is rich with eggs and has a light, airy texture — perfect for French Toast).*

TURKEY TORTILLA WRAPS

Preparation time: 15 minutes *Chef: Pamela Carter*
Serves: 4 *Yacht: Conquest II*

4	**Large flour tortillas**
2 Tblsp	**Mayonnaise**
	Salt and freshly ground pepper
3/4 lb/340 g	**Sliced cooked turkey**
1	**Large tomato, sliced**
4	**Lettuce leaves, torn**

Spread mayonnaise on tortillas then sprinkle with salt and pepper. Divide turkey, tomato and lettuce on tortillas and roll up.

Hint: Keep the ingredients simple. Wrap each one in a cloth napkin and store in ziplock bags or plastic containers and place in a cooler. When ready to serve simply open the top of the napkin and the guests can eat with one hand and keep on fishing!

CHOCOLATE CHIP COOKIES

Preparation time: 20 minutes *Chef: Pamela Carter*
Cooking time: 10 minutes *Yacht: Conquest II*
Makes: 2 dozen

1-1/4 cups	**Unbleached all purpose flour**
1/2 tsp	**Baking soda**
Pinch	**Salt**
8 Tblsp	**Unsalted butter (1 stick), softened**
6 Tblsp	**Granulated sugar**
6 Tblsp	**Light brown sugar, packed**
1/2 tsp	**Vanilla**
1	**Egg**
8 oz/225 g	**Good quality semi-sweet chocolate, hand chopped**

Preheat oven to 375°F/190°C. Lightly grease baking sheets or use silpat (non stick baking liners). In a small bowl stir together the flour, baking soda and salt. In a mixing bowl combine the butter, both sugars and vanilla: beat until light. Beat in the egg. Slowly add the flour mixture, beating until smooth. Then stir in the chocolate pieces. Drop the batter by small ice cream scoop, 3 inches (7.5 cm) apart, onto the prepared baking sheets. Bake 8-10 minutes. Remove from oven, let stand. The cookies should be dry on top and golden. You may return them to the oven for a couple more minutes, but be careful not to overcook them.

CRACKED CONCH

Preparation time: 30 minutes   *Chef: Pamela Carter*
Cooking time: 30 minutes   *Yacht: Conquest II*
Serves: 4

4	**Conch**
	Salt and pepper
1/4 cup	**Flour**
2 cups	**Panko***
2	**Eggs, beaten**
2 Tblsp	**Half and half**
	Peanut oil for frying
1	**Lime, sliced in wedges**

Season conch with salt and pepper. Place the flour and Panko on separate plates. In a bowl whisk the eggs and half and half together. Dredge the cracked conch in the flour then in the egg wash and finally in the panko. Heat peanut oil in a large skillet and fry in batches until nicely browned. Drain and chop in pieces. *Serve with lime wedges.*

Note: Conch is a speciality of the Bahamas. If you do not have time to go out and gather your own then seek out a "local" to help you. My favorite place to order conch is from Percy (Grey Ghost) at Great Harbor, Berry Island. The conch is always fresh! Preparing fabulous Cracked Conch is simple. I use the conch for three different purposes. The foot is long, round and tough. Cut this part off and save for Conch Chowder. Clean the main body, removing the orange color and save this for bottom fishing (remember we are on a yacht). The main body must be pounded (cracked) with a meat tenderizer until you don't feel any firm places.

Tip: When you purchase conch in the United States remember that it has been frozen. It is better to purchase frozen conch in 5 lb boxes, rather than thawed conch, as you never know how long it has been thawed!

*Panko: *Bread crumbs used in Japanese cooking for coating fried foods. They are coarser then thoses normally used in the United States and create a deliciously crunchy crust. Panko is sold in Asian and gourmet markets.*

TARTAR SAUCE

Preparation time: 10 minutes   *Chef: Pamela Carter*
Makes: 1 -1/2 cups   *Yacht: Conquest II*

3	**Egg yolks**
1 Tblsp	**Champagne vinegar**
1/2 cup	**Virgin olive oil**
1/2 cup	**Canola oil**
1-1/2 Tblsp	**Seeded and minced pickled Scotch bonnet chilies, reserve 1 tsp juice**
3 Tblsp	**Sweet butter pickles, diced small**
2 Tblsp	**Finely diced red onion**
1	**Hard boiled egg**
	Salt and pepper to taste

In a blender, or whisking by hand, beat the egg yolks until they turn pale. Whisk in the vinegar and the Scotch bonnet pickling juice. Very slowly whisk in the olive and canola oils until they are incorporated. Transfer to a bowl (if using a blender) and stir in the Scotch bonnets, butter, pickles, and onion. Finely dice the egg white and sieve the egg yolk through a fine mesh strainer. Stir both the egg white and yolk into the sauce and season with salt and pepper. *Keep covered in the refrigerator until needed.*

CONQUEST SALAD

Preparation time: 20 minutes   *Chef: Pamela Carter*
Standing time: 15 minutes   *Yacht: Conquest II*
Serves: 4

1	**English cucumber, diced**
1	**Yellow bell pepper, diced**
1	**Red onion, diced**
1	**Tomato, seeded and diced**
6 oz/170 g	**Crumbled feta cheese**
	Salt and pepper
2 cups	**Shredded iceberg lettuce**
2	**Lemons, juiced**

Chill salad plates in freezer. In a bowl place cucumber, bell pepper, onion, tomato, feta cheese, salt and pepper. Let rest for 5 minutes. In another bowl place iceberg lettuce, pour lemon juice over and toss. Place equal amounts of lettuce on each plate, then top with salad mixture. *This is a colorful and refreshing salad.*

GRILLED DOLPHIN WITH CARAMELIZED ONIONS

Preparation time: 20 minutes
Marinating time: 15 minutes
Cooking time: 25 minutes
Serves: 4

Chef: Pamela Carter
Yacht: Conquest II

4 - 8 oz/225 g	Dolphin fish (Mahi Mahi)
1/4 cup	Olive oil
1/4 cup	Soy sauce
1	Orange
1	Lemon
1	Lime
1	Bay leaf
6	Peppercorns
1/2	Red onion, thinly sliced
5 cloves	Garlic, thinly sliced
1	Piece ginger (1/2 inch/1 cm) thinly sliced
4	Sprigs thyme

Preheat oven to 400°F/200°C. In a large mixing bowl put the olive oil and soy sauce. Squeeze in the juice of orange, lemon and lime. Add remaining ingredients and mix well. Add the dolphin fish to the marinade at least 15 minutes before cooking. Remove fish from marinade and place in a baking dish. Bake for about 10 minutes. Most important, do NOT overcook. Top with **Caramelized Onions.** *Serve with* **Oven Roasted New Potatoes.**

Hint: *I use a grill pan in the galley and put grill marks on the fish, about 2 minutes, then put in oven.*

CARAMELIZED ONIONS:

2 Tblsp	Olive oil
2 Tblsp	Butter
2	Red onions, peeled and sliced
1 Tblsp	Sugar
1/4 cup	Red wine vinegar
	Salt and pepper to taste

Heat olive oil and butter in a large sauté pan over high heat; when butter begins to foam add the onions and stir once to coat. Sauté about 8-10 minutes, or until caramelized, stirring only occasionally. Reduce heat to medium and sauté for another 10 minutes. Sprinkle the onions with the sugar and stir gently. Cook for 1 minute, stir in the vinegar and reduce 1 or 2 minutes, or until the liquid has almost completely evaporated. Season with salt and pepper.

OVEN ROASTED NEW POTATOES

Preparation time: 10 minutes   *Chef: Pamela Carter*
Cooking time: 40 minutes   *Yacht: Conquest II*
Serves: 4

12	New potatoes, cut into wedges
	Olive oil to cover potatoes
2	Sprigs rosemary
2	Sprigs thyme
2	Cloves garlic, sliced
	Salt and fresh ground pepper

Preheat oven to 425°F/220°C. Put all ingredients in a deep roasting pan. The olive oil should just cover the potatoes. Place in the oven and roast for about 40 minutes or until cooked through. Strain and reserve oil for another use.

BANANAS FOSTER ICE CREAM PIE
WITH CARAMEL SAUCE

Preparation time: 10 minutes   *Chef: Pamela Carter*
Freezing time: 4 hours   *Yacht: Conquest II*
Serves: 4

4 Tblsp	Butter
4	Ripe bananas
1/2 cup	Brown sugar
2 Tblsp	Dark rum
4 cups	Vanilla ice cream, softened
1	Graham cracker pie crust
12.25 oz/345 g	Jar caramel sauce

In a skillet melt butter and sauté bananas, add brown sugar and rum, cook until bananas are tender. Place all in a blender and blend until smooth. Let cool. Using a pastry brush, coat caramel on graham cracker crust. Blend together the banana mixture and ice cream and pour into pie crust. Using a fork dip into the caramel and make designs onto the pie. Freeze at least 4 hours.

Note: This is a very popular dessert. I make it from scratch but have developed this version for those who have less time. Make a day in advance. Bananas are the first fruit to become overripe, so this is a good way to use them.

CORAL SEA SHOPPING LIST

VEGETABLES:
Avocados 2
Carrots, baby .... 1 lb
Cauliflower .... 1 head
Celery stalks 2
Chives .... garnish
Jalapenos 8
Romaine .... 3 hearts
Onions, small 1
Green bell pepper 1
Potatoes 3

FRUITS:
Lemon 1
Lime 1

FRESH HERBS:
Dill .... 1 Tblsp
Ginger, grated .... 1/4 cup

DRIED SPICES:
Cayenne .... pinch
Curry .... 3/4 tsp
Garlic salt .... 1/2 tsp
Paprika .... 2 tsp

CONDIMENTS:
Horseradish .... 1 Tblsp
Mustard, country Dijon .. 1 Tblsp
Dijon mustard .... 2 Tblsp
Extra virgin olive oil .... 3/4 cup
Shortening .... 1 cup
Mayonnaise .... 1-1/4 cups
Soy Sauce .... 1/2 cup
Cocoa .... 2/3 cup
Vanilla extract .... 1-1/2 Tblsp

DRY GOODS:
Flour .... 1-1/2 cups
Sugar .... 2 cups

Sugar, confectioners' ...... 1 lb
Marshmallows, mini ...... 16 oz pkg
Triscuits .... 1 box

BREAD/DOUGH/PASTA:
English muffins 6
Bread, white .... 6 slices

CANS AND JARS:
Honey .... 1 Tblsp
Chicken broth .... 2 cups
Cream of mushroom ...... 1 can
Black olives, chopped ..... 1 cup
Pimento .... 7 oz

DAIRY/MILK/CHEESE/BUTTER
Butter .... 3/4 lb
Cream .... 1/2 cup
Whipping cream .... 1/2 cup
Eggs 18
Sour cream .... 1 cup
Cheddar, sharp .... 1-1/2 cups
Cream cheese .... 8 oz
Gruyère, grated .... 1/4 cup
Jalsberg, grated .... 3 cups

NUTS:
Pecans, chopped .... 2-1/4 cups

SEAFOOD/FISH:
Crab meat .... 12 oz
Tuna steaks 6

MEAT:
Ham slices 6

LIQUORS/WINE/SPIRITS:
Dark rum .... 5 Tblsp
Tequila .... 2 Tblsp

S/Y CORAL SEA

Captain and Chef Darla Holmes
Engineer Jack Holmes

MENU
Serve 6

Breakfast

Fresh Fruit Platter
*Eggs Coba
Coffee, Tea, Juice

Lunch

*Chilled Avocado Soup
*Crab Circles

Hors d'oeuvres

*Huevos Stuffed Jalapeños
*Black Olive Cheddar Spread

Dinner

*Romaine Ting
*Xcalak tuna
*Tequila Carrots
*Cauliflower Mash

*Rio Grande Mud Pie

Darla Holmes is captain and cook on board the CORAL SEA, a lovely 68-foot Palmer Johnson schooner taking 6 guests. Her husband, Jack Holmes, is engineer. Darla and Jack gathered a store of knowledge sailing the waters of Mexico, Central America and the Caribbean and her menus reflect the many ports they have visited. For both Darla and Jack acting as charter-boat hosts comes naturally. She was formerly a public relations manager, he a former CEO of an international corporation.

*Indicates recipe provided

EGGS COBA

Preparation time: 20 minutes
Cooking time: 15 minutes
Serves: 6

Chef: Darla Holmes
Yacht: Coral Sea

14 oz/390 g	**Can cream of mushroom soup**
1/4 cup	**Whipping cream**
1	**Green bell pepper, finely chopped**
7 oz/195 g	**Jar chopped pimento**
12	**Hard boiled eggs, sliced**
6 slices	**Ham**
	Toast triangles

In a saucepan heat soup. Dilute slightly with cream. Add green pepper and pimento, then sliced eggs. Cook on low until heated through. During this time warm ham slices in microwave. Serve soup mixture over ham slices with toast triangles.

Hint: Minced jalapeños and onions may be added. If no ham is available, serve over toast.

CHILLED AVOCADO SOUP

Preparation time: 20 minutes
Chilling time: 1 hour
Serves: 6

Chef: Darla Holmes
Yacht: Coral Sea

2	**Ripe avocados**
1	**Lime, juiced**
2 cups	**Chicken broth**
1/2 tsp	**Salt**
3 Tblsp	**Dark rum**
1/2 tsp	**Curry power**
	Fresh ground pepper
1 cup	**Sour cream**
Garnish:	**Chopped chives**

Put all ingredients except sour cream and chives into a blender and blend thoroughly. Add sour cream running blender momentarily. Chill at least one hour. *Serve with chopped chives on top.*

Hint: If avocados are unavailable use prepared guacamole.

Note: *This soup cannot be frozen.*

CRAB CIRCLES

Preparation time: 20 minutes
Cooking time: 20 minutes
Serves: 6

Chef: Darla Holmes
Yacht: Coral Sea

2 - 6 oz/170 g	**Cans crab, or fresh if available**
1/2 cup	**Chopped celery**
1/2 cup	**Chopped onion**
3/4 cup	**Mayonnaise**
3 cups	**Grated jarlsberg or swiss cheese**
6	**English muffins, halved and toasted**
Garnish:	**Paprika**

Preheat oven to 375°F/190°C. Mix crab, celery, onion, mayonnaise and 1 cup cheese. Mound mixture on lightly toasted English muffin halves. Top with remaining cheese. Bake in oven until cheese is almost bubbling. Sprinkle with paprika and serve with soup for lunch.

Hint: Sometimes I serve this at breakfast with kiwi fruit and melon. For hors d'oeuvre, it's finger food, like a little pizza.

HUEVOS STUFFED JALAPENOS

Preparation time: 20 minutes
Chilling time: Overnight
Serves: 6 - 8

Chef: Darla Holmes
Yacht: Coral Sea

1 lb/450 g	**Fresh jalapeños**
8 oz/225 g	**Cream cheese, softened**
2	**Hard boiled eggs, mashed**
1/2 tsp	**Garlic salt**
1/4 cup	**Chopped pecans**
1 tsp	**Salad seasoning or paprika**
	Mayonnaise

Halve jalapeños lengthwise and de-seed. Soak overnite in ice water in the refrigerator. Beat cream cheese with mashed eggs, garlic salt, pecans and salad seasoning. Add mayonnaise to make consistency of paste. Fill jalapeños, mounding stuffing slightly. Sprinkle tops with paprika or salad seasoning.

Tip: These can be made a day ahead, covered with plastic wrap and kept in the refrigerator. Do not freeze.

BLACK OLIVE CHEDDAR SPREAD

Preparation time: 15 minutes   *Chef: Darla Holmes*
Cooking time: 15 minutes   *Yacht: Coral Sea*
Serves: 6

1 cup	**Chopped black olives**
1-1/2 cups	**Grated sharp cheddar cheese**
1/2 cup	**Mayonnaise**
1/4 tsp	**Salt**
1/4 tsp	**Curry powder**
	Triscuit crackers, or your choice

Preheat oven to 400°F/200°C. Mix together olives, cheese, mayonnaise, salt and curry powder. Spread on crackers of your choice. Heat about 15 minutes. *Serve immediately.*

ROMAINE TING

Preparation time: 15 minutes   *Chef: Darla Holmes*
Chilling time: 3 hours   *Yacht: Coral Sea*
Serves: 6

3	**Hearts romaine lettuce**
1/4 cup	**Extra virgin olive oil**
2 Tblsp	**Fresh lemon juice**
2 Tblsp	**Dijon mustard**
1 Tblsp	**Country Dijon mustard**
1 Tblsp	**Honey**
1 Tblsp	**Prepared horseradish**
	Salt and fresh ground pepper

Separate lettuce into leaves, wash and pat dry. Cover and refrigerate to crisp for up to 3 hours. In small bowl whisk together the remaining ingredients. Chill. *Dress lettuce just before serving.*

XCALAK TUNA

Preparation time: 15 minutes
Marinating time: 45 minutes
Cooking time: 10 - 15 minutes - BBQ
Serves: 6

Chef: Darla Holmes
Yacht: Coral Sea

6	**Tuna steaks, 1 inch/2.5 cm thick**
1/4 cup	**Fresh grated ginger**
1/4 cup	**Minced jalapeños**
1/2 cup	**Extra virgin olive oil**
1/2 cup	**Soy sauce**
2 Tblsp	**Dark rum**

Place tuna steaks in shallow baking pan (not metal). Mix all other ingredients together. Pour over steaks and marinate for at least 45 minutes in refrigerator, turning steaks 2 or 3 times. BBQ on hot grill 5 to 7 minutes each side. Do not overcook.

Note: An old Mayan woman in Xcalak, Mexico gave me this recipe. Simple and yummy! A couple extra steaks make wonderful tuna salad for another day. You will never want to eat canned tuna again.

TEQUILA CARROTS

Preparation time: 5 minutes　　　　　　　　*Chef: Darla Holmes*
Cooking time: 15 minutes　　　　　　　　　　*Yacht: Coral Sea*
Serves: 6

1 lb/450 g	**Baby carrots**
2 Tblsp	**Butter**
1 Tblsp	**Dill weed, fresh if available**
2 Tblsp	**Tequila**

Place carrots in a skillet with butter. Cook with lid on over medium heat for about 10 minutes stirring a few times. Reduce heat, add fresh chopped dill weed and cook for 5 minutes more. Carrots should be soft but not mushy. Bring heat up, pour in Tequila and flame. *Serve immediately.*

CAULIFLOWER MASH

Preparation time: 30 minutes　　　　　　　*Chef: Darla Holmes*
Cooking time: 15 minutes　　　　　　　　　　*Yacht: Coral Sea*
Serves: 6

1	**Cauliflower, broken in florets**
1-1/2 cups	**Mashed potatoes**
1/4 cup	**Heavy cream**
4 Tblsp	**Butter, divided**
	Salt and fresh ground pepper
1/4 cup	**Grated gruyère or emmenthaler cheese**
Pinch	**Cayenne**

Preheat oven to 425°F/220°C. Boil cauliflower until tender, or microwave. Drain well and purée in blender. Mix mashed potatoes and cauliflower together, add cream, 2 Tblsp butter, salt and pepper. Put in oven proof casserole. Sprinkle with cheese and dot with remaining butter. Bake 15 minutes or until top is brown.

Hint: Use hot milk when mashing potatoes to keep them from becoming heavy or soggy. Add 1 tsp baking powder to make them light and creamy.

RIO GRANDE MUD PIE

Preparation time: 20 minutes
Cooking time: 40 - 45 minutes
Cooling time: 30 minutes
Serves: 6 - 10

Chef: Darla Holmes
Yacht: Coral Sea

1 cup	Shortening
2 cups	Sugar
4	Eggs
1-1/2 cups	Flour
1/3 cup	Cocoa
1 Tblsp	Vanilla
1 cup	Chopped pecans
16 oz/450 g	Package miniature marshmallows

Icing:

1/3 cup	Cocoa
1 lb/450 g	Powdered sugar
1/2 cup	Butter, melted
1/2 cup	Cream
1 tsp	Vanilla
1 cup	Chopped pecans

Preheat oven to 375°F/190°C. Cream shortening and sugar. Add eggs and beat. Sift flour, cocoa and salt and add to mixture. Add vanilla and nuts. Pour into 9 x 13 inch (23 x 32.5 cm) pan. Bake 40-45 minutes. While still warm cover with marshmallows. When cool spread with icing.

Icing: Sift cocoa with powdered sugar. Add butter to dry ingredients, then cream, vanilla and nuts. Blend and spread over cake.

Note: *There is often a little left over when serving 6 but never any left by the end of the charter.*

DELPHINA SHOPPING LIST

VEGETABLES:
Celery, stalk 1
Garlic .... 1 bulb
Curly lettuce .... 1 head
Green onions 2
Yellow onions 2
Red onions 2
Tomato 1

FRUITS:
Strawberries .... 1 pint

FRESH HERBS:
Cilantro, chopped .... 2 Tblsp
Marjoram, crumbled ...... 1 Tblsp

DRIED SPICES:
Bay leaves 3
Curry .... 1/2 tsp
Nutmeg .... 1/2 tsp
Poppy seeds .... 1 tsp

CONDIMENTS:
Dates, pitted 27
Dijon mustard .... 2 Tblsp
Oil, salad .... 1/4 cup
Olive oil .... 6 Tblsp
Hot pepper .... 1/8 tsp
Crystallized ginger .... 2 Tblsp

DRY GOODS:
Linguine .... 1 lb
Long grain rice .... 3/4 cup
Sugar, granulated .... 1/2 cup

CANS AND JARS:
Mandarin oranges .... 11 oz can
Beef broth .... 1 cup
Chicken broth .... 2 cups

DAIRY/MILK/CHEESE/BUTTER
Butter .... 1 Tblsp
Eggs 7
Gruyère .... 4 oz

NUTS:
Almonds, slivered .... 1/3 cup

MEAT/POULTRY:
Bacon .... 1/2 lb
Chicken breast, boneless 1 - 1/2 lbs
Ham, diced .... 1/4 lb
Pork tenderloin .... 2 lbs

FROZEN:
Spinach, half of .... 10 oz pkg

LIQUORS/WINE/SPIRITS:
Amaretto .... 1/4 cup
White wine .... 1 cup

S/Y DELPHINA

Chef Nancy Heinesen
Captain Lars Heinesen

MENU
Serves 6

Breakfast

Fresh Squeezed Orange Juice
*Spinach and Ham Frittata
Raisin Bread Toast

Lunch

*Curried Rice, Ginger and Chicken Salad
with *Poppy Seed Dressing

Hors d'oeuvre

*Bacon Date Roll Ups

Dinner

Caesar Salad
*Seasoned Pork Tenderloin and Peppers
over Linguine or
Mashed Potatoes

*Tasty Fruit

Captain Lars Heinesen grew up in Denmark; his wife Nancy in San Francisco. In 1992 they sailed their yacht DELPHINA, a 41-foot Islander, on the long journey from California through the Panama Canal to the Caribbean and entered the charter-boat business. Nancy says, "We love the expressions of pleasure on our guests faces when we put up the spinnaker for a great downwind sail, or serve a memorable meal". With Nancy in the galley memorable meals are an everyday occurrence.

*Indicates recipe provided

SPINACH AND HAM FRITTATA

Preparation time: 5 minutes　　　　　　　　*Chef: Nancy Heinesen*
Cooking time: 20 minutes　　　　　　　　　　　*Yacht: Delphina*
Serves: 4

2 Tblsp	Olive oil
2 cloves	Garlic
1/2 pkg	Frozen spinach, thawed and drained
4 oz/115 g	Ham, diced
7	Eggs
1/2 Tblsp	Dijon mustard
4 oz/115 g	Gruyère cheese, grated

Heat oil in skillet, add garlic and cook until fragrant. Mix in ham and spinach. In a separate bowl mix eggs with mustard and pour over ham and spinach. Stir to even out ham and spinach. Cook about 8 minutes. or until eggs start to set. Sprinkle gruyère cheese on top. Put skillet in oven under medium broiler until eggs are set and cheese has started to brown. *Serve with sliced Kiwi fruit, peaches, and toasted raisin bread.*

CURRIED RICE GINGER AND CHICKEN SALAD WITH POPPY SEED DRESSING

Preparation time: 10 minutes
Cooking time: 20 minutes
Serves: 4

Chef: Nancy Heinesen
Yacht: Delphina

2 cups	Chicken broth
3/4 cup	Long grain rice
1 Tblsp	Butter
1/2 tsp	Curry powder
1/2 cup	Chopped celery
1/2 cup	Sliced green onion
2 Tblsp	Chopped crystalized ginger
2 dashes	Hot pepper sauce
2 Tblsp	Snipped cilantro
1-1/2 lbs/675 g	Chicken breasts, boneless and skinless
1 tsp	Black pepper
1/2 tsp	Salt
1 Tblsp	Cooking oil
11 oz/310 g	Can Mandarin oranges, drained, save juice
1	Curly lettuce

In a small saucepan combine broth, rice, butter, and curry powder. Bring to a boil, reduce heat and simmer 15 minutes. Remove from heat and stir in celery, onion, ginger, hot sauce, and cilantro. While rice is cooking put oil in skillet and season chicken with salt and pepper. Cut chicken into bite size strips and brown in skillet 2 to 5 minutes. Line salad bowl with curly lettuce and mound rice in center. Arrange chicken pieces around top and then decorate with oranges and pour over ***Poppy Seed Dressing.***

POPPY SEED DRESSING:
Makes: about 1/3 cup

1/3 cup	Mandarin orange juice
3 Tblsp	Salad oil
1 Tblsp	Dijon mustard
1 tsp	Poppy seeds
1/8 tsp	Hot pepper sauce

Combine all ingredients and either whisk until blended, or put in a jar and shake until blended.

Note: *I make this recipe while preparing breakfast and serve it cold under sail. Add a few slices of French bread to each bowl. Easy to assemble while heeling.*

BACON DATE ROLL UPS

Preparation time: 15 minutes　　　　　　　*Chef: Nancy Heinesen*
Cooking time: 15 minutes　　　　　　　　　*Yacht: Delphina*
Serves: 4

9 slices	**Bacon**
27 ·	**Pitted dates**

Preheat oven to 375°F/190°C. Wrap each piece of bacon around a date, secure with a toothpick. Put on baking tray until bacon is crispy, about 15 minutes. *Serve.*

TASTY FRUIT

Preparation time: 10 minutes　　　　　　　*Chef: Nancy Heinesen*
Cooking time: 5 minutes　　　　　　　　　*Yacht: Delphina*
Serves: 6

1/3 cup	**Slivered almonds**
1/2 cup	**Sugar**
1 pint	**Strawberries***
1/4 cup	**Amaretto**

Put almonds and sugar in nonstick skillet and cook over low heat until sugar melts and caramelizes. Cool and break in pieces. Clean, hull and slice the strawberries; pour amaretto over them and chill. Serve in attractive wine glasses and sprinkle with almond pieces. *Delicious and light.*

*You may use any fruit.

SEASONED PORK LOIN
AND RED PEPPERS OVER PASTA

Preparation time: 90 minutes   *Chef: Nancy Heinesen*
Cooking time: 55 minutes (pressure cooker)   *Yacht: Delphina*
Marinating time: 24 hours
Serves: 6

2-1/2 lbs/1.1 kg	Pork loin
1 tsp	Salt
1 tsp	Ground pepper
1	Bay leaf, crumbled
1 clove	Garlic, crushed
1/2 tsp	Nutmeg
3 Tblsp	Olive oil
2	Onions, sliced
4	Cloves garlic, chopped
2	Red bell peppers, seeded and sliced
1 cup	White wine, dry
1/2 cup	Chopped tomatoes
1 cup	Beef broth
2	Bay leaves
1 Tblsp	Marjoram
1 lb/450 g	Pasta

Make a paste with salt, pepper, bay leaf, garlic and nutmeg. Rub on pork loin. Put in a ziplock bag and refrigerate overnight. In a pressure cooker, sauté pork loin in 2 Tblsp olive oil until brown on all sides. Remove pork and add 1 Tblsp of oil, onions, peppers and garlic. Sauté until onions are soft. Add wine, tomatoes, beef broth, bay leaves and marjoram. Return pork and juices to pot. Cover and simmer for 45 minutes.

Cook pasta as per directions (I use linguine). Slice pork and serve over pasta with the sauce.

Note: *Sometimes I make mashed potatoes instead of pasta. Put a large scoop on each plate and lay slices of pork around the potatoes and then pour sauce over. A nice variation.*

DESIRADE II SHOPPING LIST

VEGETABLES:
Cucumbers 2
Garlic .... 1 lg bulb
Shallots 2
Red onion 1
Yellow onions 2
Red bell peppers 2
Yellow bell peppers 2
Butternut squash .... 3 lbs
Tomatoes 6

FRUITS:
Granny Smith apples .... 3 lbs
Bananas 3
Limes 2
Lemons 3
Mangos 3
Raspberries .... 3 cups
Strawberries .... 3 cups

FRESH HERBS:
Cilantro, chopped .... 1-1/2 tsp
Dill .... 1 bunch
Mint, chopped .... 2 Tblsp
Italian parsley .... 10 leaves

DRIED SPICES:
Cayenne .... 1-1/8 tsp
Cinnamon .... 2 tsp
Cloves .... 3/4 tsp
Cumin .... 1 tsp
Ginger .... 1/2 tsp
Mustard .... 2 tsp
Vanilla bean 1

CONDIMENTS:
Baking soda .... 2 tsp
Cocoa .... garnish
Mustard, Dijon .... 2 tsp
Molasses .... 2/3 cup
Cornstarch .... 1/3 cup
Sugar .... 1 cup
Sugar, brown .... 1-2/3 cups
Oil .... 2 Tblsp

Corn oil .... 3 cups
Extra virgin olive oil .... 1-1/2 cups
Olive oil .... 3 Tblsp
Tabasco .... to taste
Vinegar, cider .... 2 Tblsp
Vinegar, red wine .... 1-1/4 cups

DRY GOODS:
Flour .... 1 cup
Flour, whole wheat .... 1 cup

CANS AND JARS:
Green peppercorns 1
Blackberry preserve .... 1/3 cup
Tomato juice .... 2-1/2 cups
Chicken broth .... 8 cups
Capers .... 4 Tblsp

DAIRY/MILK/CHEESE/BUTTER
Butter .... 2 Tblsp
Unsalted butter .... 8 Tblsp
Cream .... 2/3 cup
Crème fraiche .... garnish
Eggs 10
Milk .... 3 cups
Sour cream .... garnish

MEAT/POULTRY/FISH/SEAFOOD:
Pork tenderloins 3
Lobster .... 2 lbs
Mussels 48

FROZEN:
Raspberries .... 16 oz

LIQUORS/WINE/SPIRITS:
Brandy .... 4 tsp

MISCELLANEOUS:
Coffee, hot brewed .... 2 cups
Instant espresso .... 2 Tblsp
Croissants 8
Puff pastry .... 3 sheets

S/Y DESIRADE II

Chef Connie Harclerode
Captain Robert Cooper

MENU
Serves 8

Breakfast

*Gingerbread Pancakes with
*Apple Cinnamon Compote

Lunch

*Gazpacho
*Cajun Lobster Salad Croissants

Hors d'oeuvre

*Mussels with Green Peppercorn Sauce

Dinner

*Roasted Butternut Squash and Red Onion Soup
*Pork Medallions with Blackberry Sauce and
*Mango Salsa
*Tattooed Potatoes

*Mixed Berry Napoleons with Espresso Cream and
*Raspberry Coulis

The 92-foot DESIRADE II is a beauty both inside and out. Launched in 1998 and designed for high performance sailing, four luxurious cabins sleep 8 guests very comfortably. Robert Cooper is her captain and Connie Harclerode runs the galley. For the past five years Connie has been cooking on various yachts sailing in the Caribbean, Mediterranean and New England. She reports her menus focus on ingredients she may find in the sailing area and on the tastes of her guests. Meals are served in the spacious cockpit or saloon.

*Indicates recipe provided

GINGERBREAD PANCAKES WITH
APPLE CINNAMON COMPOTE

Preparation time: 20 minutes   *Chef: Connie Harclerode*
Standing time: 10 - 15 minutes   *Yacht: Desirade II*
Cooking time: 40 minutes
Serves: 8

2 cups	Hot brewed coffee
1 cup	Brown sugar
2	Large egg
8 Tblsp	Unsalted butter, melted
1 cup	Whole wheat flour
1 cup	Flour
1-1/2 tsp	Baking soda
1 tsp	Ground ginger
1 tsp	Ground cinnamon
1/2 tsp	Ground cloves
1/2 tsp	Salt
	Vegetable oil for brushing griddle

In a large bowl combine coffee and brown sugar. Mix until sugar is dissolved. When coffee is cooled to room temperature, whisk in egg and butter. Add remaining ingredients except oil and whisk until just blended. Batter will be thin. Let batter stand at room temperature for 10 minutes or so, to thicken a little.

Heat griddle over medium-high heat. Brush with oil and ladle batter onto griddle to form pancakes, about 5-inches (12.5 cm) in diameter. Cook pancakes until bubbles appear on surface and undersides are golden brown, about 1 minute. Flip pancakes and cook until golden brown and cooked, about another minute. Place on a warm platter and repeat process until all batter is used.

APPLE CINNAMON COMPOTE:
Makes: 3 cups

3 lbs/1.4 kg	Apples
1 cup	Water
1/3 cup	Brown sugar
2-1/2 Tblsp	Fresh lemon juice
1/2 tsp	Ground cinnamon

Peel, core and cut apples in 3/4 inch (2 cm) pieces. In a saucepan combine the apples with the water and brown sugar. Bring to a boil, stirring occasionally. Reduce heat, cover and simmer until apples are very tender, about 25 minutes. Uncover and simmer until almost all liquid in the saucepan has evaporated, about 6 minutes. Remove from heat and stir in lemon juice and cinnamon.

CAJUN LOBSTER SALAD CROISSANTS

Preparation time: 20 minutes　　　　　　*Chef: Connie Harclerode*
Chilling time: 30 minutes　　　　　　　　　*Yacht: Desirade II*
Serves: 8

4	Eggs
2 Tblsp	Cider vinegar
2 tsp	Dry mustard
2 tsp	Minced garlic
1 tsp	Cumin
1 tsp	Cayenne pepper
1/2 tsp	Salt
3 cups	Corn oil
2	Yellow bell peppers
4 Tblsp	Capers
1-1/2 tsp	Chopped cilantro
2 lbs/900 g	Cooked lobster, cut in chunks
8	Croissants

Combine the eggs, vinegar, mustard, garlic, cumin, cayenne, and salt in a blender. Slowly add the corn oil until emulsified. Seed and finely chop the bell peppers and stir them into the mayonnaise. Add the capers, cilantro and lobster, mix thoroughly. Slice croissants and stuff with lobster salad.

MUSSELS WITH GREEN PEPPERCORN SAUCE

Preparation time: 15 minutes　　　　　　*Chef: Connie Harclerode*
Cooking time: 20 minutes　　　　　　　　　*Yacht: Desirade II*
Serves: 8

48	Fresh mussels
4 tsp	Green peppercorns, drained
4 tsp	Brandy
2/3 cup	Cream
2 tsp	Dijon mustard

Scrub and debeard the mussels. In a saucepan, bring two cups of water to boil. Add the mussels, cover and cook for about 10 minutes or until shells are open. Drain (discard any unopened mussels). Remove top half of each open mussel.

Combine peppercorns, brandy, cream and mustard in a small saucepan and bring to a simmer. Cook for about 5 minutes or until sauce thickens. *Spoon over mussels and serve.*

ROASTED BUTTERNUT SQUASH AND RED ONION SOUP

Preparation time: 30 minutes   *Chef: Connie Harclerode*
Cooking time: 90 minutes   *Yacht: Desirade II*
Serves: 8

3 lbs/1.4 kg	**Butternut squash**
3 lbs/1.4 kg	**Red onion, peeled and quartered**
3 Tblsp	**Olive oil**
1 tsp	**Salt**
1 bulb	**Garlic, peeled**
8 cups	**Chicken stock**
	Tabasco or other hot sauce to taste

Preheat oven to 400°F/200°C. Peel and seed the butternut squash. Cut into pieces (about 2 inches/5 cm) Put squash and red onion into a large roasting pan. Drizzle with olive oil and salt. Roast for 60 minutes. Add garlic, toss and roast for another 30 minutes. Heat chicken stock in saucepan. Add roasted vegetables. Purée in a blender or food processor. Return to saucepan and add tabasco, salt and pepper to taste.

Hint: *The roasted vegetables give the soup a richer flavor than the traditional butternut soup.*

TATTOOED POTATOES

Preparation time: 30 minutes   *Chef: Connie Harclerode*
Cooking time: 90 minutes   *Yacht: Desirade II*
Serves: 8

4 cup	**Extra virgin olive oil**
1 tsp	**Salt**
1 tsp	**Freshly ground pepper**
10	**Italian parsley leaves**
5	**Russet potatoes, unpeeled, cut in half lengthwise**

Preheat oven to 400°F/200°C. Pour olive oil into a glass baking dish, add salt and pepper. Stir to combine. Press parsley leaf on cut side of each potato half and place cut side down in pan. Bake until potatoes are brown, about 45 minutes. While potatoes are roasting gently move them every now and again to keep them from sticking.

GAZPACHO

Preparation time: 20 minutes　　　　　*Chef: Connie Harclerode*
Chilling time: 4 hours　　　　　　　　　　*Yacht: Desirade II*
Serves: 8

1/2 cup	**Red wine vinegar**
1/2 cup	**Extra virgin olive oil**
2-1/2 cups	**Canned tomato juice**
6	**Tomatoes, peeled and seeded**
2	**Red bell peppers, seeded and chopped**
2	**Onions, peeled and quartered**
2	**Shallots, peeled and cut**
2	**Cucumbers, peeled and quartered**
1/8 tsp	**Cayenne pepper**
	Salt and pepper, to taste
3 Tblsp	**Chopped fresh dill**
Garnish:	**Sour cream or crème fraiche**
	Sprigs of dill

Whisk together vinegar, olive oil, and tomato juice. In batches, process the vegetables to coarse mixture, add a small amount of the juice mixture each time. Do not purée completely so that you have some texture. Add cayenne, salt, pepper and the fresh dill. Mix well. Chill at least 4 hours. Serve in chilled bowls with garnish.

Hint: *This soup keeps well.*

PORK MEDALLIONS WITH BLACKBERRY SAUCE AND MANGO SALSA

Preparation time: 20 minutes
Chilling time: 2 hours
Cooking time: 30 minutes
Serves: 8

Chef: Connie Harclerode
Yacht: Desirade II

MANGO SALSA:

1 cup	Ripe mango, peeled and diced
1	Red onion, finely chopped
2	Limes, juiced
2	Limes, zested
2 Tblsp	Chopped fresh mint
	Salt and pepper to taste

BLACKBERRY SAUCE:

3/4 cup	Red wine vinegar
1/3 cup	Blackberry preserves, seedless
1/4 tsp	Salt
3	Pork tenderloins, trimmed and cut into medallions
2 Tblsp	Butter
2 Tblsp	Oil

Salsa: Stir together mango, red onion, lime juice, zest, mint, salt and pepper to taste. Chill. *Better if made ahead of time for flavors to mingle.*

Sauce: In a saucepan, simmer vinegar until reduced to 2/3 cup. Whisk in preserves and salt. Keep warm.

Season pork with salt and pepper. Melt half the butter with half the oil in a heavy skillet over medium-high heat. Sauté pork until cooked through, about 5 minutes on each side, then repeat process.

To serve: Divide **Blackberry Sauce** on 8 warmed plates. Place the pork medallions on the sauce then top with the **Mango Salsa.**

MIXED BERRY NAPOLEON WITH ESPRESSO CREAM AND RASPBERRY COULIS

Preparation time: 30 minutes
Chilling time: 3 hours
Serves: 8

Chef: Connie Harclerode
Yacht: Desirade II

ESPRESSO CREAM:

3 cups	Whole milk
1	Vanilla bean, split lengthwise
8	Large egg yolks
1/2 cup	Sugar
1/2 cup	Brown sugar
1/3 cup	Cornstarch, sifted
2 Tblsp	Instant espresso dissolved in 1 Tblsp hot water

RASPBERRY COULIS:

16 oz/450 g	Pkg unsweetened frozen raspberries
	Sugar syrup to taste

Pastry and Filling:

8	2-1/2 inch (6 cm) commercial puff pastry rounds
6 cups	Mixed berries
3	Bananas, peeled and sliced
Garnish:	Cocoa

Espresso Cream: Pour milk into a heavy saucepan. Scrape seeds from vanilla bean and add seeds and bean to milk. Bring to a simmer, remove from heat and discard bean. In a bowl beat egg yolks and both sugars with an electric mixer, until very thick, about 3 minutes; add cornstarch and blend well. Gradually whisk half of hot milk into egg mixture then add back to saucepan. Whisk over low heat until it thickens and simmer about 4 minutes. Remove from heat and pour in espresso. Transfer to a bowl. Place plastic wrap directly onto surface of cream. Chill at least 3 hours. Bake puff pastry rounds according to instructions. **Raspberry Coulis:** Blend raspberries and sugar syrup together until liquid.

To assemble: Pour a portion of the raspberry coulis on each plate. Cut the pastry circle in half horizontally and place bottom half on plate. Divide pastry cream among each pastry. Top with mixed berries and banana slices, reserving some for garnish. Place top half of pastry on fruit. *Dust with cocoa and garnish with remaining berries and banana slices.*

ELETHEA SHOPPING LIST

VEGETABLES:
Carrots 2
Celery, stalks & leaves 2
Mushrooms .... 1 lb
Onion 1
Shallots 3
Yellow onions 2

FRESH HERBS:
Parsley .... garnish

DRIED SPICES:
Cayenne .... pinch
Curry, Madras .... 2 Tblsp
Garlic powder .... pinch
Marjoram......................... pinch
Paprika .... garnish
Bouquet garni* 1

CONDIMENTS:
Raisins .... 1/4 cup
Mustard .... 1/4 cup
Worchestershire sauce .... 3 Tblsp
Catsup .... 1/4 cup
Beef bouillon .... 1 cube

DRY GOODS:
Flour .... 1/8 cup
Mashed potato, instant ... 1 box
Sugar, brown .... 1/4 cup

CANS AND JARS:
Beef broth .... 1 can
Chicken broth .... 2 cups
Corn, kernel .... 1 can, sml

DAIRY/MILK/CHEESE/BUTTER
Butter .... 1/3-1/2 lb
Parmesan, grated .... 1/4 cup

MEAT/POULTRY/FISH/SEAFOOD:
Beef, ground .... 1 lb
Chicken thighs 12
Rabbit, whole 1

LIQUORS/WINE/SPIRITS:
Red wine .... 2 bottles

MISCELLANEOUS:
Mousseline purée de
pommes de terre .... 9 oz
Green seasoning .... 1/3 cup

*Peppercorns, parsley, bay leaves and thyme.

S/Y ELETHEA

Chef Steven Durban
Captain Robert Birtles

CRUISING 'DOWN ISLAND'

MENU
Serves 4

Breakfast

Breakfast Quiche
Coffee and Tea

Lunch 1

Croissants with Ham and Emmenthaler
Simple Green Salad

Lunch 2

*Deluxe Shepherd's Pie

Dinner 1

*Lapin A La Manfred

Dinner 2

*Harpoon Saloon's Sweet Curried Chicken

ELETHEA, a 40-foot Beneteau sloop, cruises in the Windward Islands every winter. Each year in the fall Captain Robert Birtles and Chef Steven Durban fly down from Canada to Antiqua to prepare their vessel for the season. Sailing, entertaining and cooking — these three endeavors are a sport for them and a favorite way of life. They share that way of life with family and friends who invariably enjoy not only their company but the chef's clever menus — straightforward, easy recipes gathered through the years.

*Indicates recipe provided

CRUISING FROM DESHAIES TO ANTIGUA

Chef: Steven Durban
Yacht: Elethea

PROVISIONING IN DESHAIES:

S/Y Eletha was on her way to Antigua, when she developed an electrical problem and had to drop anchor in Deshaies, Guadeloupe. Steven was going to 'dress up' some canned creation but decided to go ashore and look around after repairing the electrical problem (he is also the boat's electrician). They had never provisioned in Deshaies before and were surprised at what was available. There is an excellent boucherie charcuterie called *La Bonne Entrecôte*, a recently expanded marché call *Ti Prix* and two small outdoor markets with a good supply of fresh fruits and vegetables.

They also found an excellent boulangerie patisserie called *L'Almondine* right at the head of the main dock. It offered a wide selection of quiches, croque monsieurs, croissants, brioches, as well as all kinds of fabulous pastries.

Note: Best to get your francs at a bank, as the merchants seem to use an exchange rate that is several years old and definitely not in your favor.

Breakfast: Breakfast quiche, warmed. Serve with local fruit, fresh baguette and butter. Inexpensive, tasty and easy on the chef.

Lunch—underway: Slice croissants, insert a slice of ham and grated emmenthaler cheese. Put in oven for a few minutes while you make a simple green salad.

Many cookbooks seem to avoid recipes for ground beef. This may be because so much of the ground beef in the Caribbean islands is coarse and often fatty. Provisioning in the French islands offers the opportunity to buy 'boeuf haché' and most butchers will let you chose your cut then grind it up for you. Remember the better the cut, the better the dish. I use the butcher at *Super H* in Fort de France, where you will also find Mousseline instant mashed potatoes, which works well with this recipe.

DELUXE SHEPHERD'S PIE

Preparation time: 30 minutes
Cooking time: 45 minutes
Serves: 6

Chef: Steven Durban
Yacht: Elethea

1 lb/450 g	**Boeuf haché (ground beef), the best cut you can afford**
2 Tblsp	**Butter**
	Garlic powder, parsley, marjoram, cayenne pepper
2	**Medium onions, chopped**
11 oz/310 g	**Small can kernel of corn**
1 cup	**Gravy (see below)**
9 oz/250 g	**Pkg Mousseline purée de pommes de terre (au fromage, if possible)**
	Parmesan cheese
	Butter
	Paprika and parsley
Gravy:	
2 Tblsp	**Butter**
2 Tblsp	**Flour**
1 cube	**Beef bouillon**
1 cup	**Boiling water**
2 Tblsp	**Worcestershire sauce**

Preheat oven to 350°F/180°C. Butter a medium size casserole dish. In a small skillet brown the 'boeuf haché' in butter and season with garlic powder, parsley, marjoram, and a pinch of cayenne pepper. Spread over bottom of casserole dish. In the same skillet add more butter and sauté chopped onions until golden and place on top of 'boeuf'. Drain corn and lay over onions. **Gravy:** In same skillet combine butter and flour into a roux. Dissolve bouillon cube with boiling water and add to skillet, then Worcestershire sauce. Cook until thickened and pour over corn in casserole dish. Make real mashed potatoes, or mousseline according to directions and put on top of gravy. Sprinkle generously with parmesan. Dot with butter, sprinkle with paprika and a little parsley. Bake for 45 minutes. *Serve with additional vegetables such as christophine and carrots or a green salad.*

The following recipe **Lapin à La Manfred** was cooked on Elethea by a Parisian named Manfred. He was an excellent amateur chef but he didn't seem to use measuring spoons and was vague about quantities. In any case, quantities within reason do not seem to matter all that much; the dish is delicious and a lot easier to prepare than it might sound.

LAPIN A LA MANFRED

Preparation time: 30 minutes   Chef: *Steven Durban*
Cooking time: all day   Yacht: *Elethea*
Serves: 6

1	**Rabbit, cut in serving pieces**
	Flour to dredge
6 Tblsp	**Lard or butter (Manfred would object)**
2	**Bottles red wine**
1 cup	**Chopped shallots or onions**
2 cups	**Chicken stock**
2	**Carrots, chopped**
2 stalks	**Celery with leaves, chopped**
1	**Bouquet garni***
1 Tblsp	**Worcestershire sauce**
1 lb/450 g	**Fresh mushrooms or canned (ouch!)**
	Salt and pepper to taste

If you are making a crossing, use a pressure cooker (but not under pressure) in case the crossing gets rough. Dredge rabbit pieces in flour then sauté in lard until lightly browned. Add one bottle red wine (save the other to drink with the meal). Add half the shallots or onions, all the stock, carrots, celery, and seasonings. Simmer and reduce; a crossing from Guadeloupe to Antigua is about the right amount of time (7-9 hours depending on weather and boat).

Twenty minutes before serving, sauté the other half of the onions and the mushrooms in butter and add to the pot. If the sauce is not reduced enough, add a little flour to the butter in the pan (make a roux) and thicken the sauce (Manfred forgive me). *Serve with mashed potatoes or pasta and a local vegetable.*

*Peppercorns, parsley, bay leaves and thyme.

After a stormy crossing from St. Lucia to Bequia, we arrived late on a Sunday evening. Tired and busy from sailing all day, we decided to have dinner ashore only to find out that no restaurants were open; so we went to the *Harpoon Saloon*. Mrs. Cambridge took pity on us and let us share her family's dinner. It was **Sweet Curried Chicken** and it was so delicious that I asked for the recipe. She said there was no recipe, but we could watch her make it the next day. I videotaped the preparation and have experimented with quantities ever since.

HARPOON SALOON'S SWEET CURRIED CHICKEN

Preparation time: 15 minutes　　　　*Chef: Steven Durban*
Cooking time: 1-1/2 hours　　　　　　*Yacht: Elethea*
Serves: 6

10	**Chicken thighs (skin on)**
2 Tblsp	**Madras curry or sweet curry**
1/4 cup	**Ketchup**
1/4 cup	**Regular prepared mustard**
1	**Small onion, chopped**
1/4 cup	**Raisins**
1/3 cup	**Green seasoning***
1/4 cup	**Brown sugar**

In large bowl mix chicken with all ingredients except brown sugar. Sprinkle brown sugar over bottom of a large nonstick frying pan; heat until sugar starts to melt. Brown chicken pieces and remove to large saucepan. Add 1/8 cup water to mixing bowl and scrape all ingredients into saucepan with chicken. Cover and simmer at low temperature. Stir chicken every 15 - 20 minutes for 1 to 1-1/2 hours. Serve with rice and vegetables and remaining sauce.

*Green Seasoning: Found easily in local stores and markets 'down island', especially south of Antigua. It comes in bottles and jars around 14 oz (290 ml) — pesto texture. The ingredients vary — shallots, celery, thyme, vinegar, etc.

ELIZA SHOPPING LIST

VEGETABLES:
Beets, medium 6
Cucumber 1
Garlic .... 2 bulbs
Jalapeños 6
Leeks, medium 6
Lettuce .... 2 cups
Romaine hearts 3
Mushrooms .... 3/4 lb
Shallot 1
Red onions 3
White onion 1
Red bell peppers, small ... 3
Potatoes, small new 12
Spinach .... 10 oz
Zucchini, medium 3
Tomatoes 12
Watercress .... 1 bunch

FRUITS:
Bananas 6
Lime 1
Orange 1
Papaya 1

FRESH HERBS:
Basil .... 1 bunch
Cilantro, chopped .... 1-1/2 Tblsp
Dill .... 1/2 tsp
Mint, minced .... 1 Tblsp
Watercress .... 1 bunch

DRIED SPICES:
Basil .... 2-1/2 tsp
Cinnamon .... 1/4 tsp
Chili powder .... 1-1/4 Tblsp
Cumin seeds .... 1/2 tsp
Ginger, grated .... 1/4 tsp
Oregano .... 1-1/2 tsp

CONDIMENTS:
Baking soda .... 1/2 tsp
Coconut .... 1/2 tsp
Honey .... 2 Tblsp
Mustard, Dijon .... 3 Tblsp
Maple syrup .... 3-4 Tblsp

Mayonnaise .... 3/4 cup
Olive oil .... 3/4 cup
Vinegar, balsamic .... 3 Tblsp
Vinegar, white wine .... 2 Tblsp
Vinegar, sherry .... 1 Tblsp

DRY GOODS:
Flour .... 1-1/3 cups
Oatmeal .... 1/2 cup
Sugar .... 2 Tblsp
Sugar, brown .... 3/4 cup
Sugar, confectioners' .... 1/2 cup

CANS AND JARS:
Anchovy filets 12
Pineapple, crushed .... 1 cup
Chicken broth .... 3/4 cup
Orange juice .... 1/2 cup
Pineapple juice .... 1/2 cup

DAIRY/MILK/CHEESE/BUTTER
Butter .... 1/2 lb
Whipping cream .... 3 Tblsp
Eggs 7
Feta .... 4 oz
Gruyère, shredded .... 1/2 cup
Mozzarella, thick slices ... 6
Parmesan, grated .... 1/4 cup
Roquefort, crumbled .... 1/3 cup

MEAT/POULTRY/FISH/SEAFOOD:
Bacon .... 1 lb
Chicken breast, smoked .. 1 lb
Pork tenderloins 3
Tuna steaks 4

LIQUORS/WINE/SPIRITS:
Rum .... 1/2 cup

BREAD/DOUGH:
English muffins 6
Bread for toast

FROZEN:
Spinach .... 20 oz

S/Y ELIZA

Chef Wendy Weller-Van Ryn
Capt. Paul Van Ryn

MENU
Serves 6

Breakfast

*Fried Eggs with New Potatoes and Spinach

Lunch

*Veggie Tucks
*Romaine and Roasted Beet Salad with
Creamy Roquefort Dressing
*Pineapple Walnut Cookies

Hors d'oeuvre

*Leek Tarts

Dinner

*Mozzarella-topped Peppers with Tomatoes and Garlic
*Grilled Pork Cutlets with
*Papaya and Red Onion Salsa
*Grilled Zucchini and Bell Pepper Couscous

*Barbecued Bananas with Tropical Sauce

Charter sailing on ELIZA, an 80-foot Southern Ocean schooner, combines luxury and superior sailing performance. A full-time crew of four make sure it's "smooth sailing" all the way whether it's sailing with the wind in the rigging, snorkeling at anchor, windsurfing or water-skiing behind one of the tenders. The captain is Paul Van Ryn and his wife is Chef Wendy Weller-Van Ryn who invariably pleases her guests throughout the day from breakfast in the cockpit to dinner in the elegant main saloon.

*Indicates recipe provided

FRIED EGGS WITH NEW POTATOES BACON AND SPINACH

Preparation time: 10 minutes　　　　　　*Chef: Wendy Weller-Van Ryn*
Cooking time: 30 minutes　　　　　　　　　　　　　*Yacht: Eliza*
Serves: 6

2-1/4 lbs/1 kg	**New potatoes, scrubbed and cut into 1/2 inch (1 cm) pieces**
1 lb/450 g	**Bacon slices, chopped**
2 Tblsp	**White wine vinegar**
2 Tblsp	**Minced garlic**
	Salt and pepper
2 - 10 oz/285 g	**Pkgs fresh spinach, stems trimmed**
6	**Large eggs**

Steam potatoes on rack over boiling water until tender, about 9 minutes. Meanwhile cook bacon in heavy large skillet over medium high heat until crisp. Using slotted spoon transfer bacon to paper towels. Pour drippings into small bowl and reserve.

Heat 1 Tblsp drippings in same skillet over medium high heat. Add potatoes and sauté until beginning to brown, about 5 minutes. Transfer to a large bowl. Drizzle with 1 Tblsp vinegar, salt and pepper. Add 1 Tblsp drippings and garlic to skillet. Stir 30 seconds. Add spinach, toss until wilted, about 3 minutes. Sprinkle with 1 Tblsp vinegar, salt and pepper. Divide between 6 plates and top with potatoes; cover loosely with foil Add remaining drippings to skillet. Break in eggs, cover and fry. *Arrange eggs on top of potatoes and sprinkle with bacon.*

VEGGIE TUCKS

Preparation time: 5 minutes   *Chef: Wendy Weller-Van Ryn*
Cooking time: 5 minutes   *Yacht: Eliza*
Serves: 6

1	**Medium red onion, sliced**
12 oz/335 g	**Mushrooms, sliced**
1 Tbslp	**Olive oil**
1 Tblsp	**Butter**
10 oz/285 g	**Fresh spinach**
6	**English muffins, split**
6 slices	**Provolone cheese**
Garnish:	**Fresh orange slices**

Sauté onions and mushrooms in oil and butter, then add spinach. Toast English muffins. Place vegetables on muffins and a slice of cheese. Put top on muffin, garnish and serve.

LEEK TARTS

Preparation time: 10 minutes   *Chef: Wendy Weller-Van Ryn*
Cooking time: 12 minutes   *Yacht: Eliza*
Serves:8

10 oz/280 g	**Refrigerated pizza dough**
6	**Medium leeks, thinly sliced**
3 cloves	**Garlic, minced**
2 Tblsp	**Olive oil**
1 tsp	**Dried basil**
2 Tblsp	**Dijon mustard**
1 Tblsp	**Water**
1 cup	**Shredded gruyère or swiss cheese**
1/4 cup	**Pine nuts or chopped almonds, toasted**

Preheat oven to 425°F/220°C. Unroll dough on greased baking sheet. Roll or press to 12 x 9 inch (30 x 23 cm). Bake for 7 minutes. Cool. Meanwhile cook leeks and garlic in oil for 5 minutes or until tender. Remove from heat and stir in basil. Stir together mustard and water, then spread over baked crust. Top with leek mixture, cheese, and nuts. Bake for 8 minutes or until bubbly. *Let stand before cutting into small pieces.*

ROMAINE AND ROASTED BEET SALAD WITH CREAMY ROQUEFORT DRESSING

Preparation time: 15 minutes
Cooking time: 1 hour 15 minutes
Serves: 6

Chef: Wendy Weller-Van Ryn
Yacht: Eliza

Dressing:

1/2 cup	Mayonnaise
1	Large shallot. minced
1 Tblsp	Sherry vinegar
1 clove	Garlic, minced
2 tsp	Dijon mustard
1/3 cup	Roquefort cheese, crumbled
3 Tblsp	Whipping cream
	Salt and pepper

Salad:

6	Medium beets, tops trimmed
3 hearts	Romaine lettuce, quartered lengthwise ends intact
1	Small red onion, thinly sliced
1 bunch	Watercress, thick stems trimmed
1/2 cup	Walnut halves, toasted

Dressing: Whisk first 5 ingredients in small bowl and blend. Fold in roquefort cheese and cream. Season dressing with salt and pepper.

Note: This can be prepared 1 day ahead. Cover and refrigerate.

Salad: Preheat oven to 400°F/200°F. Wrap beets tightly in foil. Bake until tender about 1 hour and 15 minutes. Cool beets; peel and cut into wedges. Arrange 2 lettuce quarters crosswise on each of 6 large plates. Surround lettuce with beet wedges. Top with some onion slices and watercress sprigs. Drizzle with dressing. *Sprinkle with walnuts.*

PINEAPPLE WALNUT COOKIES

Preparation time: 20 minutes　　　*Chef: Wendy Weller-Van Ryn*
Cooking time: 12 minutes　　　　　　　　　　　　*Yacht: Eliza*
Serves: 10

8 oz	Unsweetened crushed pineapple, drain, reserve juice
1/3 cup	Butter, softened
2/3 cup	Brown sugar, firmly packed
1	Egg white
1/2 tsp	Coconut extract
1-1/4 cups	All purpose flour
1/2 tsp	Baking soda
1/4 cup	Walnuts, chopped

Glaze:

2 Tblsp	Sugar
1 Tblsp	Butter
1/2 cup	Powdered sugar, sifted
1-1/2 Tblsp	Pineapple juice

Preheat oven to 350°F/180°C. Pat pineapple with paper towel to remove excess moisture; set aside. Cream 1/3 cup butter, gradually adding brown sugar at medium speed. Add egg white and coconut extract. Mix well. Combine flour and soda and add to creamed mixture, beat well at medium speed. Stir in pineapple and walnuts. Shape dough into cookies, place on baking tray and bake for 10 to 12 minutes.

Glaze: Combine sugar and butter in small pan. Cook on low stirring constantly until butter melts. Add juice and bring to a boil. Remove from heat and add powdered sugar. *Glaze cookies.*

MOZZARELLA TOPPED PEPPERS WITH TOMATOES AND GARLIC

Preparation time: 10 minutes
Cooking time: 53 minutes
Serves:6

Chef: Wendy Weller-Van Ryn
Yacht: Eliza

2 Tblsp	Olive oil
3	Small red bell pepper, halved lengthwise, seeded, stems left intact
3 cups	Tomatoes, chopped and seeded
1 Tblsp	Minced garlic
	Salt and pepper
12	Anchovy fillets, drained
6	1/3 inch (8 mm) thick slices fresh mozzarella
Garnish:	Chopped fresh basil

Preheat oven to 375°F/190°C. Oil baking sheet. Arrange peppers, cut side up. Mix tomatoes and garlic in a medium bowl. Season with salt and pepper. Fill pepper cavities with tomato mixture. Drizzle 1 tsp oil over each. Place 2 anchovy fillets atop of each. Bake until peppers are tender about 50 minutes. Arrange chesse on top of anchovies. Bake until cheese melts about 3 minutes. Transfer peppers to platter. *Sprinkle with basil and serve.*

GRILLED PORK TENDERLOIN CUTLETS WITH PAPAYA RED ONION SALSA

Preparation time: 20 minutes　　　　*Chef: Wendy Weller-Van Ryn*
Marinating time: 24 hours　　　　　　　　　　　　　*Yacht: Eliza*
Cooking time: 10 minutes
Serves:6

2 Tblsp	**Salt**
3 cups	**Water**
3 - 1-1/2 lbs/675 g	**Pork tenderloins**

Glaze:

2-1/4 Tblsp	**Water**
2-1/4 Tblsp	**Pure maple syrup**
1-1/4 Tblsp	**Chili powder**

In a large covered bowl or large ziplock bag, mix together salt and water until salt is dissolved. Add pork making sure it is completely covered by brine. Marinate pork covered and chilled for 24 hours.

Prepare grill. In a small bowl stir together syrup and chili powder. Discard brine; diagonally cut pork into 3/4 inch (2 cm) pieces. Put pork between sheets of plastic wrap and flatten with rolling pin to make 1/4 inch (5 mm) thick cutlets. Pat pork dry. Grill pork lightly on oiled rack set 6 inches (15 cm) over glowing coals until cooked through, about 2 to 3 minutes on each side. Brush pork with glaze and grill 15 seconds more on each side. *Serve with* **Papaya Red Onion Salsa.**

Note: Alternatively, pork may be cooked in a hot well seasoned ridged grill pan over moderately high heat.

PAPAYA AND RED ONION SALSA:
Preparation time: 20 minutes

2/3 cup	**Chopped firm ripe papaya**
2 Tblsp	**Minced red onion**
1/2 Tblsp	**Minced fresh jalapeños**
1-1/2 Tblsp	**Chopped fresh cilantro**
1 Tblsp	**Fresh lime juice**
1-1/2 tsp	**Pure maple syrup**

In a bowl, mix all ingredients and season with salt.

Note: *Salsa may be made a day ahead. Keep chilled and covered.*

GRILLED ZUCCHINI AND BELL PEPPER COUSCOUS

Preparation time: 15 minutes   Chef: Wendy Weller-Van Ryn
Cooking time: 15 minutes   Yacht: Eliza
Serves: 6

3	**Zucchini**
2	**Small red bell peppers**
1-1/2 tsp	**Olive oil**
3 cloves	**Garlic**
1/2 tsp	**Salt**
1/2 tsp	**Cumin seeds**
3/4 cup	**Chicken broth**
1-1/8 cups	**Water**
1-1/8 cups	**Coucous**

Prepare grill. Trim zucchini and cut each lengthwise into 1/4 inch (5 cm) slices. Quarter bell peppers lengthwise discarding seeds, stem, and ribs. Brush zucchini with oil and grill with red peppers on lightly oiled rack set 6 inches (15 cm) over glowing coals until zucchini is tender and peppers are crisp and tender, about 5 minutes each side.

Hint: You can also cook in a hot well seasoned ridged pan over moderately high heat. Cut zucchini into 1 inch (2.5 cm) wide pieces and peppers into 1/4 inch (5 mm) wide strips.

Mince garlic and mash to a paste with salt. Set aside. In a dry 1-1/2 quart (1.4L) heavy saucepan toast cumin seeds over moderately low heat, swirling pan occasionally until fragrant, about 1 minute. Add broth and water and bring to a boil. Add coucous and immediately cover pan. Let stand 5 minutes.With a fork fluff coucous and toss in a bowl with vegetables, garlic paste, and salt to taste.

BARBECUED BANANAS WITH TROPICAL SAUCE

Preparation time: 10 minutes
Cooking time: 30 minutes
Serves: 6

Chef: Wendy Weller-Van Ryn
Yacht: Eliza

2 Tblsp	**Butter**
2 Tblsp	**Honey**
1/2 cup	**Rum**
1/2 cup	**Pineapple juice**
1/2 cup	**Orange juice**
1/4 tsp	**Cinnamon**
1/4 tsp	**Ground ginger**
8	**Bananas, ripe but firm**
1/2 cup	**Oatmeal**
2 Tblsp	**Brown sugar**
1 Tblsp	**Flour, may be less**
	Nuts, crushed, optional

Heat grill. In a saucepan melt the butter and honey, Stir in the rum, juices, cinnamon and ginger. Bring to a boil and simmer for a few minutes. Leave in saucepan until ready to serve.

BBQ bananas over coals for about 7 minutes. Remove from heat and peel (be careful as they are very hot). Place on plate and pour sauce over bananas. *Serve immediately.*

Note: *Bananas may be baked. Place peeled uncooked bananas in a baking dish. Sprinkle with oatmeal mixture, then pour sauce over. Bake in moderate oven until bananas are soft, about 10 to 15 minutes at 350°F/180°C.*

ENDLESS SUMMER SHOPPING LIST

VEGETABLES:
Cucumber 1
Garlic .... 1 bulb
Salad greens .... 2 cups
Rocket lettuce .... 2 cups
White onion 1
Potatoes, small 12
Tomatoes 8

FRESH HERBS:
Basil .... 1 bunch
Dill .... 1/2 tsp
Mint .... 1 bunch

DRIED SPICES:
Basil .... 1 tsp
Oregano .... 1-1/2 tsp

CONDIMENTS:
Olive oil .... 1/2 cup
Vinegar, balsamic .... 3 Tblsp
Mayonnaise .... 1/4 cup
Mustard .... 1/4 cup

DAIRY/MILK/CHEESE/BUTTER
Butter .... 6 oz
Feta .... 4 oz
Parmesan, shaved .... 1/4 cup

MEAT/POULTRY/FISH/SEAFOOD:
Chicken breast, smoked
.... 1 lb
Tuna steaks 4

BREAD/DOUGH:
Bread, loaf 1
Toast slices 16

S/Y ENDLESS SUMMER

Chef and Captain Penny Whiting

A SAILING DAY IN NEW ZEALAND

MENU
Serves 4

Breakfast

Plunge Coffee
Juice
*Tomatoes on Toast
Fresh Fruit
More Coffee

Lunch

*Smoked Chicken Sailing Sandwich
Potato Chips
Assorted Drinks

Dinner

*Seared Tuna and
*Potato Wedges Rangitoto Style
Rocket Salad
Fresh Fruit

More Coffee

Learn to sail and have fun at the same time. Captain/Chef Penny Whiting gives 5 lessons lasting 3 hours each on her 50-foot yacht ENDLESS SUMMER out of Auckland in New Zealand (summer months only, November through March). At the same time, along with all the comforts and pleasures of a cruising vacation, Penny has gained fame as a teacher, having run her unique and successful sailing school for the past 33 years.

*Indicates recipe provided

TOMATOES ON TOAST

Preparation time: 5 minutes   *Chef: Penny Whiting*
Cooking time: 5 minutes   *Yacht: Endless Summer*
Serves: 4

1 Tblsp	**Garlic butter**
1 tsp	**Olive oil**
1/2 tsp	**Celery salt**
1 tsp	**Ground black pepper**
2	**Tomatoes, sliced**
1/2 tsp	**Dill**
1 Tblsp	**Chopped fresh basil**
1 Tblsp	**Chopped fresh mint**
8 slices	**Toast**
Garnish:	**Basil or mint leaves**

In a saucepan, melt garlic butter and olive oil. Season with salt and pepper. Add tomatoes. Stir, cover and reduce heat. Cook 2 minutes, then add dill, basil and mint. Turn off heat and leave 2 minutes longer. *Serve on toast. Garnish. Serve with pots of coffee!*

SMOKED CHICKEN SAILING SANDWICH

Preparation time: 10 minutes   *Chef: Penny Whiting*
Serves: 4   *Yacht: Endless Summer*

8 slices	**Bread, toasted**
	Mustard
	Mayonnaise
1 lb/450 g	**Smoked chicken breast, sliced**
	Salt and pepper, to taste
	Salad greens
4 oz/115 g	**Feta cheese**
	Cucumber, peel and sliced

Spread mustard on 4 slices of bread. Spread mayonnaise on the other 4. Add chicken on mustard side, sprinkle with salt and pepper. Add salad greens, feta cheese and cucumber. Cover with mayonnaise slice of bread. *Serve with potato chips.*

SEARED TUNA

Preparation time: 5 minutes   *Chef: Penny Whiting*
Marinating time: 15 minutes   *Yacht: Endless Summer*
Cooking time: 6 minutes
Serves: 4

4	**Tuna steaks**
	Freshly ground pepper
1/3 cup	**Olive oil**
3 Tblsp	**Balsamic vinegar**
2 tsp	**Garlic paste, or crushed garlic**
	Rocket or kos lettuce, or lettuce
	of your choice
1	**White onion, sliced**
	Fresh shaved parmesan
	Salt and pepper to taste
	Vinaigrette dressing of your choice

Heat BBQ or hot iron pan to high. Season tuna with pepper on both sides. Place oil and vinegar in flat dish. Add tuna and spread with garlic paste. Marinate for 10 minutes, turn tuna and marinate another 5 minutes. Cook about 3 minutes on each side. Only turn once "let it cook". Do not overcook. *Best cooked rare.* Wash, dry and tear lettuce. Place in a bowl, add onion, plenty of fresh parmesan, salt and pepper. *Pour over vinaigrette dressing.*

POTATO WEDGES RANGITOTO STYLE

Preparation time: 5 minutes   *Chef: Penny Whiting*
Cooking time: 20 minutes   *Yacht: Endless Summer*
Serves: 4

12	**Small potatoes, washed**
1/2 cup	**Garlic butter**
2 Tblsp	**Olive oil**
1 Tblsp	**Dried herbs of your choice**
	Salt and pepper

Boil potatoes until just about cooked, but still firm. Drain. In a saucepan heat garlic butter, oil and dried herbs. Cut potatoes in quarters and add to saucepan. Cook on high with lid on. Do not stir. Let brown a little, then shake or toss to coat other side.

EQUITY SHOPPING LIST

VEGETABLES:
Eggplant .... 1-1/2 lbs
Garlic cloves 7
Mushrooms 3
Red onion 1
White onions 4
Yellow bell pepper, small 1
Potatoes, medium 4
Potatoes .... 3 lbs
Zucchini 3
Tomatoes, large 9
Watercress .... 1 bunch

FRUITS:
Limes 2
Lemons 2
Strawberries .... 1 cup
Strawberries .... garnish

FRESH HERBS:
Basil, chopped .... 6 Tblsp
Mint, chopped .... 1/4 cup
Mint .... garnish
Nutmeg .... garnish
Parsley, chopped .... 1/2 cup

DRIED SPICES:
Herbes de Provence .... 1/8 tsp
Mustard .... 1 tsp

CONDIMENTS:
Coconut, shredded .... 3/4 cup
Vanilla .... 1 tsp
Mustard, Dijon .... 1/2 tsp
Oil .... 1/2 cup
Olive oil .... 1-3/4 cups
Vinegar, balsamic .... 2 Tblsp
Vinegar, cider .... 1/4 cup
Tabasco .... 2 tsp
Worchestershire .... 3-1/2 tsp

DRY GOODS:
Sugar .... 1 tsp
Sugar, brown .... 1/4 cup

CANS AND JARS:
Black olives, pitted 12
Capers .... 3 Tblsp
Sweetened condensed milk 1 cup

DAIRY/MILK/CHEESE/BUTTER
Butter .... 1/4-1/2 lb
Garlic butter .... 9 Tblsp
Whipping cream .... 3 Tblsp
Eggs 13
Feta .... 4 oz
Gruyère, shredded .... 1/2 cup
Mozzarella, thick slices ... 6
Parmesan, grated .... 1/4 cup
Roquefort, crumbled .... 1/3 cup

MEAT/POULTRY/FISH/SEAFOOD:
Bacon slices 6
Mahi Mahi .... 2-1/2 lbs
Shrimp, large 24

BREAD/DOUGH:
Sour dough loaf 1

S/Y EQUITY

Chef Bronwyn Carrick
Captain Richard Stevens

MENU
Serves 6

Breakfast

*Omelette Savoyarde

Lunch

*Hot and Sour Pickled Shrimp
*Roasted Tomato Salad
Crusty Bread

Hors d'oeuvres

*Baked Brie in Bread
Bread Sticks

Dinner

*Italian Baked Mahi Mahi
*Duchess Potatoes
*Grilled Zucchini

*Coconut Custard with Strawberry Lemon Sauce

EQUITY is a 56-foot state of the art cruising catamaran. Her captain is Richard Stevens, her chef Bronwyn Carrick, both having sailed to the Caribbean from South Africa. Richard has an impressive background, having competed in some of the world's most famous yacht races. Bronwyn's culinary skills have developed from the great chefs she has worked with in the past and her travels in the Mediterranean, the Atlantic and the Pacific. Her desserts always gain applause from Equity's guests, and the crew!

*Indicates recipe provided

OMELETTE SAVOYARDE

Preparation time: 15 minutes   *Chef: Bronwyn Carrick*
Cooking time: 30 minutes   *Yacht: Equity*
Serves: 6

4	**Medium size potatoes**
2 Tblsp	**Butter**
1 Tblsp	**Olive oil**
6 slices	**Bacon**
2	**Medium onions, chopped**
8	**Eggs, lightly beaten**
1 cup	**Coarsely grated gruyère cheese**
	Salt and freshly milled black pepper

Peel and cut the potatoes into small cubes. Pat them dry. Use an 8 inch (20 cm) diameter skillet, two if available. Melt the butter and oil together over medium heat. Add the potatoes, tossing until they begin to turn golden and are almost cooked. Add the bacon and onion and cook for a few more minutes, until the onion is soft.

Preheat the grill/broiler to its highest setting. Heat the two skillets over high heat. Divide the potato mixture and put in the two skillets. Divide the eggs and pour over the potato mixture, adding a little salt and pepper. Sprinkle the cheese over the top of each. Using a palette knife, or fork, pull the outside of the omelette inward, allowing the liquid egg to flow around the edges. Place the skillet under the grill/broiler for a few moments to set the top.

Note: If you only have one small skillet, cook half the mixture at a time.

Hint: *This can also be prepared as one large omelette. Slice and serve hot or cold with a crisp green salad for lunch.*

HOT AND SOUR PICKLED SHRIMP

Preparation time: 10 minutes   *Chef: Bronwyn Carrick*
Marinating time: 48 hours   *Yacht: Equity*
Serves: 6

24	Large shrimp
1/2	Yellow bell pepper
1/2	Red bell pepper
1/4 cup	Chopped red onion
1/2	Lemon, sliced thin
1 Tblsp	Capers
1/2 cup	Olive Oil
1 tsp	Dry mustard
1/4 cup	Cider vinegar
1/4 cup	Lime juice
1 Tblsp	Worcestershire sauce
1-1/2 tsp	Tabasco
	Salt and pepper
1 tsp	Sugar

Remove heads from shrimp and peel, leaving tails on. Slice the peppers and lemon very thin. In a flat non reactive dish, layer the shrimp, peppers, onion, and capers. In a separate bowl whisk the oil, mustard, vinegar, lime juice, worcestershire sauce and tabasco, adding salt, pepper, and sugar. Pour over shrimp. Cover and refrigerate for at least 48 hours. Stir occasionally. *Serve the shrimp with lots of marinade and fresh crunchy French bread.*

Hint: *For those who prefer the shrimp cooked, remove the shrimp from the marinade, heat a little oil and butter in a skillet and cook until they turn pink.*

ROASTED TOMATO SALAD

Preparation time: 15 minutes   *Chef: Bronwyn Carrick*
Cooking time: 50 minutes   *Yacht: Equity*
Serves: 6

6	**Large tomatoes**
	Salt and pepper, to taste
4 cloves	**Garlic, minced**
6 Tblsp	**Extra virgin olive oil**
1/4 cup	**Chopped fresh basil**
2 Tblsp	**Balsamic vinegar**

Preheat oven to 400°F/200°C. Blanch and skin tomatoes. Leave for 1 minute. Cut each tomato in half and place in roasting pan, cut side up. Sprinkle tomatoes with salt and pepper, garlic, 4 Tblsp olive oil, and basil. Place pan in top half of the oven and roast for 50 minutes, or until edges are slightly blackened. Remove from oven and allow to cool. Whisk 2 Tblsp olive oil and balsamic vinegar and drizzle over tomatoes. *Serve with lots of crusty bread.*

BAKED BRIE IN BREAD

Preparation time: 10 minutes   *Chef: Bronwyn Carrick*
Cooking time: 20 minutes   *Yacht: Equity*
Serves: 6

1 loaf	**Sour dough bread, round shape**
1 Tblsp	**Butter**
1	**Onion, finely chopped**
1 clove	**Garlic, minced**
8 oz/225 g	**Cream cheese**
8 oz/225 g	**Brie, skinned**
1 Tblsp	**Brown sugar**
2 Tblsp	**Sour cream**
	Worcestershire sauce

Preheat oven to 350°F/180°C. Cut top off the bread and remove the center. In a saucepan melt butter, add onion and garlic. Cook until onion is softened. Add cheeses, sugar, sour cream, and worcestershire sauce; continue cooking until sugar is melted. Pour mixture into center of the bread and bake for 15-20 minutes. *Serve with crudités or bread sticks.*

ITALIAN BAKED MAHI MAHI

Preparation time: 10 minutes   *Chef: Bronwyn Carrick*
Cooking time: 50 minutes   *Yacht: Equity*
Serves: 6

2-1/2 lbs/1.1 kg	Mahi Mahi, or 6 thick fillets
2 Tblsp	Olive oil
1	Medium onion, chopped
2 cloves	Garlic, crushed
2 - 16 oz/450 g	Cans Italian style tomatoes
	Salt and pepper to taste
1/2 cup	Thinly sliced mushrooms
2 Tblsp	Chopped fresh basil
2 Tblsp	Chopped capers
1	Lemon, juiced
12	Pitted black olives

Preheat oven to 375°F/190°C. Heat the olive oil in a saucepan over medium heat. Sauté onion and garlic for a few minutes. Add tomatoes, season with salt and pepper; bring to simmer and cook gently, uncovered, for 15 minutes. Stir occasionally. Add mushrooms, simmer 10 minutes until the mixture looks like a thick sauce. Stir in the basil and capers.

Place the fish in a shallow baking dish. Season with pepper and squeeze a little lemon juice on each piece. Spoon an equal quantity of the sauce on each piece of fish and arrange a few olives on top. Cover with foil and bake on a high shelf for about 25 minutes, depending on the thickness of the fish. Do not overcook.

Hints: Fish is cooked when it flakes easily. Do not overcook, it will be dry and tough. *You may use any white fish.*

DUCHESS POTATOES

Preparation time: 10 minutes   *Chef: Bronwyn Carrick*
Cooking time: 1 hour   *Yacht Equity*
Serves: 6

3 lbs/1.4 kg	**Potatoes, halved**
6 oz/170 g	**Butter**
2	**Egg yolks, divided**
	Salt and black pepper
	Nutmeg

Place potatoes in a saucepan of water, cover and bring to a boil. Cook gently for 20 minutes or until tender.

Preheat oven to 375°F/190°C. Drain potatoes and mash until free of lumps. Mix in the butter, 1 egg yolk, salt and pepper. Put the potato mixture into a piping bag fitted with a large star nozzle. Pipe onto greased baking trays into "coils". Brush with egg wash and sprinkle with nutmeg. Bake for about 30 minutes or until golden brown.

Hint: *When filling bag with potatoes, place bag in a jug.*

GRILLED ZUCCHINI

Preparation time: 1 hour   *Chef: Bronwyn Carrick*
Cooking time: 10 minutes   *Yacht: Equity*
Serves: 6

3	**Zucchini**
	Olive oil
	Italian herbs or herbes de Provence

Slice zucchini as thin as possible lengthwise (a mandolin slicer works well). Rinse and cover the zucchini with paper towels and leave to dry. Heat grill or skillet; brush zucchini with olive oil, sprinkle with herbs and cook until lightly browned on both sides.

COCONUT CUSTARD WITH STRAWBERRY LEMON SAUCE

Preparation time: 10 minutes　　　　　*Chef: Bronwyn Carrick*
Cooking time: 25 minutes　　　　　　　　　　*Yacht: Equity*
Cooling time: 45 minutes
Serves: 4 - 6

2	**Eggs**
1	**Egg yolk**
1 cup	**Sweetened condensed milk**
2 cups	**Whole milk**
1 tsp	**Vanilla extract**
3/4 cup	**Shredded coconut**

STRAWBERRY-LEMON SAUCE:

1 cup	**Strawberries**
1/4 cup	**Confectioners' sugar**
1/2	**Lemon, juiced**
Garnish:	**Small strawberries and fresh mint leaves**

Preheat oven to 350°F/180°C. Butter 6 ramekins, place in refrigerator. In a medium bowl, beat the eggs and yolk until frothy. Beat in condensed milk, whole milk and vanilla extract. Fold in coconut. Pour custard mixture into ramekins and place in Bain-Marie (baking dish filled with water 2/3 the height of the ramekins). Bake for 25 minutes or until custard is set and golden brown. Remove ramekins from oven and water. Let cool at room temperature, about 45 minutes.

In a blender purée strawberries with confectioners' sugar, add lemon juice and pulse until incorporated.

To serve: *Pour an equal amount of the strawberry-lemon sauce on each plate. Unmold the custard onto the sauce and decorate with small strawberry and mint leaf.*

FLAMBOYANCE SHOPPING LIST

VEGETABLES:
Broccoli .... 1-1/2 cups
Garlic .... 2 bulbs
Jalapeños 2
Mesclun .... 10 cups
Crimini mushrooms .... 1/2 lb
Shallots, large 20
White onions 5
Tomatoes, roma 4

FRUITS:
Limes 2
Lemons 2
Mangos 2
Strawberries .... 1 cup
Strawberries .... garnish

FRESH HERBS:
Basil, chopped .... 1/2 cup
Cilantro, chopped .... 1/4 cup
Ginger, grated .... 1/4 tsp
Rosemary sprig 1

DRIED SPICES:
Bay leaf 1
Oregano .... 1/4 tsp

CONDIMENTS:
Maple syrup .... 1 bottle
Canola oil .... 3/4 cup
Olive oil .... 4 Tblsp
Peanut oil .... 1/2 cup
Vinegar, balsamic .... 1/3 cup

DRY GOODS:
Flour .... 1/2 cup
Rice, long grain .... 1-1/2 cup
Sugar .... 4 Tblsp
Sugar, confectioners' .... garnish

CANS AND JARS:
Cannelloni beans .... 1 can
Beef consommé .... 1 can
French onion soup .... 1 can

DAIRY/MILK/CHEESE/BUTTER
Butter .... 1/2 lb
Eggs 9
Whole milk .... 1/2 cup
Brie, medium wheel 1
Mixture of several cheeses 3/4 lb
Yogurt, different flavors 2-3

MEAT/POULTRY/FISH/SEAFOOD:
Pork tenderloin .... 3 lbs

LIQUOR/WINE/SPIRITS:
Cassis .... 3 Tblsp
Tequila .... 1/4 cup
Wine, red .... 1 cup

MISCELLANEOUS:
Butter crackers .... 1 pkg
Tortillas, corn 10
Walnuts, chopped .... 3/4 cup
Cookies or cake .... 3 cups

FROZEN:
Raspberries .... 12 oz pkg

S/Y FLAMBOYANCE

Chef Teresa Dancy
Captain Jim Fritz

MENU
Serves 4

Breakfast

*German Oven Pancake

Lunch

*Brie Salad with Raspberry Vinaigrette
*Clean Out Quiche

Hors d'oeuvres

*Easy Tortilla Chips
*Tropical Tomato Mango Salsa
*Drunken Mushrooms

Dinner

*Cannelloni Beans and Tomato Salad
*Pork Tenderloin Medallions with
*Caramelized Shallots and Cassis
*Rice Mélangé
Steamed Spinach

*Quick Parfait Ideas

FLAMBOYANCE, a custom-built for charter 60-foot schooner, is named after the brilliantly flowered tree that is symbolic of the Caribbean. Captain Jim Fritz, a native New Englander, has realized his dream of living a sailing life. He is also a PADI scuba instructor. Chef Teresa Dancy, described as the perfect hostess, plans her menus with care and imagination and often seats her 8 guests in the cockpit for drinks, hors d'oeuvres and dinner under the deep blue Caribbean sky with its twinkling stars.

*Indicates recipe provided

GERMAN OVEN PANCAKE

Preparation time: 5 minutes   *Chef: Teresa Dancy*
Chilling time: 2 hours   *Yacht: Flamboyance*
Cooking time: 20 minutes
Serves: 4

1/2 cup	**Flour**
3	**Eggs, slightly beaten**
1/2 cup	**Milk**
2 Tblsp	**Melted butter**
1/4 tsp	**Salt**
Garnish:	**Fresh strawberry slices, lemon wedges, powdered sugar, maple syrup**

Note: Chill a 10 inch (25 cm) greased Pyrex baking dish 2 hours before adding mixture. Preheat oven to 450°F/230°C. In a bowl beat flour and eggs together, using a rotary beater or whisk. Stir in remaining ingredients and pour into the chilled baking dish. Bake for 20 minutes. Pancake will puff. Cut into wedges. Garnish with sliced strawberries, fresh lemon slices, butter and powdered sugar. Serve with maple syrup.
Hint: *Also terrific with apple pie filling as a topping.*

BRIE SALAD WITH RASPBERRY VINAIGRETTE

Preparation time: 10 minutes   *Chef: Teresa Dancy*
Cooking time: 4 minutes   *Yacht: Flamboyance*
Serves: 4

12 oz/336 g	**Pkg frozen raspberries**
1/3 cup	**Balsamic vinegar**
2/3 cup	**Canola oil**
2 Tblsp	**Sugar**
1/8 tsp	**Salt**
6 cups	**Mesclun greens or attractive lettuce**
1	**Medium size wheel of brie cheese**
3/4 cup	**Chopped walnuts**

Preheat oven to 400°F/200°C. Blend first 5 ingredients in the food processor. Strain to remove seeds. Divide greens on salad plates. Spray baking tray with liquid butter (e.g. Pam). Cut brie into 16 wedges and place on baking tray and soften brie in oven, about 4 minutes. Watch closely. Remove brie to plates with spatula and place on center of greens. Drizzle dressing over brie and greens. Sprinkle with chopped nuts.

Hint: *For an entree add grilled chicken or salmon. Also you can substitute a good mozzarella or goat cheese for the brie.*

CLEAN OUT QUICHE

Preparation time: 15 minutes
Cooking time: 40 minutes
Serves: 6 - 8

Chef: Teresa Dancy
Yacht: Flamboyance

1-1/2 cups	Fresh or frozen spinach, broccoli, zucchini or yellow squash
1	Medium onion. chopped
1 Tblsp	Olive oil
6	Eggs, beaten
3/4 lb/336 g	Cheddar, muenster, swiss, monterey jack, mozzarella, havarti, or american cheese, shredded
1/8 tsp	Salt
1/8 tsp	Pepper

Heat oven to 325°F/160°C. In a skillet with olive oil, cook vegetables of choice with chopped onion over medium heat until tender. Let cool slightly, then beat in eggs with cheese of choice. Stir in salt and pepper. Pour into a 9 inch (23 cm) baking dish and cook for 40 minutes. *Cut into wedges.*

Hint: *This is a great way to use up everything—eggs, cheeses, veggies, ham or lunch meats.*

EASY TORTILLA CHIPS

Preparation time: 2 minutes　　　　　　*Chef:Teresa Dancy*
Cooking time: 20 minutes　　　　　　　*Yacht: Flamboyance*
Serves: 8

	Peanut oil
10	**Tortillas, regular or flavored**
	Salt

Heat a little oil in a heavy skillet over medium-high heat. Cut tortillas in wedges with pizza cutter or kitchen shears. Lay a few in skillet. Fry quickly, turning when brown. Salt after turning. Drain on paper towels. Repeat process until all wedges are cooked. Add oil as needed.

TIP: They are great with dips. Make up a batch quickly for happy hour. Cheaper and better than store bought chips. Keep tortillas in freezer to have on hand to thaw and cook when needed.

TROPICAL TOMATO MANGO SALSA

Preparation time: 2 minutes　　　　　　*Chef:Teresa Dancy*
Makes: 2 cups　　　　　　　　　　　　*Yacht: Flamboyance*

2 Tblsp	**Lime juice**
1/4 tsp	**Salt**
1/4 tsp	**Pepper**
1/4 tsp	**Fresh grated ginger**
1 cup	**Diced mango**
1/2 cup	**Chopped seeded tomato**
1/4 cup	**Chopped fresh cilantro (Do not omit this!)**
2 Tblsp	**Chopped shallots**
2 Tblsp	**Minced jalapeño pepper**

In a bowl, combine first 4 ingredients. Gently stir in the rest of the ingredients.

Hint: *Use on fish or pork, or serve with chips for hors d'oeuvre.*

DRUNKEN MUSHROOMS

Preparation time: 10 minutes　　　　　　　*Chef: Teresa Dancy*
Chilling time: 8 hours　　　　　　　　　　*Yacht: Flamboyance*
Serves: 4

1/4 cup	Tequila
1/4 cup	Fresh squeezed lemon juice
2 Tblsp	Sugar
1/2 tsp	Cracked pepper
1/4 tsp	Salt
1/4 tsp	Dried or 1 Tblsp fresh chopped oregano
2 cloves	Garlic, halved
1	Bay leaf
1	Sprig Rosemary
8 oz/224 g	Crimini (Italian) or other mushrooms

Combine all ingredients in a non metal bowl and stir well. Cover and marinate in refrigerator at least 8 hours. Discard bay leaf. Serve with toothpicks.

Hint: Serve mushrooms antipasto style on lettuce with other veggies.

CANNELLONI BEAN AND TOMATO SALAD

Preparation time: 10 minutes　　　　　　　*Chef: Teresa Dancy*
Chilling time: 8 hours　　　　　　　　　　*Yacht: Flamboyance*
Serves: 4

15.8 oz/440 g	Can Cannelloni beans, drained, rinsed (aka white northern beans)
	Chopped fresh roma tomatoes
2 Tblsp	Olive oil
3 cloves	Garlic, minced
1/2 cup	Chopped fresh basil or parsley
4 cups	Mesclun greens

Mix all ingredients together (except mesclun greens) and let marinate for 2 hours. *Serve at room temperature over greens.*

Hint: Can also be used as an hors d'oeuvre. Serve with crostini or small bread rounds.

PORK TENDERLOIN MEDALLIONS WITH CARAMELIZED SHALLOTS AND CASSIS

Preparation time: 15 minutes
Cooking time: 55 minutes
Resting time: 10 minutes
Serves: 4

Chef: Teresa Dancy
Yacht: Flamboyance

3 lb/1.4 kg	Pork tenderloin
	Canola oil
2	Thickly sliced onions
1 cup	Red wine, or water

CARAMELIZED SHALLOTS AND CASSIS:

20	Large shallots or 5 onions
1 Tblsp	Olive oil
1 Tblsp	Butter
2 Tblsp	Sugar
	Salt and freshly ground pepper
3 Tblsp	Cassis, or Blackberry wine, or blackberry jelly (not jam)

Preheat oven to 350°F/180°C. Rub the tenderloin with enough canola oil to coat. In a roasting pan place tenderloin on top of sliced onions (or on a roasting rack). Pour over red wine and bake in oven until meat thermometer shows 160°F/70°C. about 50 minutes. *Place foil over tenderloin if it becomes too dark in the last few minutes of cooking.* When cooked remove from oven and let sit, covered with foil to preserve warmth and allow juices to settle before slicing into medallions.

While pork is cooking peel the shallots and cut lengthwise into 1/8 inch (3 mm) slices. Heat oil in a sauté pan over medium heat. Add the butter and the shallots. Sprinkle with sugar and add salt and pepper. Cook the shallots until they begin to brown evenly, then turn the heat down to low and continue to cook until shallots are very soft, about 10 minutes. Add Cassis and stir, heating through. *Serve over medallions arranged on a plate in arc fashion or across middle of plate.*

Serve with a steamed green vegetable.

RICE MELANGE

Preparation time: 10 minutes
Cooking time: 1 hour 10 minutes
Serves: 4

Chef: Teresa Dancy
Yacht: Flamboyance

11.5 oz/320 g	**Can beef consommé**
10.5 oz/295 g	**Can French onion soup**
1/4 cup	**Butter, melted**
1-1/2 cups	**Uncooked long grain rice**
1-1/2 cups	**Chopped yellow onion**

Preheat oven to 325°F/160°C. Combine above ingredients in a 2 quart (1.9 L) greased casserole dish, cover and bake.

Hint: *Easy preparation allows time for mingling with guests.*

QUICK PARFAIT IDEAS

Preparation time: 10 minutes
Chilling time: 1 hour
Serves: any number

Chef: Teresa Dancy
Yacht: Flamboyance

Shortbread cookies, lemon cookies, sugar cookies, cubed pound cake, angel food cake, coconut yogurt, lemon yogurt, lime yogurt, pina colada yogurt, vanilla yogurt, toasted coconut, candied lemon peel, cinnamon hearts, chocolate chips, etc.... you get the idea

Layer any of the above into a pretty stemmed glass beginning and ending with yogurt. Finish with whipped topping.

Hint: A very light and delicious dessert (and easy) that is just right after a filling meal. Let your imagination run and dig into that refrigerator for ideas. This is a great way to use a bag of cookies that was tossed into the bottom of the shopping cart, the dinghy, and the cockpit during provisioning. Also good to use the cake that broke in pieces!

FREE INGWE SHOPPING LIST

VEGETABLES:
Baby carrots .... 1 lb
Garlic .... 1 bulb
Green chilis...................... 2
Salad greens .... 12 cups
Yellow onions, large 7
Baby peas .... 1 lb

FRUITS:
Lemons 3
Mangos 4

FRESH HERBS:
Coriander leaves .... garnish
Parsley .... 1 bunch

DRIED SPICES:
Coriander .... 2 tsp
Cumin .... 1 tsp

CONDIMENTS:
Peppercorns, black .... 1 Tblsp
Gravy mix, instant .... 2 Tblsp
Olive oil............................ 1/4 cup
Worchestershire .... 2 tsp
Vinegar, red wine .... 1 cup
Vinegar, white wine .... 1/4 cup

DRY GOODS:
Flour .... for coating
Sugar, brown .... 6 Tblsp
Sugar............................... 1 Tblsp

CANS AND JARS:
Apricot jam .... 1 Tblsp
Corn kernels .... 14 oz can

DAIRY/MILK/CHEESE/BUTTER
Butter .... 1/4 lb
Cream .... 1 cup
Eggs 8
Whole milk .... 1 cup
Sour cream .... 1/2 cup
Yogurt .... 2 cups
Camembert .... 8 oz
Cream cheese................... 8 oz
Feta, crumbled .... 1-1/2 cups
Gruyère, shredded............. 1/3 cup

MEAT/POULTRY/FISH/SEAFOOD:
Whole chicken 1
Beef tenderloin .... 4 lbs
Ham slices 6

MISCELLANEOUS:
Bread crumbs .... 1 Tblsp
Tortilla chips .... 1 bag
Round loaf bread 1

FROZEN:
Whipped topping............. 16 oz

S/Y FREE INGWE

Chef Rose Stride
Captain Norman Welthagen

MENU
Serves 8

Breakfast

*Baked Ham and Cheese Soufflé Omelette
Coffee, Tea, Milk

Lunch

*Spiced Chicken Salad with Corn Salsa

Hors d'oeuvre

*Camembert Baked in Bread

Dinner

*Stuffed Beef Tenderloin with
*Red Wine Gravy
*Potato Croquettes
Baby Carrots and Peas

*Creamy Mangoes

The South African built 45-foot Leopard catamaran is appropriately named FREE INGWE, an African name for the leopard, in honor of the boat's designer. She accommodates 6 guests in 3 air conditioned cabins. Captain Norman Welthgen, formerly in the South African navy, is the captain of this swift, smooth-sailing craft and Rose Stride, who once managed a hotel in London, England, runs the galley. Rose loves to cook; so does Norman who often adds one of his own recipes to the menu.

*Indicates recipe provided

BAKED CHEESE AND HAM SOUFFLE OMELETTE

Preparation time: 10 minutes
Cooking time: 25 minutes
Serves: 8

Chef: Rose Stride
Yacht: Free Ingwe

1/2 cup	Cream
1/2 cup	Milk
2 Tblsp	Flour
8	Eggs, beaten
8	Slices ham, chopped
2 Tblsp	Fresh chopped parsley
2/3 cup	Gruyère cheese or any other strong cheese
	Salt and pepper

Preheat oven to 220°F/100°C. Mix first 4 ingredients. Stir in ham, parsley, 1/4 cup cheese, salt and pepper. Butter soufflé dish or 8 ramekins. Pour in egg mixture. Sprinkle remaining cheese on top and bake 25 minutes. *Serve with hot toast or English muffins.*

Hint: A good breakfast dish or lunch served with a green salad.

CREAMY MANGOES

Preparation time: 8 minutes
Chilling time: 1 hour
Serves: 8

Chef: Rose Stride
Yacht: Free Ingwe

4	Large ripe mangoes
16 oz/450 g	Tub natural yogurt
16 oz/450 g	Tub Whipped topping
4 Tblsp	Brown sugar

Cut mangoes in slices over a bowl to save the juice. Mix yogurt and whipped topping together. Pour over mangoes. Sprinkle sugar over and chill in refrigerator for at least an hour.

Hint: This may be prepared ahead of time. Tastes great and leftovers are wonderful for breakfast.

SPICED CHICKEN SALAD WITH CORN SALSA

Preparation time: 10 minutes
Cooking time: 1 hour
Chilling time: 15 minutes
Serves: 8

Chef: Rose Stride
Yacht: Free Ingwe

1	**Whole chicken or pieces**
2 tsp	**Ground coriander**
1 tsp	**Ground cumin**
	Salt and pepper
4	**Large onions, sliced**
	Olive oil for roasting

CORN SALSA:

1	**Medium onion, finely chopped**
1 Tblsp	**Olive oil**
14 oz	**Can sweet corn kernels, drained**
1/4 cup	**White wine vinegar**
1/4 cup	**Lemon juice**
	Salt and pepper, to taste
2 tsp	**Chopped green chiles**
12 cups	**Salad greens**
Garnish	**Coriander leaves**

Preheat oven to 350°F/180°C. Cut open whole chicken. Lay flat on roasting pan, cut side down. Mix coriander, cumin, salt and pepper and spread over chicken; surround with onions and pour over olive oil. Roast 1 hour; onions must be caramalized. Remove from oven and let cool. Bone the chicken and cut meat into pieces.

In a skillet sauté onions in olive oil until just tender, add corn, vinegar, lemon juice, salt, pepper, and chilies; heat through.

Divide salad greens between dinner plates and place chicken pieces on top. Spoon over corn salsa and roasted onions. Sprinkle with coriander leaves. Serve with French bread. *This makes a colorful and delicious salad.*

CAMEMBERT BAKED IN BREAD

Preparation time: 15 minutes   *Chef: Rose Stride*
Cooking time: 40 minutes   *Yacht: Free Ingwe*
Serves: 8

1	**Onion, chopped**
2 Tblsp	**Finely chopped garlic**
1 Tblsp	**Butter**
8 oz/225 g	**Camembert**
8 oz/225 g	**Cream cheese**
1/2 cup	**Sour cream**
1 Tblsp	**Lemon juice**
1 Tblsp	**Brown sugar**
1 Tblsp	**Apricot jam**
2 tsp	**Worcestershire sauce**
	Salt and pepper, to taste
1	**Round loaf bread**
1	**Bag tortilla chips**

Preheat oven to 400°F/200°C. Sauté onion and garlic in butter. Cut camembert (without skin) into pieces. Mix with cream cheese, add onion and garlic mixture, sour cream, lemon, sugar, apricot jam, worcestershire sauce, salt and pepper. Cut top off round bread and scoop out the middle. Spoon mixture into loaf. Bake for 40 minutes. Serve with tortilla chips.

POTATO CROQUETTES

Preparation time: 30 minutes   *Chef: Rose Stride*
Cooking time: 45 minutes   *Yacht: Free Ingwe*
Serves: 8

3 lb/1.4 kg	**Large potatoes**
2	**Large onions, chopped**
1 Tblsp	**Olive oil**
1/2 tsp	**Salt, or to taste**
1 Tblsp	**Black pepper**
2	**Eggs, lightly beaten**
3/4 cup	**Chopped fresh parsley**
	Flour for coating
	Oil for cooking croquettes

Boil potatoes until soft, cool. Sauté onion in oil. Mash potatoes, then add onions, salt, pepper, eggs and parsley. Mix well. Using about 1/4 cup of mixture for each croquette, shape each in a 2 inch/5 cm pattie. Coat each pattie with flour. Heat a little oil in a large skillet and cook croquettes until golden brown on both side, about 4 minutes per side.

Note: *Patties made be made 8 hours ahead of time. Keep refrigerated.*

STUFFED BEEF TENDERLOIN
WITH RED WINE GRAVY

Preparation time: 20 minutes　　　　　*Chef: Rose Stride*
Cooking time: 25 minutes　　　　　　*Yacht: Free Ingwe*
Serves: 8

4 lbs/1.8 kg	Beef tenderloin
10 oz/280 g	Spinach leaves or 1 cup defrosted spinach

Stuffing

1	Onion, finally chopped
1 Tblsp	Butter
3/4 cup	Bread crumbs
1 Tblsp	Fresh lemon juice
1/2 tsp	Salt, or to taste
1/2 tsp	Black pepper
1-1/2 cups	Crumbled feta cheese

Preheat oven to 425°F/220°C. Butterfly tenderloin. Pound to flatten. Lay spinach over meat. Sauté onion in butter, add bread crumbs, lemon juice, salt, pepper and feta cheese; cool. Place filling along middle of meat, over the spinach, roll up. Tie to hold meat together. Heat skillet and brown tenderloin to seal. Bake in oven for 25 minutes for medium. Adjust cooking time to your preference. *Serve with **Red Wine Gravy** made from roasting pan.*

RED WINE GRAVY:

1 cup	Red wine
1 Tblsp	Crushed peppercorns
1 Tblsp	Lemon juice
1/2 cup	Fresh chopped parsley
2 Tblsp	Instant brown gray mix

Add about 1 cup of red wine to roasting pan and mix with the meat juice. Add crushed peppercorns, lemon juice, and fresh chopped parsley. If gravy needs to be thicker add 2 Tblsp instant brown gravy.

FREE LANCE CHEF SHOPPING LIST

VEGETABLES:
Garlic .... 2 bulbs
Mushrooms 6
Mixed veggies .... 2 cups
Green onions .... 1 bunch
Red onion 1
Yellow onion 1
Green bell peppers 1-1/2
Red bell pepper 1/2
Potatoes, large 2
Tomatoes, Italian 3
Tomatoes, plum................ 3

FRUITS:
Granny Smith apples........ 2
Lime juice .... 1/4 cup
Mangos 3

FRESH HERBS:
Basil, chopped .... 3 Tblsp
Dill .... garnish
Ginger, grated................... 5 Tblsp
Mint .... 2 Tblsp
Mint .... garnish
Oregano, chopped .... 1 tsp
Parsley, chopped .... 2 Tblsp

DRIED SPICES:
Cardamom .... 1/4 tsp
Cayenne .... 1-1/8 tsp
Cumin .... 1/2 tsp
Oregano .... 1/2 tsp
Red pepper flakes .... 1/2 tsp
White pepper .... 3/8 tsp

CONDIMENTS:
Tabasco .... to taste
Raisins .... 1/2 cup
Almond extract .... 1/2 tsp
Vanilla extract .... 1 tsp
Olive oil.............................. 5 Tblsp
Vegetable oil .... 3 Tblsp
Oil .... 1 Tblsp
Soy sauce .... 3 Tblsp
Worchestershire .... 1/2 tsp
Vinegar, cider .... 1 cup

DRY GOODS:
Linguine............................ 10 oz
Flour .... 2 Tblsp
Sugar, brown .... 1/4 cup
Sugar, confectioners' .... 3/4 cup
Sugar .... 1 cup

CANS AND JARS:
Black beans .... 2-15 oz cans
Pineapple, crushed .... 20 oz can
Cherry pie filling.............. 21 oz can
Evaporated milk .... 1 cup
Cream of chicken .... 2 cans
Chicken broth .... 14.5 oz can
Artichoke hearts .... 14 oz can
Green chiles .... 4 oz can
Smoked mussels .... 3.75 oz can

DAIRY/MILK/CHEESE/BUTTER
Butter .... 2 oz
Heavy cream .... 1/2 cup
Sour cream .... 1-1/4 cups
Cheddar, sharp, grated ..... 1/2 cup
Jack, grated .... 1/2 cup
Mozzarella, grated .... 1/2 cup
Parmesan, grated .... 1/4 cup

MEAT/POULTRY/FISH/SEAFOOD:
Swordfish steaks............... 6-7 oz

LIQUOR/WINE/SPIRITS:
Sherry, dry .... 1/4 cup
White wine .... 1 bottle

FROZEN:
Spinach .... 2 cups

MISCELLANEOUS:
Knorr vegetable soup .... 1 pkt
Pizza crust 1
Short crust pastry shell 1
Sesame crackers 24

FREE LANCE CHEF

Pamela Pandella

MENU
Serves 6

Breakfast

*Veggie Frittata

Lunch

*Garden Pie with Three Cheeses
*Green Chili Soup

Hors d'oeuvres

*Smoked Mussels and Veggie Dip on
Sesame Crackers

Dinner

*Black Bean Soup with Marsala
*Grilled Swordfish Steaks in
*Lime Soy Marinade with
*Mango Sauce
Linguine
Steamed Broccoli tossed with Butter and Tamari

*Cream Cheese Pie with Cherry Topping

Since 1995 Pamela Pandella has been a free lance chef on both private and charter yachts sailing the waters of the Virgin Islands and Puerto Rico. She enjoys introducing her guests to local flavors, using the freshest possible ingredients and produce — creating cajun, creole, and island cuisine; with special attention to those requiring low fat, vegetarian or heart smart menus. She also loves to bake breads, muffins and make desserts!

*Indicates recipe provided

VEGGIE FRITTATA

Preparation time: 15 minutes　　　　　*Chef: Pamela Pandella*
Cooking time: 10 minutes
Serves: 6

2 Tblsp	Olive oil
2 Tblsp	Butter
2	Large cooked cold potatoes, diced
1/2	Yellow onion, chopped
1	Red bell pepper, chopped
2 cloves	Garlic, minced
1 cup	Left over veggies – squash, broccoli, etc.
3	Italian tomatoes, diced
2	Green onions, chopped
1 Tblsp	Fresh basil and parsley
1 tsp	Dried oregano
12	Large eggs
2 dashes	Tabasco
	Black and white pepper, to taste
Garnish:	Fresh fruit slices

In a large skillet, over medium heat, add butter and oil and sauté potatoes. Add onions, bell pepper, and garlic; cook until soft. Add any leftover veggies you may have. When heated through add parsley, basil, oregano. Cook until it smells really good! Beat eggs with tabasco and black and white pepper. Pour over veggies and cook slowly until eggs are set. When cooked, cut in wedges. Garnish the plate with fruit. *Serve with toast.*

Hint: Grated cheddar or monterey jack is good melted on top. This recipe is also good in a breakfast burrito along with refried beans, garnished with salsa and sour cream.

GARDEN PIE WITH THREE CHEESES

Preparation time: 20 minutes   *Chef: Pamela Pandella*
Cooking time: 25 minutes
Serves: 6

1/2	**Green bell pepper, diced**
1/2	**Red bell pepper, diced**
3	**Green onions, sliced**
6	**Mushrooms, chopped**
6	**Thin slices red onion rings**
3	**Plum tomatoes, chopped**
14 oz/390 g	**Can artichoke hearts**
1 Tblsp	**Fresh parsley**
1 Tblsp	**Fresh basil**
	Salt, pepper, cayenne
	Olive oil, or cooking spray
1	**12 inch (30 cm) pizza crust**
2 Tblsp	**Butter**
2 Tblsp	**Flour**
1 cup	**Evaporated milk**
2 cups	**Frozen spinach, thawed and drained**
1/2 cup	**Shredded monterey jack cheese**
1/2 cup	**Shredded mozzarella cheese**
1/2 cup	**Shredded cheddar**
1/4 cup	**Shredded parmesan**

Preheat oven to 450°F/230°C. Place all vegetables (except spinach) in a large bowl; toss with herbs and spices, set aside. Spread oil or cooking spray on pizza crust.

Cream sauce: Melt butter over medium heat, whisk in flour until smooth, add 3/4 cup milk slowly, whisking until smooth and thick. Add spinach, and stir until thoroughly mixed. Add extra milk if sauce becomes too thick. Spread mixture on crust. Cover with vegetables and top with cheeses. Sprinkle parmesan on top. Put in oven for about 20 minutes until heated through. Cut in wedges and *serve immediately.*

Hint: To speed up cooking time heat crust first. Make sure spinach mixture is hot. Add toppings then put it back in the oven to finish cooking.

GREEN CHILI SOUP

Preparation time: 5 minutes   *Chef: Pamela Pandella*
Cooking time:10 minutes
Serves: 6

2 - 14 fl.oz/400 ml	**Cans cream of chicken soup**
2 - 14 fl.oz/400 ml	**Cans of chicken stock or water**
4 oz/110 g	**Can green chilies, diced, save liquid**
1/2 tsp	**Worcestershire sauce**
1/4 tsp	**Cayenne pepper**

In a saucepan put soup, chicken stock, chilies and liquid, worcestershire sauce, and cayenne pepper. Whisk until hot over medium heat.

Hint: A cup of soup makes a nice addition to a sandwich for lunch.

SMOKED MUSSELS AND VEGGIE DIP

Preparation time: 5 minutes   *Chef: Pamela Pandella*
Chilling time: 6 hours
Serves: 6

1 envelope	**Knorr vegetable soup and dip mix**
3 dashes	**Tabasco**
1 cup	**Mayonnaise**
1 cup	**Sour cream**
24	**Sesame crackers**
3.66 oz/104 g	**Can smoked mussels**
Garnish:	**Chopped dill weed**

Mix soup mix with Tabasco, mayonnaise and sour cream. Refrigerate for at least 6 hours, make sure veggies have softened. Spread on sesame crackers, top each cracker with one mussel. Garnish with dill weed.

Note: This makes 2 cups of dip. Use leftovers for filling celery, sandwiches or with crudités.

BLACK BEAN SOUP WITH MARSALA

Preparation time: 15 minutes   *Chef: Pamela Pandella*
Cooking time: 15 minutes
Serves: 6

1/4	**Finely chopped yellow onion**
3 cloves	**Garlic, minced**
1 Tblsp	**Oil**
1 Tblsp	**Butter**
1/2 tsp	**Cumin**
1/2 tsp	**Oregano**
1/2 tsp	**Ground black pepper**
1/4 tsp	**Ground white pepper**
1/4 tsp	**Cayenne pepper**
2 - 15.5 oz/435 g	**Cans black beans**
14.5 fl oz/400 ml	**Can chicken stock**
1/4 cup	**Marsala or dry sherry**
1/4 cup	**Sour cream or plain yogurt**
	Finely chopped green onion

Sauté onion and garlic in oil and butter; add cumin, oregano and peppers. Add black beans with liquid, then chicken stock, enough to make about 5 cups. Bring to a boil then simmer for about 10 minutes, set aside. When ready to serve, reheat. Stir in Marsala or dry sherry. Serve with a dollop of sour cream in center and sprinkle with green onion.

Hint: Good served with slices of French bread spread with brie and roasted garlic.

GRILLED SWORDFISH WITH LIME AND SOY MARINADE

Preparation time: 10 minutes
Marinating time: 30 minutes
Cooking time: 10 minutes
Serves: 6

Chef: Pamela Pandella

1/4 cup	Fresh lime juice
2 cloves	Garlic, minced
3 Tblsp	Vegetable oil
3 Tblsp	Soy sauce
1/4 tsp	Ground black pepper
1/4 tsp	Ground white pepper
1/4 tsp	Cayenne pepper
	Tabasco to taste
2 Tblsp	Dill weed
6 - 7 oz/200 g	Swordfish steaks

Mix together lime juice, garlic, oil, soy and peppers. Pour over fish steaks in glass or non-reactive pan. Sprinkle dill weed over top of fish. Marinate for 30 minutes. Then give them to your captain to grill! Use the marinade to baste with. *Serve with **Mango Sauce.***

Hint: This marinade works well with all fish.

MANGO SAUCE OR CHUTNEY

Preparation time: 5 minutes   *Chef: Pamela Pandella*
Cooking time: 45 minutes and 1-1/2 hours
Makes: 5 cups

1 cup	Cider vinegar
1 cup	White sugar
1/4 cup	Dark brown sugar
1/2 cup	Raisins
3	Fresh mangos peeled and diced, or canned or frozen
1 - 20 oz	Can crushed pineapple with juice
2	Granny smith apples, peeled and diced
1/4 tsp	Cayenne pepper, or to taste
5 cloves	Garlic, crushed
1/4 tsp	Ground cardamom

Combine all ingredients in non-reactive sauce pan. Simmer for about 45 minutes for sauce and 1-1/2 hours for chutney.

Hint: The sauce is excellent with fish. The chutney is also good served with cream cheese and crackers for an hors d'oeuvre or as a topping on a small wheel of brie. It keeps well in the refrigerator.

CREAM CHEESE PIE WITH CHERRY TOPPING

Preparation time: 15 minutes   *Chef: Pamela Pandella*
Chilling time: 2 hours
Serves: 6

8 oz/225 g	Cream cheese, room temperature
3/4 cup	Powdered sugar
1/2 cup	Whipping cream
1 tsp	Vanilla extract
1/2 tsp	Almond extract
1	Graham cracker crust
21 oz/590 g	Can cherry pie filling, or blueberry

Beat cream cheese, sugar, cream, and extracts in mixing bowl or in a food processor until smooth. Pour into crust and chill at least 2 hours; you can also freeze it. *When ready to serve, top with pie filling.*

Hint: For more decadence, garnish with whipped cream.

GALE WINDS SHOPPING LIST

VEGETABLES:
Asparagus, large 18
Carrot 1
Celery, stalk 1
Cucumber 1
Garlic cloves 2
Sweet potatoes .... 1-1/2 lbs
Scallion 1
Chives, chopped .... garnish
Shallots 6
Yellow onion 1
Pumpkin, medium 1
Tomatoes .... garnish

FRUITS:
Coconuts 4
Kiwi 3
Lemons 2
Lemon zest .... 1 tsp
Mangos .... garnish
Nectarines 2
Orange 1
Papaya .... garnish
Peaches 4
Pineapple 1
Plums 2
Raspberries .... 1 cup
Strawberries 6

FRESH HERBS:
Ginger .... 3 inch pc
Mint sprigs .... garnish
Sage sprigs .... garnish
Sage, chopped .... 1 Tblsp
Nutmeg, grated .... 1/8 tsp

DRIED SPICES:
Bay leaf 1
Cayenne .... to taste
Cinnamon .... 1 Tblsp
Black peppercorns 3
Thyme .... 1/4 tsp

CONDIMENTS:
Coconut .... 1-3/4 cups
Sesame seeds .... 3 Tblsp
Vanilla extract .... 1 tsp
Mustard, Dijon .... 6 Tblsp
Red pepper flakes .... 1/2 tsp
Corn oil .... 5 cups
Extra virgin olive oil .... 5 Tblsp
Olive oil .... 1 Tblsp
Grapeseed oil .... 2 Tblsp

Peanut oil .... 2 Tblsp
Sesame oil .... 2 Tblsp
Truffle oil .... 1 Tblsp
Vinegar, white wine .... 1 Tblsp
Vinegar, white .... 2 Tblsp
Soy sauce .... 3 Tblsp
Tabasco .... to taste

DRY GOODS:
Cornmeal, fine .... 2 cups
Flour .... 1 Tblsp
Arborio rice .... 2 cups
Sugar, confectioners' .... 3 Tblsp
Sugar .... 8 cups

CANS AND JARS:
Coconut unsweetened milk
.... 12 oz can
Coconut unsweetened .... topping
Macademia, chopped .... 1/2 cup
Water chestnuts .... 8 oz can
Chicken broth .... 11-12 cups

DAIRY/MILK/CHEESE/BUTTER
Butter .... 2 Tblsp
Butter, unsalted .... 1/2 lb
Eggs 19
Heavy cream .... 2-3/4 cup
Crème fraiche .... 1/2 cup
Boursin .... 1 pkg
Gruyère, grated .... 1 cup

MEAT/POULTRY/FISH/SEAFOOD:
Pork, boneless .... 1 lb
Oxtails, small .... 10 *or*
Oxtails, large 3

LIQUOR/WINE/SPIRITS:
Amaretto .... 3 Tblsp
Pimms #1 .... 1 bottle
Red wine .... 1 cup
White wine, dry .... 1/2 cup

MISCELLANEOUS:
Graham cracker crumbs ...... 1 cup
Passion fruit purée .... 1 Tblsp
Sparkling cider .... 1 bottle
White bread slices 10

FROZEN:
Cool Whip .... 1 cup

M/Y GALE WINDS

Chef Betsy Millson
Captain Walter Wettmore

MENU
Serves 6

Breakfast

*Fresh Peaches with Cinnamon Crème Fraiche
*Caribbean Hash Eggs Benedict with
*Passion Fruit Hollandaise

Lunch

*Steamed Asparagus Salad with
Truffle Soy Vinaigrette
*Pumpkin Risotto
*Summer Ambrosia

Hors d'oeuvres

Cocktail Suggestion: *Pimm's Cup
*Gruyère Bites

Dinner

*Seared Sea Scallops in Passion Fruit Sauce
*Braised Oxtails over
*Fungi

*Coconut Cheesecake with Toasted Coconut and
Mango, Kiwi or Papaya Coulis

GALE WINDS, a splendid 124-foot mega yacht, has it all, including a large Jacuzzi hot tub and a fitness room. Four staterooms provide for eight guests. Captain Walter Wettmore has a caring crew, among them talented Chef Betsy Millson. Her job ranks with the captain's in pleasing guests. With the exception of some short-term apprentices (often in Europe), Betsy has worked as a chef on private yachts for 8 years. In 1999 she won the Mega Yacht Concourse de Chef Competition in Antigua.

*Indicates recipe provided

CRUISING 'DOWN ISLAND'

Chef: Betsy Millson
Yacht: Gale Winds

PROVISIONING IN ANTIGUA:

Antigua is great for provisioning, because everybody delivers. The place to go, however, is the local market on the way to St. John. There is a woman there, Sister Grant, who has her own stand and has her name posted. Her rasta son will deliver to you but it is so much better to go and see her. Her fruits and vegetables are exotic and fresh — passion fruits, sorrel, tea grass, miniature eggplants, boniato potatoes, and banana leaves, to name a few. Sister Grant prefers EC dollars and is great about writing out detailed receipts. Most of the ingredients used in this menu are availble through Sister Grant, with the exception of the fresh seafood...try Gary at **TCM.**

FRESH PEACHES WITH CINNAMON CREME FRAICHE

Preparation time: 15 minutes
Cooking time: 15 seconds
Serves: 6

Chef: Betsy Millson
Yacht: Gale Winds

1/2 cup	**Crème fraiche**
2 Tblsp	**Sugar**
1 Tblsp	**Cinnamon**
4	**Peaches, peeled***
Garnish:	**Mint sprigs**

Combine crème fraiche, sugar, and cinnamon; divide evenly among six plates. Cut peaches in half, remove stone and arrange on top. Garnish with mint sprigs.

*Hint: *For easy peeling drop the peaches into boiling water for 15 seconds, then plunge into ice water.*

Hint: *To substitute crème fraiche use plain yogurt and increase the sugar to 3 Tblsp.*

CARIBBEAN HASH EGGS BENEDICT WITH PASSION FRUIT HOLLANDAISE

Preparation time: 30 minutes   *Chef: Betsy Millson*
Cooking time: 15 minutes   *Yacht: Gale Winds*
Serves: 4 - 6

HASH PATTIES:

1-1/2 lbs/680 g	Sweet potatoes, peeled and diced
8 oz/225 g	Can water chestnut, rinsed, drained and chopped
1	Scallion, finely chopped
1 lb/450 g	Boneless pork loin
1	Small shallot, finely chopped
2 cloves	Garlic, minced
2 Tblsp	Asian sesame oil
3 Tblsp	Sesame seeds
1/2 tsp	Dried red pepper flakes

POACHED EGGS:

2 Tblsp	Distilled white vinegar
8	Large eggs
2 Tblsp	Peanut oil

Passion Fruit Hollandaise: (see recipe)
Cook sweet potatoes in boiling water for 3 minutes or until just tender; drain well. Trim fat from pork and cut in 1 inch (2.5 cm) pieces. In a food processor put pork and 'pulse', add shallot and garlic until coarsely chopped. In a large bowl lightly knead together pork mixture, potato, water chestnuts, scallion, and remaining ingredients. Form hash into 6 patties*. (Prepare the *Passion Fruit Hollandaise Sauce).*

In a 10 -12 inch (25 -30 cm) skillet heat 1 Tblsp peanut oil over moderate heat and cook patties, 4 minutes each side. Keep warm while poaching eggs. Divide hash patties among 6 plates, top patties with poached eggs and hollandaise sauce.

* Patties may be made the day before, covered and chilled.

PASSION FRUIT HOLLANDAISE

Preparation time: 10 minutes   *Chef: Betsy Millson*
Cooking time: 5 minutes   *Yacht: Gale Winds*
Serves: 6

1	**Small shallot, finely chopped**
3	**Black peppercorns, crushed**
3/4 cup	**Unsalted butter, melted**
1 Tblsp	**White wine vinegar**
4	**Large egg yolks**
1 Tblsp	**Passion fruit purée**
	Fresh lemon juice, to taste
	Cayenne, to taste
	Tabasco, to taste

Have ready a medium size saucepan of hot water on the stove. In another saucepan combine shallot, peppercorns, and white wine vinegar. Bring to a boil and reduce to about 1 tsp. Pass through fine mesh strainer. Add liquid to blender. Add yolks and purée. With the blender running, add the melted butter in a slow steady drizzle until fully incorporated. Add passion fruit purée, lemon juice and spices. Keep hollandaise in blender and in a pan of warm water until ready to use.

STEAMED ASPARAGUS SALAD WITH SOY TRUFFLE VINAIGRETTE

Preparation time: 10 minutes   *Chef: Betsy Millson*
Cooking time: 5 minutes   *Yacht: Gale Winds*
Serves: 6

18 Large asparagus spears

SOY TRUFFLE VINAIGRETTE:

1 Tblsp	**Truffle oil**
3 Tblsp	**Soy sauce**
3 Tblsp	**Lemon juice**
5 Tblsp	**Extra virgin olive oil**
Garnish:	**Tomato slices and snipped chives**

Peel asparagus and break off bottoms. Place asparagus on steamer in boiling water and cook until tender about 5 minutes, then plunge into ice water; drain and pat dry. Combine all ingredients for vinaigrette. Arrange asparagus on a platter and pour over vinaigrette. *Decorate with tomato slices and snipped chives. Vinaigrette covered will keep for days.*

PUMPKIN RISOTTO

Preparation time: 10 minutes   *Chef: Betsy Millson*
Cooking time: 40 minutes   *Yacht: Gale Winds*
Serves: 6

1	Medium pumpkin
5 - 6 cups	Chicken stock
2 Tblsp	Unsalted butter
1 Tblsp	Olive oil
4	Shallots, minced
2 cups	Arborio rice
1/2 cup	Dry white wine
1 Tblsp	Fresh sage
1/2 cup	Freshly grated parmesan
1 Tblsp	Sage, chopped
	Freshly grated nutmeg
	Salt and pepper, to taste
Garnish:	Sage sprigs

Cut the pumpkin into eighths and discard the seeds. Steam for 10 minutes or until tender. Scoop the flesh and mash lightly. In a large saucepan, heat stock to a simmer. In a large, heavy sauce pan over medium heat, melt 1 Tblsp butter. Add oil and shallots and cook for 2 minutes. Add rice; cook, stirring for 5 minutes. Add wine to rice and cook, stirring until wine is nearly absorbed. Stir in a cup of stock and the pumpkin, simmer until liquid is nearly absorbed. Continue stirring in stock, a ladle at a time, until rice is creamy and firm but not hard in the center, 15-20 minutes. Add nutmeg, salt and pepper to taste. Add chopped sage. Stir in the remaining butter and most of the parmesan. *Garnish with sage sprigs and remaining cheese.*

SUMMER AMBROSIA

Preparation time: 40 minutes　　　　　　　　　　*Chef: Betsy Millson*
Cooking time: 20 minutes　　　　　　　　　　　*Yacht: Gale Winds*
Chilling time: 45 minutes
Serves: 8

3 inch/7.5 cm	**Piece fresh ginger**
1 cup	**Sugar**
4	**Coconuts**
2	**Plums, cut in 1/4 inch (5 mm) wedges**
2	**Nectarines, cut in 1/4 inch (5 mm) wedges**
2	**Kiwis, peeled and cut lengthwise**
1 cup	**Raspberries**
1/4	**Pineapple, peeled, cut in 1 inch (2.5 cm) cubes**
3	**Oranges, peeled and sectioned**
1-3/4 cups	**Shredded coconut, sweetened**
2 cups	**Heavy cream**
3 Tblsp	**Confectioners' sugar**
3 Tblsp	**Amaretto**

Heat oven to 350°F/180°C. Slice ginger into 1/8 inch (3 mm) rounds and place in 2 cups of water in a medium saucepan. Add sugar and bring to a simmer; stir to dissolve sugar. Continue to simmer until mixture tastes strongly of ginger, about 20 minutes. Strain, refrigerate to chill.

In a large bowl, toss the plums, nectarines, kiwis, blackberries, pineapples, and oranges with 1 cup shredded sweetened coconut and the reserved ginger syrup. Whip cream, confectioners' sugar and amaretto in a chilled mixing bowl. Place 2 Tblsp coconut and a dollop of whipped amaretto cream into the bottom of each coconut half*. Spoon fruit mixture and syrup into coconut halves; top each with another additional dollop of cream. *Garnish with a handful of toasted coconut.*

*Use a decorative glass if you do not have time to prepare the coconuts. See page 366.

PIMM'S CUP

Preparation time: 2 minutes
Serves: 6

Chef: Betsy Millson
Yacht: Gale Winds

1	**Cucumber, peel on, cut into sticks**
1	**Orange, cut into rounds**
6	**Strawberries, stems removed, cut in half**
1 bottle	**Pimm's #1**
1 bottle	**Sparkling apple cider, ginger ale or ginger beer**

Place all fruits into 2 quart (1 litre) pitcher. Add the remaining ingredients and stir once to combine. Ladle the drink into 8 ounce glasses, dividing the fruit among all the glasses. Fill each glass with ice and serve.

Note: *This cocktail has been popular with the English people for 300 years. It is delicious and refreshing.*

GRUYERE BITES

Preparation time: 20 minutes
Cooking time: 20 minutes
Serves: 6

Chef: Betsy Millson
Yacht: Gale Winds

1 cup	**Grated gruyère cheese**
1 Tblsp	**Flour**
2	**Eggs**
	Salt and white pepper
1/4-1/2 cup	**Heavy cream**
10	**Slices white bread, cut into 20 1 inch (2.5 cm) circles**
5 cups	**Corn oil**
6 Tbslp	**Dijon mustard**

Combine cheese, flour, eggs, salt and white pepper to taste. Add the cream—mixture should not be too runny. Spread cheese mixture onto the bread rounds, fry in batches, until golden, about 1 minute. Drain on paper towels. Serve warm with mustard.

Hint: *Mixture will keep for several days in refrigerator if stored in an airtight container.*

SEARED SEA SCALLOPS IN PASSION FRUIT SAUCE

Preparation time: 5 minutes   *Chef: Betsy Millson*
Cooking time: 20 minutes   *Yacht: Gale Winds*
Serves: 6

18	**Large sea scallops**
3 Tblsp	**Butter**
	Salt and pepper to taste

PASSION FRUIT SAUCE:

1 Tblsp	**Unsalted butter**
2	**Shallots, coarsely chopped**
1 qt/1 litre	**Passion fruit juice**
1/2 cup	**Unsalted butter, softened**
	Salt and pepper to taste
3	**Whole passion fruit for garnish**

In a saucepan melt 1 Tblsp of butter, add the shallots and cook until translucent. Add the juice and reduce sauce to 1 cup. Season with salt and pepper. Bring sauce to a boil then transfer to a blender. With blender running add the remaining butter 1 Tblsp at a time until the butter is emulsified. Place blender in a pot of warm water to keep warm. Meanwhile heat a skillet, hot but not smoking. Add 1 tsp of butter. Add 4 or 5 scallops at a time, do not crowd pan. Sear the bottom, do not shake or move scallop. After 2-3 minutes, flip scallop and sear other side. Remove first batch and start 4 more until all the scallops are cooked. Pour a nice circle of sauce in the center of plate. Slice scallops in half. Arrange in a circle around passion fruit halves (cut side up). Serve immediately.

Note: *Sauce can be made a day ahead and refrigerated.*

COCONUT CHEESECAKE

Preparation time: 30 minutes
Cooking time: 1 hour 20 minutes
Chilling time: 24 hours
Serves: 12

Chef: Betsy Millson
Yacht: Gale Winds

Crust:

1 cup	Graham cracker crumbs
1/2 cup	Macadamia nuts, chopped
1/4 cup	Sugar
4 Tblsp	Unsalted butter, melted

Filling:

32 oz /908 g	Cream cheese, room temperature 1-1/2
cups	Sugar
12 oz/676 g	Unsweetened coconut milk
1 tsp	Fresh lemon zest
1 tsp	Vanilla
Pinch	Salt
5	Eggs
Topping:	Toasted unsweetened coconut
Garnish:	Papaya, kiwi and mango coulis

Preheat oven to 375°F/190°C. Prepare the crust, combine all ingredients and press into 11 inch (27.5 cm) spring form pan, bake 10 minutes. Remove from oven and let cool. Reduce oven temperature to 350°F/180°C. Prepare the filling. Using an electric mixer with the paddle attachment, whip the cream cheese, add the sugar and whip until fluffy, scraping the sides down. Slowly add the coconut milk until combined. Add the vanilla, lemon zest, salt and combine. On slow speed, add the eggs, one at a time until incorporated, scraping the sides down. Pour the filling into the cooled crust. Wrap the bottom of the pan with foil and place in larger pan. Add water to the larger pan and bake Bain Marie style for 1 hour and 20 minutes. Remove, let cheesecake cool before serving. Top with shredded toasted coconut and tropical coulis.

Hint: Use dental floss to cut the cheesecake.

Note: It can be refrigerated up to 3 days.

This is the dessert I entered in the Concourse de Chef in Antigua. My boss borrowed it for his restaurant chain.

IMPULSE SHOPPING LIST

VEGETABLES:
Asparagus .... 1-1/2 lbs
Cucumber 1/4
Garlic cloves 2
Yellow onions 4
Green bell pepper 1
Red bell pepper .... garnish
Spinach .... 8 oz

FRUITS:
Lemon 1

FRESH HERBS:
Cilantro, chopped .... 1 Tblsp
Parsley, chopped .... 1 Tblsp
Mint, chopped .... 2 Tblsp

DRIED SPICES:
Bay leaf 1
Cinnamon .... 1/2 tsp
Chili powder .... 1 tsp
Curry .... 2 tsp
Garam masala .... 1 tsp
Paprika .... 2 tsp

CONDIMENTS:
Baking powder .... 1-1/2 tsp
Coconut .... 1-1/4 cups
Walnuts, finely chopped . 2-1/4 cups
Honey .... 3/4 cup
Mustard, Dijon .... 2 tsp
Oil .... 1/3 cup
Vegetable oil .... 1/4 cup
Tandoori paste .... 1 Tblsp
Vinegar, white wine .... 2 Tblsp

DRY GOODS:
Flour .... 1/2 cup
Flour, whole wheat .... 3/4 cup
Flour, self rising .... 3/4 cup
Long grain rice .... 2 cups
Sugar .... 2/3 cup

CANS AND JARS:
Pineapple pieces .... 4 oz can
Chicken broth .... 3-1/2 cups
Tomatoes, chopped .... 15 oz can

DAIRY/MILK/CHEESE/BUTTER:
Butter .... 1-1/4 lb
Cream .... 3/4 cup
Heavy cream .... 1/2 cup
Eggs 14
Whole milk .... 1-1/3 cup
Yogurt .... 1 cup
Brie .... 6 oz
Cheddar, grated .... 1 cup
Cream cheese .... 9 oz

MEAT/POULTRY/FISH/SEAFOOD:
Chicken .... 1/2 cup
Shrimp, cooked .... 1 cup

LIQUOR/WINE/SPIRITS:
Cassis .... 3 Tblsp
Tequila .... 1/4 cup
Wine, red .... 1 cup

MISCELLANEOUS:
Brown bread crumbs .... 2 cups
Gelatin .... 1 pkg
Digestive biscuits .... 8 oz
Short crust pastry shell ... 1

FROZEN:
Strawberries .... 10 oz pkg
Peas .... 1/2 cup

S/Y IMPULSE

Chef Kelly Thomas
Capt. Simon Thomas

MENU
Serves 6

Breakfast

Fresh Grapefruit Halves
*Whole Wheat Honey Muffins

Lunch

*Quick Spanish Paella
Green Salad
*Pineapple and Coconut Loaf

Hors d'oeuvres

*Tandoori Chicken with Minted Cucumber Dip
*Spinach Cakes

Dinner

*Brie Tart
*Walnut Croquettes
with Fresh Tomatoes
Wild Rice
*Asparagus with Hollandaise Sauce

*No Bake Strawberry Cheesecake

IMPULSE, a Dynamique 62-foot yacht, is all about sailing pleasure, and gourmet menus. Captain Simon Thomas and Chef Kelly Thomas have sailed extensively around the Mediterranean and in the Caribbean from Venezuela to the Caymans. This beautiful yacht with its sophisticated on-board equipment is so well contained that remote areas can be visited extensively. And Kelly, a Cordon Bleu chef, can still turn out the same delicious menus without benefit of extra shopping. Impulse accommodates 6 guests.

*Indicates recipe provided

WHOLE WHEAT HONEY MUFFINS

Preparation time: 20 minutes　　　　　　　　*Chef: Kelly Thomas*
Cooking time: 20 minutes　　　　　　　　　　　　*Yacht: Impulse*
Serves: 6

3/4 cup	**Whole wheat flour**
1 tsp	**Baking powder**
1	**Egg, beaten**
3/4 cup	**Milk**
3/4 cup	**Honey**
1/4 cup	**Vegetable oil**
1/4 cup	**Chopped walnuts**

Preheat oven to 400° F/200° C. Blend dry ingredients together. Combine remaining ingredients and add to flour mixture. Stir quickly until just mixed and batter is still lumpy. Fill greased muffin tins 2/3 full and bake.

QUICK SPANISH PAELLA

Preparation time: 20 minutes　　　　　　　　*Chef: Kelly Thomas*
Cooking time: 20 minutes　　　　　　　　　　　　*Yacht: Impulse*
Serves: 6

1 Tblsp	**Cooking oil**
1	**Large onion, chopped**
2	**Cloves garlic, crushed**
1	**Green bell pepper, chopped**
3-1/2 cups	**Chicken stock**
14.5 oz/411 g	**Can chopped tomatoes**
2 cups	**Long grain rice**
2 tsp	**Paprika**
1/2 cup	**Cooked chicken, chopped**
	Salt and pepper, to taste
1 cup	**Cooked prawns**
1/2 cup	**Frozen peas**

Heat oil in saucepan until very hot. Add onion, garlic, and pepper; cook for about 5 minutes, stirring until soft. Add stock, tomatoes, rice, paprika, chicken, salt and pepper. Bring to a boil then cover and simmer for 20 minutes. Uncover and stir in prawns and peas. Cook for another 5 minutes and *serve with a fresh garden salad.*

Note: *This is a good low fat recipe.*

PINEAPPLE AND COCONUT LOAF

Preparation time: 10 minutes　　　　　　*Chef: Kelly Thomas*
Cooking time: 45 minutes　　　　　　　　　*Yacht: Impulse*
Serves: 6

3/4 cup	Self raising flour
1/2 tsp	Cinnamon
4 Tblsp	Butter
1/4 cup	Sugar
4-1/2 oz/126 g	Can pineapple pieces
2	Eggs, well beaten
1-1/4 cups	Shredded coconut

Preheat oven to 300° F/150°C: Grease and line 1 lb loaf pan. Stir flour and cinnamon into a large bowl. Add butter and mix in until mixture resembles fine bread crumbs, then stir in sugar. Drain pineapple reserving 1 Tblsp of juice. Beat eggs into flour with pineapple juice. Fold in pineapple pieces and coconut. Pour into loaf pan and bake for 40 to 45 minutes until well risen and firm to touch.

TANDOORI CHICKEN WITH MINTED CUCUMBER DIP

Preparation time: 30 minutes　　　　　　*Chef: Kelly Thomas*
Cooking time: 10 minutes　　　　　　　　*Yacht: Impulse*
Chilling time: overnight
Marinating time. overnight
Serves 6

1 cup	Yogurt
1 Tblsp	Tandoori paste
1 tsp	Garam masala
1 tsp	Chili powder
1	Lemon, juiced
4	Boneless, skinless, chicken breasts
2 Tblsp	Chopped mint
1/4	Cucumber

Mix together half the yogurt, tandoori paste, garam masala, chili powder, and lemon juice. Cut the chicken into bite size pieces and put into the marinade. Cover and chill overnight. For the dip mix together the mint and remaining yogurt. Peel, seed, and finely chop the cucumber and fold in. Season to taste.

Take chicken out of marinade and grill under high setting for 10 minutes, turning occasionally. *Spear on cocktail sticks and serve with dip.*

SPINACH CAKES

Preparation time: 20 minutes
Cooking time: 20 minutes
Serves: 6

Chef: Kelly Thomas
Yacht: Impulse

1	Egg
1 Tblsp	Chopped onion
2 Tblsp	Melted butter
10 oz/289 g	Pkg fresh spinach*
1/2 cup	Flour
1/2 cup	Bread crumbs
1/2 tsp	Salt
1/2 tsp	Baking powder
1/2 cup	Milk

In a bowl, beat egg, then add onion, melted butter and spinach. Stir in flour, bread crumbs, salt, and baking powder; mix well. Add some milk and make mixture just firm enough to drop from spoon.

Heat oil in a saucepan. Drop rounded spoonfuls in hot oil until lightly browned. Drain on paper towel and serve.

*Hint: If using frozen spinach, first thaw and drain it.

Note: This is a great vegetarian recipe.

BRIE TART

Preparation time: 10 minutes
Cooking time: 30 - 40 minutes
Serves: 6

Chef: Kelly Thomas
Yacht: Impulse

6 oz/170 g	Brie cheese
1	Egg yolk
3	Eggs
2 tsp	Dijon mustard
3/4 cup	Cream
1 cup	Milk
	Salt and pepper, to taste
1	8 inch (20 cm) short crust pastry shell

Preheat oven to 400°F/200° C. Mix in blender or food processor the cheese, eggs, mustard, cream, milk and seasoning. Pour into a pastry shell and bake until set and golden brown, about 40 minutes.

WALNUT CROQUETTES

Preparation time: 15 minutes
Cooking time: 15 minutes
Serves: 4

Chef: Kelly Thomas
Yacht: Impulse

6 Tblsp	**Butter**
2	**Medium onions, chopped**
2 tsp	**Curry powder**
2 cups	**Finely chopped walnut pieces**
1 cup	**Grated sharp cheddar cheese**
1-1/2 cups	**Fresh brown bread crumbs**
2 Tblsps	**Fresh chopped herbs**
2	**Eggs**
2 Tblsp	**Milk**
	Salt and pepper, to taste
	Oil

Melt butter in medium size saucepan and cook onion until soft. Add curry powder and cook for a further minute. Remove from heat, stir in nuts, cheese, bread crumbs, herbs, egg and enough milk to bind to a firm mixture. Season. Heat skillet. Shape mixture into croquettes and sauté gently until browned.

Note: A wonderful vegetarian main course meal. Delicious served with a fresh tomato sauce or mango chutney.

ASPARAGUS WITH HOLLANDAISE SAUCE

Preparation time: 10 minutes
Cooking time: 15 minutes
Serves: 6

Chef: Kelly Thomas
Yacht: Impulse

1-1/2 lbs/680 g	**Fresh asparagus**

HOLLANDAISE SAUCE:
Makes: about 1 cup

2 Tblsp	**White wine vinegar**
1 Tblsp	**Water**
1	**Bay leaf**
4	**Egg yolks**
8 oz/225 g	**Butter, softened**
	Salt and pepper
Garnish:	
1	**Red pepper, very finely chopped**

Prepare asparagus, blanch, drain and refresh. Arrange on vegetable platter. Meanwhile make Hollandaise sauce by putting vinegar, water, and bay leaf in saucepan and boil gently until liquid is reduced by half. Set aside and cool. Put egg yolks and reduced vinegar into a double boiler and whisk until light and fluffy. Gradually add butter whisking after each addition. Season with salt and pepper and pour over asparagus. Garnish and serve at once.

Note: This is a good recipe to impress the guests. It tastes delicious and the contrast in colors looks wonderful.

Hint: Instead of the wine vinegar, try using 2 Tblsp of fresh lemon juice.

Tip: An easy version—Place egg yolks and lemon juice in a food processor or blender and process until light and frothy. Melt butter until it is hot and bubbling. With processor or blender running, slowly pour in hot melted butter and process until thick. *No cooking is required if you make sure that the butter is hot and bubbling when you add it to the egg mixture.*

NO BAKE STRAWBERRY CHEESECAKE

Preparation time: 20 minutes
Chilling time: overnight
Serves: 6

Chef: Kelly Thomas
Yacht: Impulse

8 oz/225 g	**Digestive biscuits/cookies**
8 Tblsp	**Butter, melted**
1 pkg	**Gelatin, approx 1 tsp**
10 oz/280 g	**Frozen strawberries***
1/3 cup	**Sugar**
9 oz/250 g	**Cream cheese**
1/2 cup	**Whipping cream**

Put digestive biscuits in a bowl and crush with a rolling pin. Add melted butter and mix well. Pour into bottom of greased springform pan and flatten with a spoon. Chill. Meanwhile sprinkle gelatin into 1/4 cup water and let sit for 2 minutes. Then microwave on high for 40 seconds, let sit for a further 2 minutes until gelatin is dissolved. Put fresh or defrosted strawberries in a blender and purée until smooth. Add sugar and cream cheese and mix well. Stir dissolved gelatin mixture into strawberries. Whip cream in a separate bowl and fold into strawberry mixture. Pour over biscuit base and chill overnight.

*This recipe is also good with raspberries or blueberries.

ISLAND DREAMS SHOPPING LIST

VEGETABLES:
Baby carrots .... 1 lb bag
Garlic .... 2 cloves
Green onion 1
Green bell pepper 1
Red bell pepper 1
Potatoes, large baking 2

FRUITS:
Limes 5
Lime wedges .... garnish
Mango 1

FRESH HERBS:
Cilantro sprigs .... garnish
Parsley sprigs .... garnish

DRIED SPICES:
All spice .... 1/4 tsp
Cumin, ground .... 1 tsp
Ginger, ground .... 1/4 tsp
Paprika .... 4 tsp

CONDIMENTS:
Baking powder .... 1 Tblsp
Raisins .... 1/2 cup
Olive oil .... 2-1/3 cups
Vinegar, balsamic .... 1/4 cup
Vinegar, white .... 1 Tblsp

DRY GOODS:
Flour .... 1-3/4 cup
White rice cooked .... 1/2 cups
Sugar .... 1/4 cup
Sugar, brown .... 1/3 cup

CANS AND JARS:
Tuna .... 6 oz can
Sweetened condensed milk
 .... 14 oz

DAIRY/MILK/CHEESE/BUTTER
Butter .... 10 Tblsp
Eggs 2
Whole milk .... 1/2 cup
American slices 8
Goat/chèvre .... 5-1/2 oz
Parmesan, grated .... 1/4 cup

MEAT/POULTRY/FISH/SEAFOOD:
Snapper filets .... 1-3/4 lbs

MISCELLANEOUS:
Pecans, chopped .... 1/4 cup
Graham cracker crust 1
Baguette 1
Hamburger buns 4

FROZEN:
Cool Whip .... 1 cup

S/Y ISLAND DREAMS

Chef Janice Brown
Captain Scott Killam

MENU
Serves 4

Breakfast

Grapefruit Halves
*Raisin Scones

Lunch

*Tuna Burgers In Paradise
*Oven Fries

Hors d'oeuvre

*Baked Goat Cheese with
Fresh Baguette

Dinner

*Caribbean Red Snapper and
*Mango Salsa
*Glazed Carrots
Wild Rice
Warm French Rolls

*Key Lime Pie

Welcome aboard ISLAND DREAMS, a 45-foot Beneteau captained by Scott Killam with Janice Brown heading the galley. Scott has been in and around the water all his life, is a PADI dive master and loves to organize any water-sports activities. Janice calls herself a "superb self taught sailboat chef" which comes from years of living on board a sailboat and learning to turn out fine dining in a small galley. Some of the magic of this accomplishment comes from creative thinking mixed with clever planning.

*Indicates recipe provided

RAISIN SCONES

Preparation time: 15 minutes　　　　　　　*Chef: Janice Brown*
Cooking time: 12-15 minutes　　　　　　*Yacht: Island Dreams*
Serves: 4-6

1-3/4 cups	**Flour**
1/4 cup	**Sugar**
1 Tblsp	**Baking powder**
1/2 tsp	**Salt**
1/2 cup	**Raisins**
1/2 cup	**Butter**
1	**Egg**
1/2 cup	**Milk**

Preheat oven to 400°F/200°C. Combine the dry ingredients then stir in raisins. Cut in butter with a pastry cutter until mixture resembles dry oatmeal. Lightly beat the egg and combine with milk. Stir into dry ingredients until moistened. Pour into lightly greased 11 x 7 inch (27.5 x 18 cm) metal pan. Bake until lightly browned. Cut into squares. *Serve warm with butter and preserves.*

Note: Baking time is for a metal pan. Glass pan or dish may need longer baking time.

Hint: Variations—cranberries, currents or grated cheddar cheese.

TUNA BURGERS IN PARADISE

Preparation time: 10 minutes　　　　　　　*Chef: Janice Brown*
Cooking time: 15 minutes　　　　　　　*Yacht: Island Dreams*
Serves: 4

1 - 6 oz/170 g	**Can tuna, drained**
1	**Egg, beaten**
1/2 cup	**Cooked rice**
1/4 cup	**Grated Parmesan cheese**
1/4 cup	**Finely chopped green pepper**
2 Tblsp	**Olive oil**
4	**Fresh hamburger buns**
8	**Slices american cheese**
	Condiments of choice

Combine tuna, egg, rice, parmesan cheese and green pepper; mix well. Form into 4 patties. Heat olive oil in non stick skillet and cook patties over medium heat 5 minutes per side or until lightly browned. Serve on burger buns with slices of cheese and condiments of your choice.

OVEN FRIES

Preparation time: 15 minutes
Cooking time: 45 minutes
Serves: 4

Chef: Janice Brown
Yacht: Island Dreams

2	**Large baking potatoes**
1-1/2 Tblsp	**Olive oil**
1 Tblsp	**Paprika**
1 tsp	**Ground cumin**
	Salt to taste

Preheat oven to 425°F/220°C. Wash potatoes, peeling is optional. Cut potatoes lengthwise into 1/2 inch (1 cm) slices. Then cut through the slices to make 1/2 inch (1 cm) strips, no bigger. Combine olive oil, paprika and cumin. In a large bowl toss potatoes with olive oil and spice mixture. Bake potatoes on a lightly greased baking sheet for 45 minutes or until golden and starting to crisp. Stir occasionally while baking. Sprinkle with salt and *serve immediately.*

BAKED GOAT CHEESE

Preparation time: 10 minutes
Cooking time: 20-25 minutes
Serves: 4

Chef: Janice Brown
Yacht: Island Dreams

5 -1/2 oz/155 g	**Block chèvre (goat) cheese**
2	**Cloves garlic, minced**
1/4 cup	**Chopped pecans**
1/3 cup	**Olive oil**
1/4 cup	**Balsamic vinegar**
1	**Fresh baguette**

Preheat oven to 200°F/190°C. This is a "to taste" recipe. Feel free to adjust quantities of garlic, olive oil and balsamic vinegar. Place cheese in an 11 x 7 inch (27.5x18 cm) oven-to-table baking dish. Cover with minced garlic and pecans. Pour olive oil and vinegar over slowly. Bake in oven for 20-25 minutes. Cheese will melt. Serve with fresh baguette. Spread cheese on bread or dip right into pan and soak up the marinade.

CARIBBEAN RED SNAPPER
WITH MANGO SALSA

Preparation time: 15 minutes
Cooking time: 10 minutes
Serves: 4

Chef: Janice Brown
Yacht: Island Dreams

4 - 7 oz/200 g	**Fillets of snapper**
1 Tblsp	**Lime juice**
1 Tblsp	**Water**
1 tsp	**Paprika**
1/2 tsp	**Salt**
1/4 tsp	**Ground ginger**
1/4 tsp	**Allspice**
1/4 tsp	**Black pepper**
Garnish	**Lime wedges**
	Parsley or cilantro sprigs

Preheat oven to 450°F/230°C. Rinse fish and pat dry. Combine lime juice and water and brush onto each fillet. Combine all spices into a small bowl and sprinkle generously over fillets. Arrange in a shallow baking and serving dish. Bake uncovered for approximately 10 minutes. Garnish with lime wedges, and parsley. *Serve with **Mango Salsa** on the side.*

MANGO SALSA:
Chilling time: 1 hour

1	**Mango, peeled, seeded and chopped**
1	**Red bell pepper, seeded and chopped**
1/4 cup	**Thinly sliced green onion**
3 Tblsp	**Olive oil**
2 Tblsp	**Lime juice**
1 Tblsp	**White vinegar**
	Salt and pepper, to taste

Combine all ingredients and let chill in refrigerator for at least 1 hour to blend flavors.

GLAZED CARROTS

Preparation time: 2 minutes
Cooking time: 12-15 minutes
Serves: 4

Chef: Janice Brown
Yacht: Island Dreams

1 lb/450 g	**Pack fresh baby carrots**
1/3 cup	**Brown sugar, packed**
1/2 tsp	**Salt**
2 Tblsp	**Butter**

Cook baby carrots in boiling water until tender. Drain. In a saucepan melt butter and stir in brown sugar and salt, cook until bubbly. Add carrots and cook over low heat until carrots are glazed and heated through, about 5 minutes.

KEY LIME PIE

Preparation time: 20 minutes
Chilling time: 4-6 hours
Serves: 6

Chef: Janice Brown
Yacht: Island Dreams

1/2 cup	**Fresh squeezed lime juice**
14 oz/390 g	**Can sweetened condensed milk**
1 cup	**Frozen whipped topping, thawed**
1	**9 inch/23 cm graham pie crust**

Mix together lime juice and sweetened condensed milk until well combined. Fold in whipped topping. Pour into pie crust and refrigerate as long as necessary to set, usually about 4 hours.

Hint: I usually make this recipe in the morning and serve it for dessert in the evening.

JAYED SHOPPING LIST

VEGETABLES:
Bok choy stalk 1
Garlic, cloves 4
Red chili peppers 3
Spring onion 1
Shallot 1

FRUITS:
Limes 3
Kaffir limes 2

FRESH HERBS:
Cilantro .... garnish
Coriander root, chop .... 1 tsp
Mint .... garnish

DRIED SPICES:
Chili powder .... 1 tsp

CONDIMENTS:
Coconut, shaved .... 3 cups
Vanilla.............................. 1/2 tsp
Peanut oil .... 1 bottle
Soy sauce .... 1 bottle
Sweet chili .... 1 bottle
Fish sauce .... 1 Tblsp
Oyster sauce .... 8 tsp
Pickled soy beans .... 1-1/2 tsp
Plum sauce .... 1 jar

DRY GOODS:
Flour .... 1 Tblsp
Sugar .... 1-1/4 cups

CANS AND JARS:
Chicken broth .... 1/2 cup

DAIRY/MILK/CHEESE/BUTTER
Butter .... 9 Tblsp
Eggs 8

MEAT/POULTRY/FISH/SEAFOOD:
Chicken breast, boneless . 1
Shrimp .... 1/4 lb
Snapper .... 5-1/4 oz

MISCELLANEOUS:
Spring roll sheets............. 2

M/Y JAYED

Chef Pam Costa
Captain Gene Costa

AN ASIAN MENU
Serves 1

Breakfast

Continental Breakfast

Lunch

*Larb Gai – Spicy Minced Chicken Salad

Hors d'oeuvre

*Goong Pan – Deep Fried Shrimp Crêpe

Dinner

*Pla Pad Kuen Chai – Stir Fried Fish
with Chinese Celery
Jasmine Rice

*Kaffir Lime and Coconut Tart

Captain Gene Costa and his wife Pam are in Italy overseeing the construction of JAYED, a new 72-foot San Lorenzo motor yacht. After chartering in the Caribbean for 8 years, they took off for farther shores and sailed half way around the world on ABSOLUTE FREEDOM to visit French Polynesia, Australia, Bali, the Philippines, Singapore and Thailand. Pam, always a good cook, reports she is now heavily influenced by Asian delicacies.

*Indicates recipe provided

LARB GAI— SPICY MINCED CHICKEN SALAD

Preparation time: 15 minutes   Chef: Pam Costa
Cooking time: 15 minutes   Yacht: Jayed
Serves: 1

5-1/4 oz/150 g   **Chicken, minced or ground**

SPICY DRESSING:
1 Tblsp	**Lime Juice**
1-1/3 Tblsp	**Fish Sauce**
2 tsp	**Sugar**
1 tsp	**Chili powder**
1 Tblsp	**Toasted rice powder***
1 Tblsp	**Sliced Shallot**
1 Tblsp	**Sliced spring onion**
Garnish:	**Mint leaves and coriander**

Cook minced chicken in a very hot pan. Add some water and stir well.

Dressing: Combine lime juice, fish sauce and sugar. Add to cooked chicken, mix well and cook a few minutes. Add chili powder, toasted rice powder, shallots and spring onion. Remove from heat. Garnish. *Serve with side dishes of string beans and coriander.*

*Toasted rice powder – whole grains of rice fried in a dry pan and then crushed.

GOONG PAN—DEEP FRIED SHRIMP CREPE

Preparation time: 30 minutes
Cooking time: 20 minutes
Serves: 1

Chef: Pam Costa
Yacht: Jayed

4-1/4 oz/120 g	**Shrimp, minced**
1	**Egg yolk, slightly beaten**
1 tsp	**Chopped garlic**
1 tsp	**Chopped coriander (cilantro)**
2 Tblsp	**Oyster sauce**
1 tsp	**Fish sauce***
	Pepper powder
2	**Pieces rice crèpe-spring roll wrapper**
	Soy oil, or peanut oil for frying
	Plum Sauce
	Sweet Chili Sauce

Combine minced shrimp, egg yolk, garlic, coriander; mix well. Add fish sauce, oyster sauce and pepper powder. Combine. Spread the filling on one crèpe, brush with egg yolk and top with remaining crèpe. Pierce well with fork. Heat oil and deep fry until golden brown. *Cut into wedges and serve with plum and sweet chili sauces.*

*Fish sauce available in Asian grocery stores.

PLA PAD KUEN CHAI
STIR FRIED FISH WITH CELERY

Preparation time: 10 minutes   *Chef: Pam Costa*
Cooking time: 15 minutes   *Yacht: Jayed*
Serves: 1

5-1/4 oz/150 g	Fillet of red snapper or sea bass
1 Tblsp	Flour
	Salt and pepper powder* to taste
1 cup	Peanut oil for frying
1 Tblsp	Chopped garlic
2 Tblsp	Chopped chinese celery**
1/2 cup	Chicken stock
1-1/2 tsp	Pickled soy beans***
2 tsp	Fish sauce
2 tsp	Oyster sauce

Cut fish in 3/8 inch (8 mm) slices; coat with flour, salt and pepper powder. Heat oil in wok and cook fish 2 - 3 minutes. Remove fish and oil, leaving about 1 Tblsp. Add chopped garlic to wok and stir well. Add celery to cook, then fish. If it is dry, add some stock. Season with pickled soy beans, fish sauce, oyster sauce and pepper powder. Garnish with red chili peppers and *serve with Jasmine rice.*

Hint: 2 tsp of grated ginger may also be added.

*pepper powder is finely ground white pepper.

** similar to baby celery leaves.

***pickled soy beans is a condiment available in Asian grocery stores.

KAFFIR LIME AND COCONUT TART

Preparation time: 15 minutes　　　　　　　　　*Chef: Pam Costa*
Cooking time: 25 minutes　　　　　　　　　　　*Yacht: Jayed*
Serves: 1

Coconut Crust

1/2 cup	Sugar
2	Egg yolks
3 cups	Shaved coconut
2	Kaffir lime leaves, finely sliced
1	Egg white
Filling:	
2	Kaffir limes*, juice and zest
2	Lemons, juice and zest
3/4 cup	Sugar
6	Egg yolks
1/2 tsp	Vanilla extract
5/8 cup	Unsalted butter, chopped
Garnish	Kaffir lime wedges

Preheat oven to 300°F/150°C. Whisk sugar and egg yolks until pale and thick. Add coconut and lime leaves; stir until well combined. Beat egg white until stiff peaks form and fold gently into yolk mixture. With damp fingers press mixture evenly over base and sides of a lightly greased 9 inch (23 cm) round tart tin with removable base. Bake for about 25 minutes, or until golden.

Filling: Whisk grated lime and lemon rinds and juice with sugar, egg yolks and vanilla extract in a heatproof bowl over simmering water, until well combined, Whisk in butter a little at a time. Stir until mixture thickens to coat the back of a spoon; do not boil. Remove and cover. Cool. Spoon filling into coconut crust, cover and refrigerate over night. Serve with wedges of kaffir lime.

*Note: Kaffir limes have a very distinct taste are not like any limes grown in the USA. Substitute with the grated zest of 1 ordinary lime and juice of 1/2 lime, or you can find dried kaffir lime leaves in Asian groceries.

LA CREOLE SHOPPING LIST

VEGETABLES:
Avocados 2
Celery stalks 2
Garlic cloves 4
Spring onions 4
Red onion 1
Yellow onions 2
Mixed greens .... 3 cups
Lettuce .... garnish
Arugula .... 1 bunch

FRUITS:
Granny Smith apples 2
Grapes, seedless .... 1/2 lb
Limes 3
Lemons 2
Mangos 2
Oranges............................. 4
Orange juice .... 3/4 cup
Pineapple .... garnish

FRESH HERBS:
Cilantro, chopped .... 3 Tblsp
Ginger, chopped .... 2 tsp
Mint .... 1 bunch
Parsley, chopped .... 2 Tblsp
Italian parsley, chopped .. 2 Tblsp
Watercress .... 1 bunch

DRIED SPICES:
Cinnamon .... 4 tsp
Curry .... 3 Tblsp

CONDIMENTS:
Peanuts .... garnish
Raisins .... 1/4 cup
Basil pesto .... 1 cup
Vanilla extract .... 1 tsp
Olive oil............................ 3/4 cup
Mayonnaise .... 1 cup
Maple syrup .... optional
Tabasco .... 1/4 tsp
Vinegar, cider .... 2 Tblsp

DRY GOODS:
Sugar, brown .... 1/3 cups
Sugar................................ 4 tsp
Sugar, confectioners' .... garnish

CANS AND JARS:
Pimento .... 1 jar
Mango chutney .... 1/2 cup

DAIRY/MILK/CHEESE/BUTTER
Butter .... 1-3/4 lbs
Eggs 7
Half and half .... 1-1/2 cups
Whole milk .... 1/2 cup
Sour cream .... 8 oz
Blue cheese .... 8 oz
Cream cheese................... 8 oz
Mozzarella, grated .... 1/2 cup
Parmesan, grated .... 1/2 cup
Ricotta .... 3 cups

MEAT/POULTRY/FISH/SEAFOOD:
Chicken breasts 4
Snapper filets.................. 4-8 oz

LIQUOR/WINE/SPIRITS:
Rum, white .... 1/2 cup

MISCELLANEOUS:
Shortbread cookies 4
Baguette 1
Club soda .... 6 pack

LA CREOLE

Chef Frances Anne Johns
Captain Oliver Deligny

MENU
Serves 4

Breakfast

*Mango Breakfast Pancakes

Lunch

*Island Curry Chicken Salad

Hors d'oeuvres

*Goat Cheese Bruschettas
*Mojito Cocktail

Dinner

*Avocado Orange Salad with Orange Vinaigrette
*Roasted Red Snapper with Salsa
*Herbed Orange Rice

*Lemon Cream Berry Trifle

Captain Oliver Deligny on the 50-foot Gulfstar ketch LA CREOLE feels sun, snorkeling, diving, exploring other islands, good sailing and gourmet meals are what cruising and chartering are all about. Chef Frances Anne Johns is there to provide the good meals, which she does with a deft hand and, often, imaginative use of local dishes and products. Oliver, one of the favorite captains in the Caribbean, is a native West Indian from St. Lucia, knows the waters and island lore like no other. La Creole takes up to 6 guests.

*Indicates recipe provided

MANGO BREAKFAST PANCAKES

Preparation time: 15 minutes　　　　　　　　*Chef: Frances Johns*
Cooking time: 20 minutes　　　　　　　　　　*Yacht: La Creole*
Serves: 6

4 Tblsp	**Butter**
2	**Mangos, sliced**
1/3 cup	**Brown sugar**
1 tsp	**Cinnamon**
1	**Lemon, juiced**
6	**Eggs**
1-1/2 cups	**Milk**
1-1/2 cups	**Flour**
1 tsp	**Vanilla**
1/4 tsp	**Salt**
	Confectioners' sugar
	Syrup or yogurt, optional

Preheat oven to 425°F/220°C. In an oven proof skillet, melt butter and sauté mango slices lightly. Sprinkle with brown sugar, cinnamon and lemon juice. In a bowl or food processor blend milk, eggs, flour, vanilla, salt and pour over fruit in hot skillet. Place in oven and bake for 20 minutes. Let stand 5 minutes. Sprinkle with confectioners' sugar. *Serve with your choice of syrup or yogurt.*

ISLAND CURRY CHICKEN SALAD

Preparation time: 30 minutes   *Chef: Frances Johns*
Cooking time: 20 minutes   *Yacht: La Creole*
Chilling time: 1 hour
Serves: 4

4	**Boneless chicken breast halves**
1/2 cup	**Half and half**
	Salt and pepper
1/2	**Onion, chopped**
1	**Green apple, chopped**
2 stalks	**Celery, chopped**
1/4 cup	**Raisins**
1 cup	**Mayonnaise, low-fat**
1/2 cup	**Mango chutney**
3 Tblsp	**Curry powder**
1 Tblsp	**Lemon juice**
1/2 tsp	**Salt**
2 Tblsp	**Parsley, chopped**
Garnish:	**Lettuce, pineapple wedge, peanuts, coconut and chopped scallions**

Preheat oven to 400°F/200°C. Season chicken breast with salt, pepper, half and half. Wrap in a foil pouch, place on a cookie sheet and bake for 20 minutes. Open pouch and let cool. Chop onion, apple, celery and add raisins in a bowl. Chop chicken and add. Make a sauce with remaining ingredients. Mix all together and stir into chicken mixture. Chill 1 hour. Serve on a bed of lettuce with a pineapple wedge. Garnish with toasted peanuts or coconut and chopped scallions.

Hint: *May also be served in pita pockets with shredded lettuce. Very colorful and easy!*

GOAT CHEESE BRUSCHETTAS

Preparation time: 5 minutes   *Chef: Frances Johns*
Cooking time: 5 minutes   *Yacht: La Creole*
Serves: 4

1	**Baguette sliced or toast rounds**
1 cup	**Basil or tomato pesto**
3/4 cup	**Goat cheese**
1	**Jar pimento, sliced**
1/2 lb/225 g	**Seedless grapes**
	Apple, sliced

Toast baguette slices until lightly browned. Spread with pesto; crumble on goat cheese. Place under broiler until cheese is slightly browned. Top with pimento slices for color. *Serve with grapes and sliced apples.*

Hint: Purchase pesto in tube or jar. Simple to prepare!

MOJITO COCKTAIL

Preparation time: 5 minutes   *Chef: Frances Johns*
Serves: 4   *Yacht: La Creole*

4 tsp	**Sugar**
4 Tblsp	**Lime juice**
3	**Sprigs of mint**
1/2 cup	**White rum**
	Club soda

Mix sugar and lime juice together. Add several sprigs of mint and mash all together with wooden spoon. Divide between four tall glasses filled with ice, add rum and fill with club soda. Stir. Garnish with fresh mint sprig. *Very refreshing!*

AVOCADO ORANGE SALAD WITH ORANGE VINAIGRETTE

Preparation time: 30 minutes
Serves: 4

Chef: Frances Johns
Yacht: La Creole

4	Oranges

ORANGE VINAIGRETTE:

1/4 cup	Olive oil
2 Tblsp	Cider vinegar
2 Tblsp	Fresh orange juice
1 tsp	Orange zest
1 tsp	Sugar
2 cloves	Garlic, minced
1/2 tsp	Cumin, ground
1/4 tsp	Tabasco
2	Avocados, ripe
1 Tblsp	Lemon juice

Greens:

3 cups	Romaine, arugula, watercress
1/2 cup	Finely chopped red onion

Grate zest from one orange and set aside. Cut peel from oranges (over a bowl to catch juice). Slice into rounds. Save juice for dressing. Combine vinaigrette ingredients in a jar and shake well. Cut avocado into sections and sprinkle with lemon juice. Arrange greens on plates and top with avocado slices, orange rounds and red onion. Drizzle with vinaigrette.

Hint: *Papaya may be substituted for orange slices.*

ROASTED RED SNAPPER WITH SALSA

Preparation time: 30 minutes
Cooking time: 20 minutes
Resting time: 20 minutes
Serves: 4

Chef: Frances Johns
Yacht: La Creole

2 Tblsp	Olive oil
2 Tblsp	Lime juice
1 Tblsp	Chopped cilantro
4 - 8 oz/225 g	Snapper fillets
	Salt and pepper to taste
1 bunch	Arugula
1 bunch	Watercress

Salsa:

2 large	Tomatoes
2 Tblsp	Scallions, chopped
2 Tblsp	Cilantro, chopped
2 cloves	Garlic, chopped
2 tsp	Lime juice
	Salt and pepper to taste

Preheat oven to 400°F/200°C. Combine oil, lime juice and cilantro in a small bowl. Place fish (skin side down) on a greased baking sheet. Brush with oil mixture and sprinkle with salt and pepper. Let rest 20 minutes. Then bake for 20 minutes. Meantime, combine salsa ingredients in food processor and pulse lightly. Arrange arugula and watercress on plates, lay snapper over greens and top with salsa.

HERBED ORANGE RICE

Preparation time: 5 minutes   *Chef: Frances Johns*
Cooking time: 20 minutes   *Yacht: La Creole*
Serves: 4

1 Tblsp	Butter
1 small	Onion, chopped
1 cup	Basmati rice
1-1/4 cups	Chicken broth
1/2 cup	Fresh orange juice
2 tsp	Minced fresh ginger
1 tsp	Orange zest
Pinch	Salt
2 Tblsp	Scallions, chopped
2 Tblsp	Italian parsley, chopped

Melt butter and sauté onion over medium heat, briefly. Add rice and cook stirring for 3 minutes. Add the broth, orange juice, ginger, zest and salt, and bring to boil. Cook covered over low heat approximately 20 minutes. Fluff with fork, cover and let rest. Stir in scallions and parsley.

LEMON CREAM BERRY TRIFLE

Preparation time: 15 minutes   *Chef: Frances Johns*
Chilling time: 2 hours   *Yacht: La Creole*
Serves: 4

1 cup	Whipped cream
1 cup	Lemon yogurt
2 cups	Mixed berries, blue, raspberries, strawberries, etc. (fresh or frozen)
4	Shortbread cookies (gingerbread or similar cookies)
Garnish:	Lemon slices or mint sprigs

Mix the whipped cream and lemon yogurt together and chill about an hour. In a glass dish or wine glass, layer berries, yogurt cream, cookie, berries, cream. Chill 1 hour or longer. *Garnish.*

LA DOLCE VITA SHOPPING LIST

VEGETABLES:
Garlic cloves 2
Yellow onions 2

FRUITS:
Bananas 5
Kiwi .... garnish
Mangos 3

FRESH HERBS:
Cilantro, chopped .... 2 Tblsp

DRIED SPICES:
Cayenne .... 1/4 tsp
Chili powder .... 1/4 cup
Cumin, ground .... 2 tsp

CONDIMENTS:
Baking powder .... 2 tsp
Baking soda .... 1/4 tsp
Bouillon cubes 2
Chocolate, semi-sweet ..... 8 oz
Cocoa .... garnish
Olive oil .... 1 Tblsp
Vegetable oil .... 5 Tblsp
Soy sauce .... 1 Tblsp

DRY GOODS:
Flour .... 1-3/4 cups
Sugar, brown .... 3 Tblsp
Sugar, confectioners' .... 5 Tblsp
Sugar .... 2/3 cup

CANS AND JARS:
Kidney beans .... 2 cans
Chicken broth .... 3/4 cup
Tomatoes, crushed .... 1 lg can

DAIRY/MILK/CHEESE/BUTTER
Butter .... 5 oz
Eggs 8
Goat/chèvre .... 5 oz

MEAT/POULTRY/FISH/SEAFOOD:
Chicken breasts 6
Ground beef .... 2 lb

LIQUOR/WINE/SPIRITS:
Rum, spiced .... 5 Tblsp

MISCELLANEOUS:
Tortillas, flour 6

FROZEN:
Spinach .... 10 oz pkg

S/Y LA DOLCE VITA

Chef Dominique Feix
Captain Tony Hutterer

MENU
Serves 6

Breakfast

Tropical Fruits with Yogurt
*Banana Bread

Lunch

*Chili Con Carne

Hors d'oeuvre

*Goat Cheese and Spinach Quesadillas

Dinner

*BBQ Chicken Breast with
*Fresh Mango Sauce
Fried Plantains
Rice

*Chocolate Rum Mousse

LA DOLCE VITA, the name given to this 52-foot Irwin cutter/ketch, means "the sweet life". And indeed it is aboard this elegant, intimate yacht. Captain Anton (Tony) Hutterer and Chef Dominique Feix do everything they can to spoil their guests and part of the spoiling is serving marvelous meals planned and executed by Dominique who was born in Strasbourg on the French-German border. She has had 20 years of experience in the Caribbean hotel and culinary industry and that French/Creole influence often appears on the menu.

*Indicates recipe provided

BANANA BREAD

Preparation time: 15 minutes　　　　　　*Chef: Dominique Feix*
Cooking time: 1 hour　　　　　　　　　　*Yacht: La Dolce Vita*
Makes: 1 loaf

1-3/4 cups	Flour
2 tsp	Baking powder
1/4 tsp	Baking soda
1/4 tsp	Salt
2/3 cup	Sugar
4 tsp	Vegetable oil
2	Eggs, well beaten
2 cups	Ripe mashed bananas

Heat oven to 350°F/180°C. Sift dry ingredients together. Combine eggs, oil, and mashed bananas; add them to dry ingredients and beat until smooth. Bake in a greased 8-1/2 x 4-1/2 x 2-1/2 inch (21 x 11 x 6 cm) pan, about 1 hour. Cool before slicing. *Serve with butter.*

Hint: Also good for an afternoon snack with a cup of tea.

Hint: Prepare banana Bread after each charter with your "too ripe left over bananas" and freeze it. Defrost the night before breakfast and warm 1 minute in microwave. My oven holds 3 loaf pans, so I often make three loaves, use one and freeze the other two.

Tip: If you don't have time to bake the bread, peel the "too ripe" bananas, place in a reclosable bag and freeze until needed.

Note: Vanessa from S/Y Shamoun adds 1/2 cup sour cream and 1 tsp vanilla essence.

CHILI CON CARNE

Preparation time: 30 minutes
Cooking time: 1 hour
Serves: 12*

Chef: Dominique Feix
Yacht: La Dolce Vita

3 Tblsp	Vegetable oil
2	Large onions, diced
2	Green bell peppers, diced
2 cloves	Garlic, chopped
2 lbs/900 g	Ground beef
2 cubes	Beef bouillon, dissolved in 2 cups water
32 oz/900 g	Can crushed tomatoes
3 Tblsp	Tomato paste
1/4 cup	Chili powder
1/4 tsp	Cayenne pepper
2 tsp	Ground cumin
1 tsp	Salt
2 - 16 oz/450 g	Cans red kidney beans, drained

Heat a large frying pan on medium-high heat, about 45 seconds. Add 1 Tblsp oil, onions, and peppers; sauté until soft, about 6 minutes. Add garlic and sauté 2 more minutes. Transfer mixture to a large soup pot.

Increase heat under frying pan to high and let the pan get very hot, about 90 seconds. Add 1 Tblsp of oil and half the ground beef. Brown the meat for about 6 minutes, then transfer to a colander to drain off excess fat. Repeat with the remaining ground beef. Then add beef, beef broth, crushed tomatoes, tomato paste and all of the spices to the soup pot.

Bring mixture to a boil over medium-high heat, then reduce heat to low and simmer for 45 minutes, stirring occasionally. Add the beans and simmer for 15 more minutes .

Serving suggestions: Prepare bowls of sour cream, grated cheddar cheese, chopped bell pepper, crumbled cooked bacon, and chopped red onion to sprinkle on top of individual servings. *Serve with corn bread.*

*Note: *This recipe is time consuming, so I prepare it for 12 servings and freeze half for the next charter. The chili is excellent reheated.*

GOAT CHEESE AND SPINACH QUESADILLAS

Preparation time: 10 minutes
Cooking time: 2 minutes
Serves: 6

Chef: Dominique Feix
Yacht: La Dolce Vita

6	**Flour tortillas**
5 oz/140 g	**Block goat cheese**
10 oz/280 g	**Pkg frozen spinach, thawed**
	Salt and pepper to taste

Spread half of each tortilla with goat cheese. Squeeze spinach and pat dry, add on top of goat cheese. Sprinkle with salt and pepper. Fold and cook in an ungreased medium-hot skillet, about 1 minute each side. *Serve immediately.*

CHOCOLATE RUM MOUSSE

Preparation time: 10 minutes
Cooking time: 2 minutes
Chilling time: 2 hours
Serves: 6

Chef: Dominique Feix
Yacht: La Dolce Vita

1/2 lb/250 g	**Semi-sweet chocolate**
5 Tblsp	**Rum (spiced is good)**
5 Tblsp	**Unsalted butter**
6	**Eggs, separated**
5 Tblsp	**Powdered sugar**
Garnish:	**Kiwi slices and a little cocoa**

Melt chocolate in rum over low heat. Whisk in butter and sugar. Remove from heat and whisk in egg yolks. In a separate bowl beat egg whites until firm then fold carefully into mixture. Chill in refrigerator for a minimum of 2 hours. *Before serving decorate with kiwi fruit slices and sift unsweetened cocoa on top.*

BBQ CHICKEN BREAST WITH FRESH MANGO SAUCE

Preparation time: 15 minutes
Cooking time: 20 minutes
Serves: 6

Chef: Dominique Feix
Yacht: La Dolce Vita

6	**Chicken breasts**
1 Tblsp	**Olive oil**
1/4 tsp	**Salt**
1/2 tsp	**Freshly ground pepper, or to taste**

Preheat the BBQ. Brush the chicken breasts with oil and sprinkle with salt and pepper. Grill about 10 minutes per side. Put aside and keep warm.

MANGO SAUCE:

2	**Large mangoes, peeled**
1 Tblsp	**Vegetable oil**
2 cloves	**Garlic, crushed**
1/3 cup	**Chopped fresh cilantro or sage leaves**
3/4 cup	**Chicken broth**
3 Tblsp	**Brown sugar**
1 Tblsp	**Soy sauce**
	Salt and pepper

Prepare mangoes and purée. Heat 1 Tblsp of oil in a skillet to medium hot. Add garlic and cilantro or sage leaves. Sauté for about 1 minute. Add the chicken broth, brown sugar, and soy sauce. Bring to a boil stirring occasionally. Reduce the heat and simmer 3 minutes. Gradually whisk in the mango purée (about 1/2 to 1 cup). Simmer until sauce thickens, about 5 minutes, season with salt and pepper and pour over chicken breasts. *Serve with rice and fresh steamed vegetables.*

Note: *Easy Caribbean recipe. Looks fantastic, low cost, and tastes terrific.*

LADY ALLISON SHOPPING LIST

VEGETABLES:
Asparagus, green .... 1/2 bunch
Asparagus, white .... 1/2 bunch
Napa cabbage .... 1 head
Garlic .... 1 bulb
Jalapeño 1
Shallot 1
Red onions 4
Red bell pepper 1
Yellow bell pepper 1
Plantains 2
Potatoes, medium 8
Snowpeas .... 1/4 cup
Bean sprouts .... 1/2 cup

FRUITS:
Lemon 1
Mango 1
Papaya 1
Pear 1

FRESH HERBS:
Parsley, chopped .... garnish

DRIED SPICES:
Cinnamon .... 1-1/2 Tblsp
Curry .... 1-1/2 Tblsp
Garlic powder .... 1-1/2 Tblsp
Ginger .... 1-1/2 Tblsp
Paprika .... 1-1/2 Tblsp
Saffron .... pinch
Turmeric .... 1-1/2 Tblsp
Kosher salt .... 1-1/2 Tblsp

CONDIMENTS:
Chocolate chips .... 1/2 cup
Honey .... 3/4 cup
Creole mustard .... 2-1/2 Tblsp
Molasses .... 1/4 cup
Canola oil .... 3/4 cup
Olive oil .... 2 cups
Peanut oil .... 1-1/2 cups

Vegetable oil .... 4 cups
Soy sauce .... 3 Tblsp
Vinegar, rice wine .... 1/4 cup

DRY GOODS:
Flour .... 1/2 cup
Rice, basmati .... 1-1/2 cups
Sugar .... 2 Tblsp
Sugar, confectioners' .... 1/2 cup

CANS AND JARS:
Chocolate sauce .... garnish
Peanut butter .... 4 Tblsp
Beef broth .... 1 cup

DAIRY/MILK/CHEESE/BUTTER
Butter .... 1 lb+2 Tblsp
Whole milk .... 1 cup
Mascarpone .... 8 oz
Ricotta .... 8 oz

MEAT/POULTRY/FISH/SEAFOOD:
Beef tenderloin 1
Duck breasts 3
Dolphin filets .... 6 - 8 oz

LIQUOR/WINE/SPIRITS:
Bourbon .... 1/4 cup
Kahlua .... 2 Tblsp
Wine, red .... 1/2 cup

MISCELLANEOUS:
Wonton wrappers .... 1 pkg
Phyllo dough .... 1 pkg

FROZEN:
Peas .... 1/2 cup

M/Y LADY ALLISON

Chef Kevin Rico

MENU
Serves 6

Breakfast

Continental Breakfast

Lunch

*Moroccan Spiced Dolphin with
*Mango Papaya Relish
*Saffron Rice and Peas

Hors d'oeuvre

*Mongolian Duck and Wonton Stack
*Asian Slaw

Dinner

*Beef Tenderloin Medallions with
*Bourbon Molasses Sauce
*Caramelized Pear and Onion Mashed Potatoes
*Green and White Asparagus

*Chocolate Chip Phyllo Napoleons

*Indicates recipe provided

MOROCCAN SPICED DOLPHIN
WITH MANGO PAPAYA RELISH

Preparation time: 10 minutes　　　　　　　　*Chef: Kevin Rico*
Cooking time:30 minutes　　　　　　　　*Yacht: Lady Allison*
Serves: 6

6 - 8 oz/225 g	**Dolphin fish filets**
1/4 cup	**Olive oil**

MOROCCAN SPICE MIX:

1-1/2 Tblsp	**Kosher salt**
1-1/2 Tblsp	**Fresh black pepper**
1-1/2 Tblsp	**Cinnamon**
1-1/2 Tblsp	**Curry powder**
1-1/2 Tblsp	**Turmeric**
1-1/2 Tblsp	**Ground ginger**
1-1/2 Tblsp	**Paprika**
1-1/2 Tblsp	**Garlic powder**

SAFFRON RICE:

1-1/2 cups	**Basmati rice**
3 cups	**Water**
Pinch	**Saffron**
1/2 cup	**Frozen peas**

PLANTAIN CHIPS:

2	**Plantains**
1/4 cup	**Flour**
2 cups	**Vegetable oil**

MANGO PAPAYA RELISH:

1	**Ripe mango, diced**
1	**Ripe papaya, diced**
1-1/2 cups	**Diced red onion**
1	**Jalapeño, diced**
1 clove	**Garlic, diced**
1/4 cup	**Honey**
1/4 cup	**Olive oil**

Preheat oven to 400°F/200°C. Coat fish filets with spice mix. Cook rice adding peas the last 3 minutes. Slice plantains in rounds about 3/8 inch (5 mm) thick, coat with flour and fry in oil until golden brown; drain on paper towels. In a glass bowl mix together mango-papaya relish ingredients. Heat 1/4 cup olive oil in a large skillet over medium-high heat. Sear filets on both sides. Transfer to a baking sheet and bake in the oven 8 - 12 minutes or until fish is cooked. *Place rice and peas in the center of each plate. Place fish on top, spoon over relish and add plantain chips around the edge.*

MONGOLIAN DUCK AND WONTON STACK WITH ASIAN SLAW

Preparation time: 20 minutes
Marinating time: 6 - 24 hours
Cooking time: 20 minutes
Serves: 6

Chef: Kevin Rico
Yacht: Lady Allison

3	Duck breasts
1	Package wonton wrappers
2 cups	Vegetable oil

Marinade:

4 Tblsp	Peanut butter
2-1/2 Tblsp	Creole mustard
2 Tblsp	Garlic
2 Tblsp	Sugar
2 Tblsp	Soy sauce
1 Tblsp	Diced jalapeño pepper
1-1/2 Tblsp	Honey
1-1/2 cups	Peanut oil
1/4 cup	Flour
1/2 cup	Olive oil
1/4 cup	Honey
Pinch	Saffron

Blend the marinade ingredients in food processor until smooth. Pour over duck breasts and marinate for 6 - 24 hours. Fry wonton wrappers in oil until crisp and drain on paper towels. Sauté duck breasts until cooked through and slice into thin strips.

ASIAN SLAW:

1/4 cup each	Julienned red and yellow bell pepper
1/4 cup	Thinly sliced onion
1/4 cup	Blanched snow peas
1/2 cup	Bean sprouts
2 cups	Napa cabbage, shredded
1/4 cup	Rice wine vinegar
2 Tblsp	Honey
1 Tblsp	Soy sauce
3/4 cup	Canola oil

Mix all ingredients in a bowl, cover and refrigerate for at least 2 hours.
To Serve: Place some Asian slaw in the center of a large platter. Stack 4 wontons, Asian slaw and duck strips. Repeat layer using 3 wrappers, then 2, then 1, creating a tower. *Garnish plate with black sesame seeds and diced red and yellow peppers. Makes a great presentation.*

BEEF TENDERLOIN MEDALLIONS WITH BOURBON MOLASSES SAUCE

Preparation time: 5 miniutes
Cooking time: 20 minutes
Serves: 6

Chef: Kevin Rico
Yacht: Lady Allison

18	**Beef tenderloin medallions 1/4 inch (5 mm) thick**
Garnish:	**Chopped parsley**

BOURBON-MOLASSES SAUCE:

1	**Shallot, diced**
1/2 cup	**Red wine**
1 cup	**Beef stock**
1/4 cup	**Molasses**
1/4 cup	**Bourbon**
8 oz/225 g	**Butter**

In a small saucepan cook shallot in red wine reduce to 1/4 cup. Add beef stock and reduce to 3/4 cup; remove from heat. Stir in molasses, bourbon and butter. Serve over **Medallions** *and* **Caramelized Pear and Onion Mashed Potatoes**

Grill **Beef Medallions** to desired temperature. Divide mashed potatoes between 6 plates, place in the center. Lay 3 beef medallions on one side of the potatoes and asparagus on other. Pour sauce over potatoes and meat. Garnish with chopped parsley.

GREEN AND WHITE ASPARAGUS

Preparation time: 5 minutes
Cooking time: 5 minutes
Serves: 6

Chef: Kevin Rico
Yacht: Lady Allison

1/2	**Bunch green asparagus**
1/2	**Bunch white asparagus**
2 Tblsp	**Fresh lemon juice**
2 Tblsp	**Olive oil**

Brush asparagus with lemon juice and olive oil and grill until just tender turning frequently.

CARAMELIZED PEAR AND ONION MASHED POTATOES

Preparation time: 10 minutes　　　　　　*Chef: Kevin Rico*
Cooking time: 30 minutes　　　　　　　*Yacht: Lady Allison*
Serves: 6

8	**Medium size potatoes**
1	**Pear, peeled and chopped**
1	**Red onion, finely chopped**
2 Tblsp	**Butter**
1	**Cup milk**
	Salt and pepper

Peel and cut potatoes. Place in a saucepan, cover with cold salted water and cook over medium high heat for 30 minutes. Sauté pear and onion in butter until brown and caramelized. Mash potatoes, add milk, pear and onion mixture, salt and pepper. Serve with ***Beef Medallions and Asparagus.***

CHOCOLATE CHIP PHYLLO NAPOLEONS

Preparation time: 30 minutes　　　　　　*Chef: Kevin Rico*
Chilling time: 30 minutes　　　　　　　*Yacht: Lady Allison*
Serves: 6

1 Pkg	**Phyllo dough**
8 oz/225 g	**Mascarpone**
8 oz/225 g	**Ricotta cheese**
2 Tblsp	**Kahlua**
1/2 cup	**Powdered sugar**
1/2 cup	**Chocolate chips**
	Butter
Garnish:	**Hershey's chocolate sauce**

Preheat oven to 375°F/190°C. Layer 4 sheets of phyllo on a cookie sheet. Brush each sheet with melted butter. Cut in half lengthwise. Slice each half into 4-5 triangles of the same size. Bake for 8-10 minutes until brown and crispy. Blend all other ingredients (except chocolate sauce) in a bowl and refrigerate for at least 30 minutes. Squirt chocolate sauce onto plate in a zigzag pattern. Place 1 layered phyllo triangle in center of plate. Spread chocolate chip/cheese mixture on triangle and repeat layers 2 more times. Dust with powdered sugar and serve.

Hint: *Serve with ICE COLD Champagne for a delicious finale!!!*

MARGE'S BARGE SHOPPING LIST

VEGETABLES:
Garlic .... 1 bulb
Leek 1
Mushrooms .... 1/3 lb
Scallion 1
Shallot 1
Yellow onions 4
Potatoes large 2

FRUITS:
Lemon 2

FRESH HERBS:
Basil, chopped .... 2 tsp
Oregano, chopped .... 2 tsp
Parsley, chopped .... 4 Tblsp
Rosemary, chopped .... 1 Tblsp
Sage, chopped .... 1 Tblsp
Tarragon, chopped .... 1 Tblsp
Thyme, chopped .... 1 Tblsp

DRIED SPICES:
Tarragon .... 1/4 tsp

CONDIMENTS:
Mustard, Dijon .... 1 Tblsp
Olive oil .... 1/3 cup
Vegetable oil .... 2 Tblsp
Soy sauce .... 2 Tblsp
Vinegar, red wine .... 2 Tblsp
Vinegar, white wine .... 2 Tblsp

DRY GOODS:
Lasagna .... 1 lb
Orzo .... 1 lb
Sugar .... 1/2 tsp

CANS AND JARS:
Chicken broth, low salt ... 7 cups
Capers .... 2 Tblsp

DAIRY/MILK/CHEESE/BUTTER
Butter .... 1 Tblsp
Butter, unsalted .... 1/4 lb
Eggs 8
Whole milk .... splash
Cheddar, shredded .... 3 cups
Mozzarella, shredded ...... 2-1/4 cups
Parmesan, grated .... 2 cups

MEAT/POULTRY/FISH/SEAFOOD:
Ground beef .... 2 lbs
Ham, chopped .... 1 cup
London broil .... 1-1/2 lbs
Italian hot sausage .... 4 links
Italian sweet sausage .... 1 lb

FROZEN:
Pastry shells, miniature .. 2 pkg

M/Y MARGE'S BARGE

Captain Ed Kalik
Captain Fernand Dionne
Chef Marge Kalik
Chef Michael Cabacungan
Chef Spring Loudenslager

MENU
Serves 6 to 12

Breakfast

Mimosas and Bloody Marys
*Hurricane Eggs

Lunch

*Prima Lasagna
Mixed Green Salad

Hors d'oeuvres

*Leek and Sausage Tartets
Cheese Platter and Assorted Crackers

Dinner

*London Broil with Ravigote Sauce
*F-du Rice

The motor yacht MARGE'S BARGE, a 48-foot Seamaster, cruises the Virgin Islands every Sunday and sometimes Monday, weather permitting. When Captain Fernand Dionne pulls into the designated anchorage of the day, usually around 10:30 am, a feast begins and continues as the guests play backgammon and card games through the day. Chefs vary as does the menu, but frequent contributors are Marge Kalik, wife of the owner, and her friends Michael Cabacungan and Spring Loudenslager.

*Indicates recipe provided

HURRICANE EGGS

Preparation time: 5 minutes
Cooking time: 30 minutes
Serves: 6

Chef: Michael Cabacungan
Yacht: Marge's Barge

8	Eggs
8 Tblsp	Butter, diced
1 cup	Shredded cheddar cheese
1 cup	Chopped ham
1	Onion, chopped
2	Large potatoes, cooked and diced
1 splash	Milk
1 splash	Water
	Salt and pepper, to taste

Preheat oven to 350°F/180°C. Grease a jelly roll baking dish 15 x 10 x 1-1/8 inch (37.5 x25 x 2.8 cm) with cooking spray. In a bowl mix all ingredients together. Pour into the baking dish and spread evenly. Bake for 30 minutes, or until eggs are set. Do not overcook.

Hint: Use your imagination with ingredients; add anything you like.

PRIMA LASAGNE

Preparation time: 30 minutes　　　　*Chef: Spring Loudenslager*
Cooking time: 2 hours*　　　　　　　*Yacht: Marge's Barge*
Serves: 12

2 lbs/900 g	Ground beef
4	Links hot sausage (take out of casing)
8 cloves	Garlic, minced
3	Small onions, minced
2 tsp	Oregano
2 tsp	Basil
1 Tblsp	Parsley
	Salt and pepper to taste
3 - 16 oz/450 g	Jars spaghetti sauce (Prego)
3 cups	Water
3 qts	Water
2 tsp	Salt
1 lb/450	Lasagne noodles
2 cups	Shredded cheddar cheese
2 cups	Shredded mozzarella cheese
2 cups	Shredded parmesan cheese
2 cups	Cottage cheese

In a 5 quart saucepan, brown ground beef and hot sausage, drain. Add garlic, onion, oregano, basil, parsley, salt and pepper. Stir frequently on medium heat. Add 3 jars spaghetti sauce and rinse jars with 3 cups water; add to sauce. Let simmer, uncovered at least 2 hours, stirring every 15 minutes. (*I cook mine 6 hours plus).

In a separate 5 quart sauce pan bring 3 quarts of water and salt to a boil. Add lasagna noodles. Cook 10 minutes. Drain noodles, lay them flat so they don't stick together.

Preheat oven to 350°F/180°C. In a 9-1/2x13 inch (24x32.5 cm) casserole pan, from bottom to top layer the following: 2 cups sauce mixture, 4 lasagna noodles (side by side), 2 cups sauce mixture. Sprinkle over 1 cup cheddar, 1 cup mozzarella cheese, 1 cup parmesan, and spoon over 1 cup cottage cheese. Repeat from 4 lasagna noodles. Then layer top with 4 lasagna noodles. Top with 1 cup sauce mixture and remaining cheese. Cover casserole with foil and place on sheet pan. Bake for 50 minutes. Remove foil and bake for an additional 10 minutes. Let set for 10 minutes before cutting into 12 squares. *Serve with a side of extra sauce.*

LONDON BROIL WITH RAVIGOTE SAUCE

Preparation time: 30 minutes
Marinating time: 1 hour or overnight
Cooking time: 16-20 minutes
Standing time: 10 minutes
Serves: 6

Chef: Marge Kalik
Yacht: Marge's Barge

2 Tblsp	Minced garlic
2 Tblsp	Soy sauce
2 Tblsp	Red wine vinegar
1 Tblsp	Vegetable oil
1/2 tsp	Sugar
1/2 tsp	Salt
1-1/2 lbs/680 g	London broil, about 1-1/2 inches (3.5 cm) thick

In a blender combine all ingredients, except London broil, and blend well. Place London broil in a strong sealable plastic bag, and pour marinade over. Seal bag. Marinate at room temperature 1 hour, or chill overnight; turn occasionally.

Preheat grill. Remove London broil from marinade and drain. Place on an oiled rack over glowing coals or on an oiled rack of a broiler about 1-inch from the heat for 8 - 10 minutes per side or until meat thermometer registers 130°F/55°C for medium-rare.

Transfer to cutting board and let stand for 10 minutes. Slice thin with knife held at 45° angle. Serve with **Ravigote Sauce.**

RAVIGOTE SAUCE:

Makes: 3/4 cup

1/3 cup	Finely chopped onion
1 Tblsp	Dijon mustard
2 tsp	White vinegar
1/3 cup	Olive oil
1 Tblsp	Minced shallot
1 Tblsp	Minced green scallion, or chives
2 Tblsp	Drained capers, chopped
2 Tblsp	Minced parsley
1/4 tsp	Dried tarragon, crumbled
	Salt and pepper, to taste

Soak onion in water for 3 minutes; drain and squeeze dry. In a small bowl, whisk together mustard and vinegar. Add oil in a slow stream, whisking until emulsified, then stir in remaining ingredients; mix well. Transfer to a container and chill.

LEEK AND SAUSAGE TARTLETS

Preparation time: 20 minutes   *Chef: Michael Cabacungan*
Cooking time: 10 minutes   *Yacht: Marge's Barge*
Makes: about 30

1 lb/450 g	Sweet sausage
1 Tblsp	Butter
1	Large leek, chopped
1/4 lb/115 g	Mushrooms, chopped
	Salt and pepper, to taste
1	Egg
1/4 cup	Shredded mozzarella cheese
2 pkgs	Frozen pastry shells

Preheat oven to 350°F/175°C. Remove and discard skin from sausage and pan fry meat until cooked. Remove and drain. Sauté leek and mushroom in butter; drain. Mix with sausage, add salt, pepper, egg, and cheese; mix well and fill shells. Bake in oven about 10 minutes or until pastry shells are lightly browned.

F-Du RICE

Preparation time: 10 minutes   *Chef: Michael Cabacungan*
Cooking time: 20 minutes   *Yacht: Marge's Barge*
Serves: 6

7 cups	Low salt-fat free chicken broth
16 oz/450 g	Orzo
1/4 cup	Fresh lemon juice
1 Tblsp	Fresh chopped Rosemary
1 Tblsp	Fresh chopped thyme
1 Tblsp	Fresh chopped sage
1 Tblsp	Parsley
1 Tblsp	Olive oil
	Salt and white pepper, to taste
1 cup	Chopped mushrooms

Preheat oven to 350°F/180°C. In a large saucepan bring broth to boil over medium heat. Add orzo and cook 10 minutes, stirring constantly. Remove from heat and add all other ingredients; mix well. Pour into a 2 quart (8x11.5x2 inch/20x27.5x5 cm) baking dish. Cover with foil and bake for 10 minutes.

MUNGL SHOPPING LIST

VEGETABLES:
Avocados 2
Garlic cloves 2
Romaine .... 1 head
Scallions 2
Red onion, small 1
Yellow onions 2
Red bell peppers 2
Portabello mushrooms ... 4
Tomatoes, plum 4

FRUITS:
Mixed fruits .... 1 cup
Kiwi 1
Lemon 1
Mango, large 1
Orange 1

FRESH HERBS:
Basil, chopped .... 5 Tblsp
Basil .... garnish
Cilantro, chopped .... 1 Tblsp
Cilantro .... 1 bunch
Ginger .... 1 inch pc

DRIED SPICES:
Cumin .... 1 Tblsp
Curry .... 1 tsp

CONDIMENTS:
Bread crumbs .... 1-1/3 cups
Coconut, flaked .... 1/2 cup
Coconut milk .... 2 Tblsp
Pistachio .... 3 oz
Mustard, Dijon .... 2 Tblsp
Oil .... 2 tsp
Olive oil .... 1/2 cup
Vinegar, balsamic .... 2 Tblsp
Vinegar, white wine .... 1 tsp
Mayonnaise .... 1/2 cup

DRY GOODS:
Cornstarch .... 1 tsp
Flour, self rising .... 2-1/2 cups
Rice, basmati .... 1-1/2 cups
Sugar .... 1-3/4 cups

CANS AND JARS:
Salsa .... 2 Tblsp
Sweet chili .... 2 Tblsp
Thai kitchen green chili dipping
 sauce .... 1 Tblsp
Coconut milk .... 1 cup
Black beans .... 1 can
Crab meat .... 1 lb
Pineapple slices .... 1 small can
Orange juice .... 1/2 cup
Pineapple juice .... 1/2 cup
Chicken broth .... 2 cups
Black olives, pitted 16

DAIRY/MILK/CHEESE/BUTTER
Butter .... 7 Tblsp
Heavy cream .... 2 cups
Eggs 9
Milk, whole .... 2/3 cup
Sour cream .... 2 Tblsp
Feta .... 4 oz
Jack with jalapeño .... 8 oz
Parmesan, grated .... 2 Tblsp

MEAT/POULTRY/FISH/SEAFOOD:
Lump crab .... 1 lb
Mahi mahi filets .... 4 - 7 oz

MISCELLANEOUS:
Burrito seasoning mix .... 2 Tblsp
Tortillas, large flour .... 1 pkg

S/Y MUNGL

Chef Vicky Schilder
Captain Rob Van Veenendaal

MENU
Serves 4

Breakfast

*Coconut and Orange Muffins

Lunch

*Portabello Feta Salad with
*Balsamic Basil Vinaigrette

Hors d'oeuvre

*Black Bean Dip with
*Cheese Avocado Quesadillas

Dinner

*Crab Cakes with Pistachio Avocado Butter
*Sautéed Mahi Mahi with
*Mango Cilantro Salsa
Coconut Curry Rice
Sautéed Vegetables

*Pavlova

Now chartering in the Caribbean, the graceful MUNGL, a 65-foot custom sailing yacht, was built and designed in New Zealand. Her owner/captain, who sailed her on the long journey, is Australian Rob Van Veenendaal. Another Australian, Vicky Schilder, is chef. Families are welcome and not all the toys are for the adults. Vicky even has a kids menu. For the grown-ups the treats and tastes come from around the world, the result of Vicky's travels in Thailand, Mexico, the Caribbean and Australia.

*Indicates recipe provided

COCONUT AND ORANGE MUFFINS

Preparation time: 20 minutes　　　　　　*Chef: Vicky Schilder*
Cooking time: 25 minutes　　　　　　　　　　*Yacht: Mungl*
Makes: 12 muffins

Wet Mix:

1/4 cup	Butter or margarine
1/2 cup	Sugar
2	Eggs
1/2 cup	Milk
1/2 cup	Orange juice (with pulp for texture)
2 Tblsp	Orange zest

Dry Mix:

2-1/2 cups	Self raising flour
1/4 cup	Desiccated coconut*

Topping:

1/4 cup	Sugar
1/4 cup	Desiccated coconut*

Preheat oven to 350°F/180°C. Grease muffin pans. Blend the butter and sugar then add eggs, milk, orange juice, and zest. Fold the combined dry mix into the wet mix. Do **not** over mix. Spoon mixture into prepared muffin tins. Combine sugar and coconut and sprinkle on top. Bake approximately 25 minutes.

*flaked or shredded coconut.

PORTABELLO FETA SALAD

Preparation time: 30 minutes　　　　　　　　*Chef: Vicky Schilder*
Cooking time:10 minutes　　　　　　　　　　　*Yacht: Mungl*
Chilling time: 20 minutes
Serves: 4

1	Egg
1 Tblsp	Milk
4	Portabello mushrooms, sliced
	Salt and freshly ground black pepper
1/3 cup	Italian style bread crumbs
2 Tblsp	Freshly grated parmesan cheese
2 Tblsp	Butter
1 Tblsp	Olive oil
1	Romaine lettuce
4	Plum tomatoes, sliced
1	Red onion, peeled and sliced
16	Black olives, pitted and halved
1/4 cup	Fresh basil chopped, or to taste
4 oz/112 g	Feta cheese, plain or seasoned
Garnish:	Fresh basil leaves and flowers
	Balsamic vinaigrette, to taste

Beat egg, milk, salt and pepper together. Dredge portabellos in egg mixture then coat in bread crumbs. Cover and leave for 1 hour. Melt butter and oil in a non stick pan over medium heat. Add mushrooms and cook for approximately 3 minutes each side. Top with freshly grated parmesan before removing from pan.

Salad: Place large lettuce leaves on serving platter. Top with torn lettuce and arrange to make an even mound. Place tomatoes around the edge of platter, then olives and onion rings. Sprinkle with feta. Place portabellos on the mound of lettuce, in a spiral form. and top with extra parmesan. *Garnish with basil leaves and flowers. Serve with a **Balsamic Basil Vinaigrette***

Note: A great vegetarian lunch. Serve with crusty garlic bread and a bottle of white burgundy

BALSAMIC BASIL VINAIGRETTE:

2 Tblsp	Balsamic vinegar
1 Tblsp	Dijon mustard
1/3 cup	Virgin olive oil
1 Tblsp	Fresh chopped basil, or 1 tsp dried
	Salt and pepper, to taste

Place vinegar and mustard in small bowl, whisk in oil, adding in a thin stream. Add basil, salt and pepper. *Serve over **Portabello Feta Salad.***

BLACK BEAN DIP AND CHEESE AVOCADO QUESADILLAS

Preparation time: 10 minutes   *Chef: Vicky Schilder*
Cooking time: 10 minutes   *Yacht: Mungl*
Serves: 4

BLACK BEAN DIP:

1/2	Onion, finely chopped
2 tsp	Oil
2 cloves	Garlic, crushed
1 Tblsp	Cumin
2 Tblsp	Burrito seasoning mix
15.5 oz/440 g	Can black beans, mashed
2 Tblsp	Salsa

Garnish:

2 Tblsp	Sour cream
1 Tblsp	Fresh chopped coriander

Cook onion in oil until clear, add garlic, cumin, seasoning mix, and cook for 2 minutes; add beans and salsa. Stir to combine and heat through. *Garnish top of Dip with sour cream and fresh coriander. Serve with* **Cheese Avocado Quesidillas** *or corn chips.*

CHEESE AVOCADO QUESADILLAS:

Preparation time: 10 minutes
Cooking time: 20 minutes

1 pkg	Large flour tortillas
8 oz/225 g	Pkg monterey jack cheese with jalapeños, shredded
1	Ripe avocado

In a heated nonstick skillet place tortilla and cover with shredded cheese and slices of avocado, top with another tortilla. Heat until the cheese is melted. Flip tortilla over and cook through until it is slightly brown. Remove from pan, slice into eight pieces with pizza cutter. Repeat process if more are wanted. *Serve with* **Black Bean Dip.**

CRAB CAKES WITH PISTACHIO AVOCADO BUTTER

Preparation time: 30 minutes
Chilling time: 30 minutes
Cooking time: 20 minutes
Serves: 4

Chef: Vicky Schilder
Yacht: Mungl

CRAB CAKES:

1 lb/450 g	Crab meat, tinned or fresh
2	Eggs, slightly beaten
1 cup	Bread crumbs
2 Tblsp	Fresh chopped cilantro
2	Scallions, finely chopped
2 Tblsp	Sweet chili sauce
1/2	Lemon, juiced and grated rind
1 Tblsp	Dijon mustard
1 Tblsp	Fresh grated ginger
	Butter and oil for frying
	Flour to coat

PISTACHIO AVOCADO BUTTER:

1 Tblsp	Butter
3 oz	Pistachio nuts, finely chopped
1	Avocado
1 tsp	Fresh lemon juice
1/2 cup	Mayonnaise
1/2 tsp	Black pepper, or to taste

In a large bowl combine drained crab, eggs, bread crumbs, cilantro, scallions, chili sauce, lemon juice, rind, mustard, and ginger; mix thoroughly. Shape into 4 large portions, refrigerate 30 minutes.

Pistachio Avocado Butter. Melt 1 Tblsp butter and cook pistachios until golden. Remove and cool. Peel and seed the avocado, mash. Add the lemon juice and mix well. Fold in nuts, mayonnaise, and pepper. Place in small serving bowl and top with extra nuts for decoration.

Crab Cakes: In a skillet, heat butter and oil. Toss cakes in flour and fry for 3 minutes or until golden. Drain. *Serve warm with* **Butter**.

Note: *Serve with a nice green salad for lunch or as an appetizer. Will make approximately 48 bite size patties. These are really nice. Can be made 6 hours ahead.*

MAHI MAHI WITH MANGO CILANTRO SALSA

Preparation time: 10 minutes
Cooking time: 8 minutes
Chilling time: 2 hours
Serves: 4

Chef: Vicky Schilder
Yacht:Mungl

MANGO CILANTRO SALSA:

1	**Large ripe mango***
1	**Bunch fresh cilantro, chopped**
1	**Small red onion, finely diced**
1/2	**Medium red bell pepper**
1 Tblsp	**Thai Kitchen Green Chili Dipping Sauce****
4 - 7 oz/195 g	**Mahi Mahi fillets**

Chop mango into small cubes. Add 2 Tblsp cilantro, onion, red pepper, and dipping sauce. Mix well and chill for at least 2 hours.

*The best way to peel a mango: Place the mango, with stalk end up, on a cutting board. Turn so the narrow side of the mango is towards you. Place a sharp knife about 1/2 inch (1 cm) from stalk and slice down close to the stone, turn the mango and cut down the other side close to the stone. Take a small butter knife and cut through the flesh evenly down to the skin(do not cut the skin) then cut along the other way to make small cubes. Do this with both pieces. You then open the flesh by bending back the skin (hedgehog style) and just slice through the flesh along the skin and the cubes will fall off easily.

** Available in gourmet supermarkets

Prepare the Mahi Mahi by lightly dredging it in seasoned flour. Shake off any excess. Heat a small amount of oil in a nonstick pan and cook fish approximately 4 minutes each side. *Serve with **Mango Cilantro Salsa** and coconut curry rice.*

PAVLOVA

Preparation time: 20 minutes
Cooking time: 55 minutes
Serves: 6 - 8

Chef: Vicky Shilder
Yacht: Mungl

4	**Egg whites**
Pinch	**Salt**
1 cup	**Sugar**
1 tsp	**Cornstarch**
1 tsp	**White wine vinegar**
	Desiccated coconut (flaked), optional

Topping:

1-1/2 cups	**Heavy cream**
1/4 cup	**Sugar**
	Fruits of your choice - kiwi, mango, strawberries, etc.

Preheat oven to 225°F/100°C. Beat egg whites with salt to stiff peaks. Gradually add sugar and continue to beat for 5 minutes. Fold in cornstarch, vinegar and coconut. Line a baking sheet with silicone or wax paper; or grease with butter or oil. Pile mixture into a round, about 9 inches in diameter (build up sides a little) on prepared baking sheet. Bake for 55 minutes, then switch oven OFF and leave Pavlova in oven overnight - to dry it out. Remove from oven and keep covered until serving. *Best served within 2 days of baking.*

Just before serving, whip cream with sugar. Spread over the Pavlova. Prepare fruits and arrange on top of cream.

Hint: I usually prepare the meringue the night before charter starts and serve it the first night.

Note: 'Pavlova' is a large meringue served with fruit and whipped cream. Australians claim it as their very own creation - believing it was invented by a Western Australian chef when the great Russian dancer, Pavlova, was touring early last century.

Note: *Jan likes to serve her Pavlova on a cake stand. It makes it look very elegant. Please note that New Zealand claims the Pavlova!!*

MUSTARD SEED SHOPPING LIST

VEGETABLES:
Garlic cloves 2
Shallots 1
Tomatoes, roma 6

FRUITS:
Kiwi .... garnish
Lemon 1
Strawberries .... garnish

FRESH HERBS:
Basil .... 1 bunch
Ginger, grated .... 2 Tblsp
Mint .... garnish

DRIED SPICES:
Cinnamon .... 1-1/2 tsp
Cinnamon .... garnish
Nutmeg .... 1 tsp

CONDIMENTS:
Wasabi .... 2 Tblsp
Vanilla extract .... 2 Tblsp
Mustard, Dijon .... to taste
Maple syrup .... 1 bottle
Extra virgin olive oil .... 1/4 cup
Soy sauce .... 1-1/3 cups
Vinegar, balsamic .... 2 Tblsp
Vinegar, white wine .... 1/4 cup

DRY GOODS:
Corn flour .... 3 Tblsp
Sugar, brown .... 4 Tblsp

CANS AND JARS:
Apricot jam .... 1/2 cup
Sweetened condensed milk
.... 1 can

DAIRY/MILK/CHEESE/BUTTER
Butter .... 1/4 lb
Eggs 9
Milk, whole .... 6-3/4 cups
Bocconcini 5
Brie, small wheel 1
Cream cheese .... 1/2 cup
Swiss, slices 4

MEAT/POULTRY/FISH/SEAFOOD:
Smoked turkey slices 4
Tuna .... 1-3/4 lb

LIQUOR/WINE/SPIRITS:
Sherry, dry .... 2/3 cup
Vermouth, dry .... 2 Tblsp

BREAD/DOUGH:
Croissants 4
Graham cracker crusts ... 2
Bread .... 8 slices

S/Y MUSTARD SEED

Chef Jean Berry
Capt. Derek Berry

MENU
Serves 4

Breakfast

Fresh Fruits and Juice
*Cream Cheese and Apple French Toast

Lunch

*Croissant Bake
Green Salad

Hors d'oeuvre

*Apricot Brie

Dinner

*Teriyaki Tuna with Wasabi Beurre Blanc
New Potatoes
*Tomato and Bocconcini Salad

*Melt Tert (Milk Tart)

Another charter yacht from far away, MUSTARD SEED is a 44-foot fast cruising catamaran from St. Francis Bay, South Africa. To reach the Caribbean, Captain Derek Berry and his wife Jean sailed through the Indian Ocean via the Cape of Good Hope, across the Atlantic to the islands off South America and to the turquoise waters of the Caribbean. Mustard Seed welcomes families and has plenty of snorkeling and fishing gear on hand as well as a sailboard and flotation sunbeds. Chef Jean Berry's special collection of delicious recipes never disappoints.

*Indicates recipe provided

CREAM CHEESE
AND APPLE FRENCH TOAST

Preparation time: 20 minutes
Cooking time: 30 minutes
Serves: 4

Chef: Jean Berry
Yacht: Mustard Seed

Filling:

2	**Granny smith apples**
2 tsp	**Brown sugar**
1 tsp	**Cinnamon**
1 tsp	**Nutmeg**
1/2 cup	**Cream cheese, softened**
8 slices	**Bread, crust removed**

Batter:

2	**Eggs, slightly beaten**
1 Tblsp	**Vanilla**
1/4 cup	**Milk**
1/2 tsp	**Cinnamon**

Garnish:	**Mint leaves**
	Maple syrup

Peel, core and dice apples; fry in butter until softened. Add brown sugar, cinnamon, nutmeg, and cream cheese. When heated through spread mixture between two slices of bread. Mix together eggs, vanilla, milk and cinnamon in a shallow dish. Heat skillet. Place prepared bread into egg mixture, turn, then pan fry until golden on both sides. Garnish with mint leaves and *serve with maple syrup.*

CROISSANT BAKE

Preparation time: 15 minutes
Cooking time: 25 minutes
Serves: 4

Chef: Jean Berry
Yacht: Mustard Seed

4	**Croissants**
	Dijon mustard, to taste
4 slices	**Smoked turkey or ham**
4 slices	**Cheese**
4	**Eggs**
1 cup	**Milk**
	Salt and pepper, to taste

Preheat oven 375°F/190°C. Half croissants lengthwise. Smear with mustard then layer with slices of ham and cheese. Put in buttered ramekins – must fit snugly. Whisk eggs and milk together, season with salt and pepper and pour half over croissants. Place top on croissants and pour remaining egg mixture over each croissant. Bake for 10 minutes then reduce heat to 325°F/160°C and continue baking until set, about 15 minutes.

APRICOT BRIE

Preparation time: 10 minutes
Cooking time: 20 minutes
Serves: 4

Chef: Jean Berry
Yacht: Mustard Seed

1	**Pillsbury croissant dough**
1	**Small wheel of brie**
1/2 cup	**Apricot jam**
3 Tblsp	**Brown sugar**
Garnish:	**Fresh strawberries and sliced kiwi fruit**

Preheat oven to 375°F/190°C. Roll out croissant dough and place in the centre of a lightly greased baking tray. Place brie in center of dough and totally cover with apricot jam. Sprinkle with brown sugar then cover with dough rectangle. Bake in centre of oven for 20 minutes. Garnish.

TERIYAKI TUNA WITH
WASABI BEURRE BLANC

Preparation time: 20 minutes
Cooling time: 30 minutes
Marinating time: 4 hours
Cooking time: 15 minutes
Serves: 4

Chef: Jean Berry
Yacht: Mustard Seed

1-3/4 lbs/780 g	Tuna fillet, cut in 4 pieces

TERIYAKI MARINADE:

1-1/3 cups	Soy sauce
2/3 cup	Sherry
2 Tblsp	Grated ginger
2 cloves	Garlic, crushed

Combine all marinade ingredients and bring to a quick boil. Then cool. Place tuna in flat glass dish or reclosable storage bag; pour in marinade and marinate in the refrigerator for at least 4 hours, turning occasionally. Preheat grill. Remove tuna steaks from marinade and grill about 5 minutes on each side for medium.

WASABI BEURRE BLANC:

1/4 cup	White wine vinegar
2 Tblsp	Lemon juice
2 Tblsp	Dry vermouth
1 Tblsp	Minced shallots
	Salt and pepper, to taste
1 cup	Chilled butter, cut in 1/4 inch (5 mm) pieces
2 Tblsp	Wasabi (Japanese horseradish)

In a saucepan, boil vinegar, lemon juice, vermouth, shallots and salt and pepper. Reduce to 2 Tblsp and remove from heat immediately. Whisk in 2 pieces of butter. As butter softens and creams in the liquid, beat in another piece. Set pan over low heat and continue to beat in pieces of chilled butter. Beat in wasabi and adjust to personal taste. Sauce should become a thick ivory coloured cream. Serve immediately over grilled tuna.

TOMATO AND BOCCONCINI SALAD

Preparation time: 15 minutes　　　　　　　　　*Chef: Jean Berry*
Serves: 4　　　　　　　　　　　　　　　　　　*Yacht: Mustard Seed*

6	**Roma tomatoes**
5	**Bocconcini***
2/3 cups	**Basil leaves, loosely packed**
1/4 cup	**Olive oil, extra virgin**
2 Tblsp	**Balsamic vinegar**

Cut the tomatoes lengthwise into 3 – 4 slices (discard the thin outside slices which won't lie flat). Slice the bocconcini lengthwise into 3 – 4 slices. Arrange some tomato slices on a serving plate, place bocconcini slice on top of each tomato and scatter some of the basil leaves. Repeat the layers until all the tomato, bocconcini and basil leaves have been used. Season with salt and pepper. Whisk the oil and vinegar together and drizzle over the salad.

*Small balls of fresh mozzarella.

MELK TERT (MILK TART)

Preparation time: 20 minutes　　　　　　　　*Chef: Jean Berry*
Cooling time: 30 minutes　　　　　　　　　　*Yacht: Mustard Seed*
Chilling time: 2 hours
Serves: 8

3 Tblsp	**Corn flour**
3 tsp	**Vanilla essence**
3	**Eggs**
	Milk, as needed
2	**9 inch (23 cm) Graham cracker crusts**
14 oz/390 g	**Can sweetened condensed milk**
5-1/4 cups	**Milk**
	Ground cinnamon

In a bowl mix together the corn flour, vanilla essence and eggs with a little milk, to make a runny paste and totally smooth. Mix the sweetened condensed milk and the milk together in a saucepan. Bring to a boil then add to the flour mixture, stirring rapidly until the mixture thickens. Pour into the crusts. Sprinkle with ground cinnamon. Allow to cool then place in the refrigerator to chill thoroughly.

Tip: Use this dessert at the end of the charter week, then you can use the other Milk Tart at the beginning of the next charter.

OF COURSE SHOPPING LIST

VEGETABLES:
Broccoli .... 1 bunch
Carrots 7
Lettuce .... 4 leaves
Mushrooms 9
Shitake 6
Scallions 6
Green bell pepper 1
Red bell peppers 2
Yellow bell pepper 1
Snowpeas .... 1 lb 12 oz
Zucchini, medium 2

FRUITS:
Lemon 1
Bosc pears 6

FRESH HERBS:
Basil, chopped .... 1 Tblsp
Basil leaves 6
Ginger, grated .... 5 Tblsp
Mint .... garnish

DRIED SPICES:
All spice .... 1/2 tsp
Cinnamon .... 1 tsp
Cloves, ground .... 1/2 tsp
Five spice .... 1 tsp
Old bay mix .... 1 tsp

CONDIMENTS:
Baking powder .... 2 tsp
Baking soda .... 1 tsp
Light coconut milk .... 14 oz can
Pecan halves 12
Sesame seeds .... 1/2 cup
Sesame seed black .... 1/2 cup
Mustard, Dijon .... 1 Tblsp
Maple syrup .... 3/4 cup
Wasabi .... 3 Tblsp
Canola oil .... 3/4 cup
Ketchup Manis .... 1/4 Cup
Sesame oil .... 1/4 cup
Soy sauce .... 2-1/4 cups
Mayonnaise .... 1/2 cup

DRY GOODS:
Flour .... 1-1/2 cups
Corn flour .... 3 Tblsp
Cornstarch .... 2 Tblsp
Sugar, brown .... 2/3 cup
Sugar .... 1/3 cup
Rice noodles .... 1/2 cup
Rice, wild & brown .... 3/4 cup

CANS AND JARS:
Honey .... 2 Tblsp
Hoisin sauce .... 7 oz jar
Hot pepper sauce .... 1 Tblsp
Sarachi .... 8 oz jar
Water chestnuts .... 8 oz can
Chocolate sauce .... 2 Tblsp
Pumpkin .... 3/4 cup
Chicken broth .... 3 cans

DAIRY/MILK/CHEESE/BUTTER
Butter .... 3 oz
Milk, whole .... 1/2 cup
Brie, small wheel 1
Cream cheese .... 4 oz
Swiss, slices 4

MEAT/POULTRY/FISH/SEAFOOD:
Chicken breasts 2
Pork tenderloin 1/2
Lump crab .... 1 lb
Shrimp .... 1/2 lb
Tuna .... 3/4 lb

LIQUOR/WINE/SPIRITS:
Sherry, dry .... 4 Tblsp
White wine .... 1 bottle

MISCELLANEOUS:
Fortune cookies 6
Spring roll sheets .... 1 pkg
Orange juice concentrate 1/2 cup
Crème anglaise .... 2 cups

S/Y OF COURSE

Chef Ann E. Brown-McHorney
Captain Jackson McHorney

MENU
Serves 6

Breakfast

Fresh Orange Juice
*Pumpkin Muffins
Eggs cooked to order

Lunch

*Oriental Crab and Rice Salad with
*Orange Ginger Marinated Snow Peas and Carrots

Hors d'oeuvre

*Spring Rolls with Hoisin Dipping Sauce

Dinner

*Thai Chicken Coconut Soup
*Sesame Seared Tuna with Wasabi Mayonnaise
Julienned Veggie Stir Fry
Steamed Rice

*Ginger Poached Pears with Crème Anglaise

Designed for four guests OF COURSE! a 72-foot Bruce Farr cutter is a magnificent sailing vessel famous for her sleek lines, racing speeds and interior luxury. Captain Jackson McHorney is the son and grandson of Chesapeake Bay sea captains. Chef Annie Brown-McHorney received a bachelor's degree in Nutrition and Restaurant Management. She added to this knowledge by further studies at Cordon Bleu in Paris. This mix means everything she serves is healthy but also delicious and gloriously presented.

*Indicates recipe provided

PUMPKIN MUFFINS

Preparation time: 10 minutes
Cooking time: 25 minutes
Serves: 6-8

Chef: Anne E. Brown-McHorney
Yacht: Of Course

1-1/2 cups	Flour
pinch	Salt
2 tsp	Baking powder
1 tsp	Baking soda
1 tsp	Cinnamon
1/2 tsp	Ground allspice
1/2 tsp	Ground cloves
6 Tblsp	Butter, room temperature
2/3 cup	Brown sugar, packed
2	Eggs
1/2 cup	Milk
3/4 cup	Maple flavored pancake syrup
3/4 cup	Canned pumpkin
Garnish:	
12	Shelled pecan halves

Preheat oven to 350°F/180°C. Grease or line muffin tins. In a large bowl sift together, flour, salt, baking powder, baking soda, cinnamon, allspice, and cloves. In another bowl cream together butter and brown sugar. Add eggs and beat well. Stir in milk, syrup and pumpkin, mix well. Make a well in center of dry ingredients, pour in pumpkin mixture. Stir until well blended. Fill muffin tins 2/3 full. *Garnish with pecan halves.* Bake approximately 25 minutes or until done. *Remove from oven and serve.*

ORIENTAL CRAB AND RICE SALAD

Preparation time: 10 minutes   *Chef: Anne E Brown-McHorney*
Cooking time: 25 minutes   *Yacht: Of Course*
Serves: 6 - 8

2 cups	Cooked wild and brown rice
1/2	Red bell pepper, finely chopped
1/2	Green bell pepper, finely chopped
1/2	Yellow bell pepper, finely chopped
1/2 cup	Finely chopped scallion
1/2 cup	Fresh chopped parsley
1-1/2 cups	Sliced fresh mushrooms
8 oz/225 g	Can water chestnuts, coarsely chopped
1 lb/450 g	Fresh or frozen jumbo lump crab

SESAME DRESSING:

1 Tblsp	Dijon mustard
1/4 cup	Canola oil
2 Tblsp	Sherry
3 Tblsp	Sesame oil
3 Tblsp	Soy sauce, or to taste
	Salt and pepper, to taste

Mix all salad ingredients together in a big bowl. Whisk together dressing ingredients. Add to salad just before serving. For individual servings serve atop a large bok choy or lettuce leaf with a fan of **Orange Ginger Marinated Snow Peas and Carrots** on the side.

ORANGE GINGER MARINATED SNOW PEAS AND CARROTS

Preparation time: 10 minutes　　　　*Chef: Ann E. Brown-McHorney*
Cooking time: 3 minutes　　　　　　　　*Yacht: Of Course*
Marinating time: 1 - 4 hours
Serves: 6

1 lb/450 g	**Snow peas**
3	**Carrots, peeled**
1/2 cup	**Orange juice concentrate**
2 Tblsp	**Freshly grated ginger**
2 Tblsp	**Honey**

Clean and blanch snow peas (about 1 minute). Make carrot daisies by cutting narrow lengthwise v-shaped slits around carrot (about 5 or so). Cut carrots crosswise – instant flowers! Blanch 2 minutes, or until just soft. Peel ginger and place in garlic or ginger press. Place peas and carrots in a bowl, add orange juice, honey, and ginger; mix well and marinate.

THAI CHICKEN COCONUT SOUP

Preparation time: 15 minutes　　　　*Chef: Ann E. Brown-McHorney*
Cooking time: 20 minutes　　　　　　　*Yacht: Of Course*
Serves: 6

2	**Chicken breasts, poached and shredded, reserve liquid**
14 oz/400 ml	**Can chicken stock**
14 oz/400 ml	**Can light coconut milk**
2 Tblsp	**Grated lemon rind**
1 Tblsp	**Finely chopped ginger**
2 Tblsp	**Fresh or dried lemon grass**
3 Tblsp	**Soy sauce**
1 Tblsp	**Dried or fresh chilies, chopped**
1 cup	**Sliced fresh shitake mushrooms, or button mushrooms**
1 Tblsp	**Chopped basil or cilantro leaves**
1	**Scallion, chopped**

In a saucepan, combine chicken stock, poaching liquid, coconut milk, lemon rind, ginger, lemon grass, soy sauce, and chilies. Simmer together for 20 minutes. Just before serving, add mushrooms and chicken. Heat through. Sprinkle with basil or cilantro, and scallions.

SPRING ROLLS WITH HOISIN DIPPING SAUCE

Preparation time: 20 minutes   *Chef: Ann E. Brown-McHorney*
Cooking time: 15 minutes   *Yacht: Of Course*
Chilling time: 2 hours
Serves: 6

1/2	**Pork tenderloin,**
1 tsp	**5 spice powder**
1/2 lb/225 g	**Large shrimp**
1 tsp	**Old bay seasoning**
1	**Pkg spring roll skins (rice paper)**
1/2 cup	**Cooked rice noodles**
4	**Shredded red leaf lettuce leaves**
6 oz/170 g	**Fresh bean sprouts**
1 cup	**Grated carrots**
	Fresh basil leaves
	Fresh cilantro or mint leaves
7 oz/195 g	**Jar hoisin sauce**
8 oz/225 g	**Jar sarachi sauce (Thai chili-garlic sauce)**

Poach pork tenderloin with 5 spice powder, about 15 minutes. Julienne poached tenderloin. Cook shrimp in water with old bay seasoning until they turn pink. Soak 2 spring roll skins in a large bowl of water until just moistened, about 1 minute. Lay on work surface while soaking next 2 skins. Place a small amount of noodle, lettuce, sprouts and pork 1/4 way up on the skin. Slice shrimp lengthwise. Lay 2 pieces of shrimp above this and sprinkle with carrot. Lay one basil and one mint or cilantro sprig above that. Roll envelope style. The shrimp and leaves should show through the top of the rolls, making them very pretty. Cover rolls and chill. They will keep for a day in the refrigerator. To serve, mix hoisin sauce with water to a dipping consistency. Let guests dip rolls into sauce and use the sarachi sauce on the side.

SESAME SEARED TUNA WITH WASABI MAYONNAISE

Preparation time: 10 minutes
Cooking time: 5 to 10 minutes
Marinating time: 30 minutes
Serves: 6

Chef: Ann E. Brown-McHorney
Yacht: Of Course

1/2 cup	Soy sauce
3 Tblsp	Prepared wasabi
1/2 cup	Mayonnaise
1 tsp	Canola oil
3-1/4 lbs/1.5 kg	Fresh tuna
1/2 cup	Sesame seeds
1/2 cup	Black sesame seeds

Cooking times: For rare—cut tuna into 1-1/2 inch (3.5 cm) chunks. For medium—cut into 3/4 to 1 inch (2 to 2.5 cm) chunks. Marinate up to 1/2 hour in soy sauce, turning frequently. Mix together prepared wasabi and mayonnaise; set aside. Heat a large skillet on medium high. Brush very lightly with oil. Mix sesame seeds in small bowl, dip tuna in sesame seeds, coat well. Place in hot skillet. For rare tuna, sear chunks briefly on all sides. For medium, cook both sides until the edge goes from red to pink. Garnish with wasabi and mayonnaise. (I put wasabi/mayonnaise mixture into a pastry bag and do a zig zag pattern).

Hint: Great served with *Julienne Stir Fry* of your favorite veggies as a lunch dish. For dinner, add rice and lemon slices.

Note: *We first had a similar meal at Pussers. The crew said to figure out how to make it or walk the plank! It is now a favorite on board.*

GINGER POACHED PEARS WITH CREME ANGLAISE

Preparation time: 20 minutes   *Chef: Ann E. Brown-McHorney*
Cooling time: 30 minutes   *Yacht: Of Course*
Cooking time: 20 minutes
Serves: 6

6	**Bosc or bartlett pears, semi ripe**
1 bottle	**Dry white wine**
2 Tblsp	**Lemon juice**
2 Tblsp	**Fresh or crystallized ginger**
2 Tblsp	**Sherry**
1/3 cup	**Sugar**
2 cups	**Crème anglaise (vanilla custard sauce)**
2 Tblsp	**Chocolate or raspberry sauce**
Garnish:	**Mint leaves**
	Fortune cookies

Peel pears, leaving stems attached. Place in saucepan just large enough to hold them. Add wine and just enough water to cover. Add lemon juice, ginger, sherry, and sugar. Simmer gently until just soft – usually about 15 minutes. Cool the pears in their cooking liquid in a glass container (do not use metal). Add 2 Tblsp cooking liquid to thin crème anglaise, if necessary.

Remove core of pear with melon scoop, make bottom of pear flat so that it stands straight, setting in center of dessert plate. Spoon crème anglaise around each pear. Place drops of chocolate or raspberry sauce around crème, running through with toothpick to make heart shapes. *Garnish with mint leaves. Serve with a fortune cookie.*

Note: For the crème anglaise I like to use the Honig or Bird's custard mixes made with skim milk as that makes this a very low calorie, low cholesterol dessert.

ORPHEE III SHOPPING LIST

VEGETABLES:
Asparagus .... 2 bunches
Napa cabbages .... 2 head
Purple cabbage .... 1 head
Garlic cloves 2
Green onions 8
Shallots 2
Red onions 2

FRUITS:
Granny Smith apples 10
Lemon 1
Mangos 3

FRESH HERBS:
Dill, chopped .... 1/4 tsp
Parsley, chopped .... 1 Tblsp
Tarragon, chopped .... 1 Tblsp

DRIED SPICES:
All spice .... 1/2 tsp
Cinnamon .... 4 tsp
Cloves, ground .... 1/2 tsp
Ginger .... 1/2 tsp
Lemon pepper .... 1 tsp

CONDIMENTS:
Baking powder .... 1/2 tsp
Baking soda .... 2 tsp
Cavenders Greek seasoning
.... 1 tsp
Almonds, sliced .... 1 cup
Sesame seeds .... 1/2 cup
Wasabi .... 1/4 tsp
Honey .... 1/4 cup
Oil .... 1/2 cup
Canola oil .... 1 cup
Shortening .... 1/2 cup
Sesame oil, hot .... 1/8 cup
Low salt soy sauce .... 1/4 cup
Vinegar, red wine .... 1/3 cup
Mayonnaise .... 2 Tblsp

DRY GOODS:
Lasagna .... 1 lb
Ramen noodles .... 1 pkg
Cornflour .... 1 tsp
Flour .... 5 cups
Rice, basmati .... 1-1/2 cups
Sugar, brown .... 1-3/4 cups
Sugar .... 1-1/2 cups
Sugar, confectioners' .... 1/2 cup

CANS AND JARS:
Crab meat .... 2 - 6 oz cans

DAIRY/MILK/CHEESE/BUTTER
Butter .... 1-3/4 lbs
Eggs 7
Half and half .... 1-1/2 cups
Whole milk .... 1/2 cup
Sour cream .... 8 oz
Blue .... 8 oz
Cream cheese .... 8 oz
Mozzarella, grated .... 4 oz
Parmesan, grated .... 4 oz
Ricotta .... 3 cups

MEAT/POULTRY/FISH/SEAFOOD:
Crab legs .... 1/2 lb
Scallops, small .... 1 lb
Shrimp, cooked .... 2 lbs
Shrimp .... 1 lb
White fish .... 1/2 lb

LIQUOR/WINE/SPIRITS:
Calvados .... 1/3 cup
Sherry, sweet .... 1/4 cup
Sherry, semi-sweet .... 1/2 cup

BREAD/DOUGH:
Puff pastry sheets .... 1 pkg
Bread, white 1

FROZEN:
Spinach .... 2 - 10 oz pkg

S/Y ORPHEE III

Chef Jan Netherland
Captain Michael White

MENU
Serves 6-8

Breakfast

*Mango Sour Cream Coffee Cake

Lunch

*Oriental Shrimp Salad

Hors d'oeuvre

*Spanikopita

Dinner

*Asparagus en Croute
*Seafood Lasagna

*Apple Pie

ORPHEE III is a classy yacht, a 90-foot wooden ketch with graceful lines and old world charm. She was designed by John Alden and built in France for the automobile tycoon, Ettore Bugatti, in 1936. Captain Michael White, a master mariner and her present owner, carried out a major refit in 1997 and now charters in the Virgin Islands and the Southern Caribbean. Chef Jan Netherland has been a respected chef in the charter industry for many years. Menus are always a pleasure for her guests.

*Indicates recipe provided

MANGO SOUR CREAM COFFEE CAKE

Preparation time: 15 minutes 　　　　*Chef: Jan Netherland*
Cooking time: 30 minutes 　　　　　　　*Yacht: Orphee III*
Serves: 8

Cake:

3 cups	Flour
2 tsp	Soda
1/2 tsp	Baking powder
1/2 tsp	Cinnamon
1/2 cup	Oil
1 cup	Sugar
8 oz/227 g	Sour cream
1/2 cup	Milk
1/2 tsp	Salt

Topping:

3/4 cup	Brown sugar
1/2 cup	Butter, melted
3	Mangos, sliced
1 Tblsp	Cinnamon

Heat oven to 325°F/170°C. In a bundt pan place brown sugar, butter, mango slices and cinnamon. Pour cake mixture over and bake for 30 minutes. Turn over on a platter and serve warm with ice cream or whipped cream.

Hints: *You can lower fat content with low fat sour cream and skimmed milk. Can be made ahead and frozen.*

ORIENTAL SHRIMP SALAD

Preparation time: 20-30 minutes   *Chef: Jan Netherland*
Cooking time: 5 minutes   *Yacht: Orphee III*
Chilling time: 30 minutes
Serves: 8

1 pkg	Ramen noodles, cooked
2 heads	Napa cabbage or Bok Choy, sliced
6	Spring onions, chopped
1	Purple cabbage, sliced
1	Red pepper, finely chopped
1 cup	Sliced almonds
1/2 cup	Sesame seeds
2 lbs/900 g	Shrimp, cooked

Dressing:

1/3 cup	Red wine vinegar
1/8 cup	Hot sesame oil
1/4 cup	Sweet sherry
4 Tblsp	Low salt soy sauce
1/4 cup	Honey
1 cup	Canola oil
1/4 tsp	Wasabi
1/4 cup	Brown sugar

Mix all dressing ingredients and chill for at least 30 minutes. Add noodles; mix well, then add remaining salad ingredients and chill for another 30 minutes.

SPANIKOPITA

Preparation time: 20 minutes　　　　　　　　Chef: Jan Netherland
Cooking time: 30 minutes　　　　　　　　　Yacht: Orphee III
Serves: 8

3 - 10 oz/280 g	**Pkgs frozen chopped spinach**
1/2	**Lemon, juiced**
1/2	**Lemon zest**
1 tsp	**Lemon pepper**
2	**Green onions, chopped**
1 clove	**Garlic, crushed**
1 tsp	**Cavenders Greek seasoning**
1/2 cup	**Chopped red pepper**
2	**Egg, slightly beaten**
2 Tblsp	**Mayonnaise**
1 tsp	**Parsley**
2 - 6 oz/170 g	**Cans crab meat**
1 pkg	**Puff pastry sheets**

Ricotta Mixture:

1	**Egg, slightly beaten**
1 Tblsp	**Chopped fresh parsley**
2 cups	**Ricotta cheese**

Preheat oven to 350°F/180°C. Thaw and squeeze all excess water from spinach. Add lemon and zest, green onions, garlic, greek seasoning, red pepper and eggs. Mix well. Add crab and mix again. Thaw puff pastry and roll out fairly thin. Cut into small squares. Add spinach mixture and top with Ricotta mixture. Fold over in triangle. Secure edges. Bake for 30 minutes or until browned.

Note: *May be made ahead.*

ASPARAGUS EN CROUTE

Preparation time: 30 minutes
Cooking time: 15 minutes
Marinating time: 15 minutes
Serves: 6

Chef: Jan Netherland
Yacht: Orphee III

2 bunches	**Asparagus spears**
1 loaf	**Wheat or white bread, crusts removed**
8 oz/227 g	**Cream cheese**
4 oz/114 g	**Blue or gorgonzola cheese, room temperature**
1/4 tsp	**Dill**
2 Tblsp	**Soft butter**

Preheat oven to 375°F/190°C. Remove crust from bread. With rolling pin, flatten each piece of bread. Mix cream cheese, gorgonzola and dill; let stand 15 minutes. Spread cheese mixture on bread, place asparagus spear on top and roll up. Spread small amount butter on top and bake until browned.

Note: *All can be made ahead; stored in refrigerator then brought to room temperature prior to baking.*

SEAFOOD LASAGNA

Preparation time: 45 minutes   Chef: Jan Netherland
Cooking time: 1-1/2 hours   Yacht: Orphee III
Serves: 8 - 10

Sauce:

1 cup	Half and half
3	Egg yolks, beaten
1 large	Shallot, peeled, sliced and sautéed in butter
1/2 cup	Sherry, semi-sweet
1 Tblsp	Tarragon
	Salt and pepper
1 clove	Garlic, crushed

Lasagna:

1 lb/450 g	Cleaned shrimp
1 lb/450 g	Small scallops
1/2 lb/225 g	White fish, cooked
1/2 lb/225 g	Crab legs, cut in bite size pieces
1 lb/450 g	Lasagna noodles
1 cup	Ricotta cheese
1/2 cup	Grated parmesan cheese
1/2 cup	Grated mozzarella cheese
1	Egg
	Salt and pepper

Preheat oven to 325°F/165°C. In a large saucepan put all sauce ingredients, then add seafood and cook lightly. Let sit 20 minutes. Boil lasagna noodles per directions on package until "almost" al dente. In a bowl, mix ricotta, egg, salt and pepper. Spray a 9 x 12 inch (23 x 30 cm) lasagna pan with cooking oil. Pour in a little sauce then start layering noodles, ricotta, seafood, mozzarella and a little parmesan, ending with layer of noodles. Pour in any left over sauce and top with mozzarella. Cover loosely with foil. Bake for 1 hour and 20 minutes; remove foil and bake for ten more minutes. *Serve.*

APPLE PIE

Preparation time: 30 minutes
Cooking time: 50-60 minutes
Chilling time: for crust, 20 minutes
Marinating time: for fruit, 20 minutes
Serves: 8

Chef: Jan Netherland
Yacht: Orphee III

Crust:

1/2 cup	**Shortening**
2 cups	**Flour**
1/2 tsp	**Salt**
1/8± cup	**Ice water**

Filling:

10	**Granny smith apples, peeled, sliced thinly**
1/3 cup	**Calvados poured over apples**
3/4 cup	**Brown sugar**
1/3 cup	**White sugar**
1/3 cup	**Butter**
1/2 tsp	**Cinnamon**
1/2 tsp	**Allspice**
1/2 tsp	**Cloves**
1/2 tsp	**Ginger**
1 tsp	**Cornflour**
2 Tblsp	**Lemon juice**
6 Tblsp	**Butter**
1/2 cup	**Half and half or cream**

Preheat oven to 375°F/190°C. In large bowl, place shortening, flour and salt; using a pastry cutter, blend until flour looks like meal. Add small amounts of ice water until pastry holds together. Divide in two and wrap each portion in plastic wrap and place in refrigerator for 20 minutes. Peel and slice apples adding 1/3 cup calvados, sugar mixture, 2 Tblsp lemon juice, cinnamon, allspice, cloves, ginger, and cornflour. Toss well and set aside. In a heavy sauce pan, melt butter. Add 1/2 cup brown sugar, 1/3 cup calvados. Let boil over medium-high heat until sugar is melted. Add half and half; bring back to boil, cook another minute and allow to cool. Roll out pastry dough and place in a deep pie pan. Add apple mixture then pour over calvados praline cream. Add top crust, seal the edges and pierce pastry for steam vents. Bake for 50-60 minutes. *Make apple leaves with pastry scraps for decoration.*

Note: Place foil or cookie sheet under pie pan before baking.

PACIFIC JEMM SHOPPING LIST

VEGETABLES:
Beets .... 1 lb
Garlic .... 1 bulb
Red onion, small 1
Hot red chile 1

FRUITS:
Lemon 1
Oranges 5
Pears 6
Selection of fresh fruits

FRESH HERBS:
Fresh herbs, chopped ...... 3 Tblsp
Ginger, sliced .... 4 Tblsp
Mint sprigs .... garnish

DRIED SPICES:
Cinnamon .... 1/4 tsp
Cumin, ground .... 1 tsp
Nutmeg .... 1/4 tsp

CONDIMENTS:
Baking powder .... 2 tsp
Wasabi .... to taste
Mustard, whole grain ...... 1 Tblsp
Mustard, Dijon .... 1 tsp
Oil .... 1/8 cup
Olive oil .... 1 cup
Peanut oil .... 1/8 cup
Vinegar, balsamic .... 1/3 cup
Vinegar, cider .... 1/4 cup
Maple syrup .... 1 bottle

DRY GOODS:
Flour .... 3-3/4 cups
Polenta .... 1/4 cup
Sugar, brown .... 1/4 cup
Sugar .... 1 cup
Sugar, raw .... 1/2 cup

CANS AND JARS:
Fruit chutney .... 1 jar
Corn, cream style .... 15 oz can

DAIRY/MILK/CHEESE/BUTTER
Butter .... 1/3 lb
Eggs 8
Whole milk .... 1 cup
Cream .... 1/2 cup
Sour cream .... 4 tsp
Goat/chèvre .... 7 oz
Ricotta .... 8 oz

MEAT/POULTRY/FISH/SEAFOOD:
Bacon .... 3/4 lb
Lamb cutlets 12
Salmon, smoked .... 4 slices
Tuna .... 1 lb
Venison loin .... 4 - 7 oz

LIQUOR/WINE/SPIRITS:
Red wine .... 1 - 2 cups

MISCELLANEOUS:
Dried nectarines, chopped
.... 7 oz

FROZEN:
Ice cream .... 2 cups
Puff pastry .... 2 sheets

M/Y PACIFIC JEMM

Chef Stephanie Parton
Captain Derek Munro

MENU FROM NEW ZEALAND
Serves 4

Breakfast

*Polenta and Ricotta Hotcakes with
Crispy Bacon and Maple Syrup

Lunch

*Grilled Lamb Cutlets with
Lemon and Cumin
Mesclun Summer Salad with
*Balsamic and Whole Grain Mustard Dressing

Hors d'oeuvre

*Corn Fritters with Smoked Salmon
and Wasabi Cream

Dinner

*Goat Cheese Tart with Nectarine Salsa and Rocket Salad
*Seared Venison Loin with
*Orange and Gingered Beetroot
Green Beans and Kumara Mash

*Roasted Pears and Butterscotch Tart with
Hokey Pokey Ice Cream

The 80-foot Falcon motor launch PACIFIC JEMM is a luxury yacht chartering out of Auckland, New Zealand. Both her captain, Derek Munro, and her chef, Stephanie Parton, are New Zealanders which means there is an abundance of Kiwi hospitality on board. There is also an abundance of fine cuisine as Stephanie has won numerous awards and received a stream of rave reviews for her menus and the beautiful meals she serves on board in the splendor and comfort and charm of Pacific Jemm.

*Indicates recipe provided

POLENTA AND RICOTTA HOTCAKES

Preparation time: 15 minutes
Cooking time: 10 minutes
Chilling time: 30 minutes
Serves: 4

Chef: Stephanie Parton
Yacht: Pacific Jemm

1/4 cup	**Polenta**
1 cup	**Flour**
1/3 cup	**Sugar**
1 tsp	**Baking powder**
1/4 tsp	**Ground nutmeg**
1/4 tsp	**Ground cinnamon**
1 cup	**Milk**
2	**Eggs**
2 Tblsp	**Butter, melted**
1 cup	**Ricotta cheese**
1	**Orange, zested**
3/4 lb/335 g	**Bacon**
	Maple syrup
	Selection of fresh fruits

Sift dry ingredients together, add polenta. Whisk together egg and milk and stir into dry ingredients. Gently fold in ricotta and orange zest. Allow to rest for at least 1/2 hour. Can be made the night before. Heat pan with a small amount of oil or butter. Spoon mix into pan. Cook until golden on both sides. *Serve with grilled bacon and maple syrup.*

GRILLED LAMB CUTLETS WITH LEMON AND CUMIN

Preparation time: 10 minutes
Cooking time: 3-4 minutes
Marinating time: 2-3 hours
Serves: 4

Chef: Stephanie Parton
Yacht: Pacific Jemm

12	Lamb cutlets
2 Tblsp	Balsamic vinegar
2 Tblsp	Lemon juice
2 Tblsp	Olive oil
2 cloves	Garlic, crushed
1 tsp	Ground cumin
	Fruit or tomato chutney

BALSAMIC AND WHOLE GRAIN MUSTARD DRESSING:

4 Tblsp	Balsamic vinegar
2/3 cup	Olive oil
1 Tblsp	Wholegrain mustard
	Salt and freshly ground pepper

Remove fat from cutlets. Scrape bones of any sinew. Combine remaining ingredients and marinate cutlets for at least 2 hours. Remove cutlets from marinade and season with salt and pepper. Grill to medium-rare. Be careful not to over cook.

Serve with chutney of your choice, and a mesclun salad with **Balsamic Dressing.**

Hint: *Cutlets can be lightly grill marked prior to serving time and reheated in oven.*

CORN FRITTERS WITH SMOKED SALMON AND WASABI CREAM

Preparation time: 5 minutes
Cooking time: 10 minutes
Serves: 4

Chef: Stephanie Parton
Yacht: Pacific Jemm

CORN FRITTERS:

3/4 cup	**All purpose flour**
1 tsp	**Baking powder**
1/2 tsp	**Salt**
	Black pepper
1	**Egg**
15-3/4 oz/440 g	**Can cream style sweet corn**
2 Tblsp	**Oil**

Sift flour, baking powder, salt and pepper into a bowl. Add egg, mix to combine, stir in sweet corn. Heat oil in frying pan. Drop tablespoonsful of mixture into pan. Cook until golden on both sides.

Hint: Mix can be made and kept in refrigerator. Fritters can also be made and reheated in oven.

SMOKED SALMON WITH WASABI CREAM:

4 slices	**Smoked salmon**
4 tsp	**Sour cream mixed with wasabi powder or paste**

Top fritters with smoked salmon and a dollop of wasabi cream, garnish with fresh herbs.

GOAT CHEESE TART
WITH NECTARINE SALSA

Preparation time: 20 minutes   *Chef: Stephanie Parton*
Cooking time: 10 minutes   *Yacht: Pacific Jemm*
Chilling time: 30 minutes
Serves: 4

GOAT CHEESE TART:

2 sheets	**Puff pastry, rolled into appropriate tart moulds**
7 oz/200 g	**Goat cheese or feta**
1/2 cup	**Cream**
4	**Eggs**

Preheat oven to 400°F/200°C. Allow pastry to rest for 30 minutes. Line pastry with grease proof paper and baking beans or rice. Bake until the pastry is cooked, about 15-20 minutes. Remove paper and beans from pastry. Lower oven temperature to 300°F/150°C. Pour in tart mix. Bake for about 30 minutes or until mix is set. Serve with salad, (preferably rocket, watercress or something tangy as the tart is very rich) and *Nectarine Salsa.*

NECTARINE SALSA:

2 Tblsp	**Peanut oil**
1/4 cup	**Very thinly sliced, peeled ginger**
3 cloves	**Garlic, crushed**
1/2 tsp	**Salt**
1	**Hot red chilli, thinly sliced**
1	**Small red onion, finely chopped**
7 oz/200 g	**Dried nectarines, roughly chopped**
1/4 cup	**Sugar**
4 Tblsp	**Cider vinegar**

Heat the oil in a pan, add ginger, garlic, salt, chillies and onion. Sauté without browning until the onion is soft. Add remaining ingredients, bring to a boil and simmer until reduced by half, about 20 minutes. Cool.

Hints: Nectarine salsa is a great standby to have on hand. Excellent with meats, cheeses, antipasto, etc. Nectarines can be substituted with other dried or fresh fruit/tomatoes.

SEARED VENISON LOIN WITH ORANGE GINGERED BEETROOT

Preparation time: 20 minutes
Cooking time: 15 minutes
Marinating time: overnight
Serves: 4

Chef: Stephanie Parton
Yacht: Pacific Jemm

4 - 7 oz/200 g	**Venison loin**
2 cups	**Red wine**
2 cloves	**Garlic, crushed**
3 Tblsp	**Fresh herbs**

Preheat oven to 400°F/200°C. Trim venison of any fat or sinew. Cut into portions. Marinate overnight in red wine, garlic, herbs. Remove venison from marinade and drain. Heat a small amount of oil in pan until very hot. Quickly sear outside of venison until golden brown. (Can be done earlier). When ready to serve place venison in oven for approximately 5 to 10 minutes, depending on size of loin. Best served rare to medium-rare.

ORANGE — GINGERED BEETROOT:

1 lb/450 g	**Fresh beetroot**
2 Tblsp	**Olive oil**
2 Tblsp	**Finely sliced fresh ginger**
1 cup	**Fresh orange juice**

Peel beetroot and trim into bite size pieces. Heat oil in pan, add ginger and beetroot. Sauté until ginger is fragrant. Add orange juice and simmer until beetroot is soft and sauce is reduced.

Serve with Kumara mash and green beans.

Hint: Use tinned baby beetroot if fresh not available. Make sauce first then add beetroot at the end.

ROASTED PEARS AND BUTTERSCOTCH TART WITH HOKEY POKEY ICE CREAM

Preparation time: 10 minutes
Cooking time: 15 minutes
Chilling time: 30 minutes
Serves: 4

Chef: Stephanie Parton
Yacht: Pacific Jemm

SWEET PASTRY:

2 cups	**All purpose flour**
5 Tblsp	**Butter**
1/4 cup	**Sugar**
1	**Egg yolk**
1 Tblsp	**Water**

PEARS

6	**Pears, peeled, cored and quartered**
1/4 cup	**Brown sugar**
1/2 cup	**Sugar**
2 Tblsp	**Butter**

HOKEY POKEY ICE CREAM:
Garnish: **Sprigs of mint or angelica**

Preheat oven to 350°F/180°C. Sift flour, cut in butter until it resembles fine breadcrumbs. Stir in sugar. Add egg yolk and water. Mix to a stiff dough. Chill for 30 minutes.While dough is chilling, prepare pears. Place pears in baking pan and toss with brown sugar and roast until cooked. Place 1/2 cup sugar, butter and water in saucepan, and bring to a boil on high heat. Boil until mixture is golden brown (caramel). Add roasted pears, remove from heat and pour into oven proof dish. Roll out pastry big enough to cover the top of the pears. Place over pears and cook in hot oven 400°F/200°C until golden. To serve turn pie onto platter so the pears sit on top of the pastry. Garnish with a large scoop of Hokey Pokey ice cream and a sprig of mint or angelica.

Hint: Pears can be made into individual tarts if desired.

Tip: Hokey Pokey ice cream can only be found in New Zealand and is vanilla ice cream with lumps of toffee through it.

PENTESILEA II SHOPPING LIST

VEGETABLES:
Cucumber .... garnish
Garlic cloves 2
Mushrooms, medium 24
Yellow onion 1
Tomatoes .... garnish

FRUITS:
Granny Smith apple 1
Mixed cut up fruits .... 2 cups
Lime 1
Mango .... garnish
Orange 1

FRESH HERBS:
Lemon grass .... 2 inch pc
Mint .... garnish
Parsley, chopped .... 1 Tblsp
Watercress .... 3.6 oz pkg

DRIED SPICES:
Cayenne .... 1/8 tsp
Cinnamon .... 1-1/3 tsp
Coriander seeds .... 1 Tblsp
Cream of tartar .... 1/4 tsp
Fennel seeds .... 2 tsp
Turmeric .... 1/2 tsp

CONDIMENTS:
Chocolate chips, semi ...... 4 oz
Almonds, ground .... 1/4 cup
Walnuts, chopped .... 1 cup
Vanilla extract .... 1/2 tsp
Sesame oil .... 1 Tblsp
Soy sauce .... 2 Tblsp

DRY GOODS:
Flour .... 2-1/4 cups
Sugar .... 6 Tblsp

CANS AND JARS:
Mustard, Dijon .... 1 Tblsp
Cranberry sauce, jellied ... 1 cup
Maraschino cherries .... garnish
Raspberry jam .... 10 oz jar
Ginger peanut sauce .... garnish

DAIRY/MILK/CHEESE/BUTTER
Butter .... 5 oz
Butter, unsalted .... 1 oz
Heavy cream .... 1/2 cup
Eggs 4
Milk, whole .... 1 cup
Yogurt .... 2 cups
Brie .... 4 oz
Gruyère, grated .... 2 Tblsp
Parmesan, grated .... 2 Tblsp

MEAT/POULTRY/FISH/SEAFOOD:
Turkey, cooked .... 1 lb
Lump crab .... 1 lb
Shrimp, large 24

LIQUOR/WINE/SPIRITS:
Sherry, dry .... 2 Tblsp

FROZEN:
Spinach .... 2 cups

MISCELLANEOUS:
Bread crumbs .... 2 Tblsp
Muesli mix .... 1 cup
Tortillas, flour 4

More Store to Shore Shopping Lists available…1-800-338-6073 –CapJan@aol.com
www.shiptoshoreinc.com

S/Y PENTESILEA II

Chef Ruth Deller
Captain Hans Deller

MENU
Serves 4

Breakfast

*Birchermuesli
(A Swiss Favorite)

Lunch

*Turkey Cranberry Wrap
*Linzertorte

Hors d'oeuvre

*Mushroom Stuffed with Crabmeat and Gruyère

Dinner

*Marinated Grilled Shrimp with
Ginger Peanut Sauce
Caribbean Rice

*Chocolate Mousse

Leaving the world behind, PENTESILEA II, a 48-foot luxury catamaran, sails away into the deep blue on weekly charters with Captain Hans Deller and wife/chef/hostess Ruth Deller. Both were born in Switzerland where they learned to sail on Lake Zurich. Eighteen years ago, they sailed to the Caribbean and stayed. With 1,000 square feet of deck space, Pentesilea's large cockpit serves as a panoramic terrace to enjoy gourmet meals prepared by Ruth who loves to introduce dishes from her native Suisse.

*Indicates recipe provided

BIRCHERMUESLI
(A Swiss Favorite)

Preparation time: 15 minutes　　　　　　*Chef: Ruth Deller*
Serves: 4　　　　　　　　　　　　　*Yacht: Pentesilea II*

2 cups	**Cut up fruit, mango,banana, strawberries, apple (depending on season)**
2 cups	**Plain yogurt**
1 cup	**Tropical fruit muesli mix***
	Milk
Garnish:	**Maraschino cherries**

Mix together fruit, yogurt, and muesli. Moisten with milk. *Decorate with cherries.*

*Or use any granola mix

TURKEY CRANBERRY WRAP

Preparation time: 25 minutes　　　　　　　*Chef: Ruth Deller*
Serves: 4　　　　　　　　　　　　　　　*Yacht: Pentesilea II*

1 cup	Jellied cranberry sauce
1	Granny smith apple, cored and diced
1 cup	Chopped walnuts
2 tsp	Orange juice
1 tsp	Grated orange zest
1 tsp	Salt
1 tsp	Fresh ground black pepper
1 Tblsp	Country-style Dijon mustard
4	Flour tortillas 8 inch (20 cm)
1 bunch	Fresh watercress
2 cups	Shredded cooked turkey
4 oz/112 g	Brie cheese, cut into strips
Garnish:	Orange slices and watercress sprigs

Combine cranberry sauce with apple, walnuts, juice, zest, salt and pepper. Set aside. Spread 1 tsp mustard over top 2/3 of each tortilla. Layer watercress, turkey, cheese, and cranberry mixture in 3 inch wide strip down center of mustard on each tortilla. Fold bottom of tortilla over filling and fold sides of each tortilla over. Secure with toothpick if necessary. Transfer to a serving platter. *Garnish.*

LINZERTORTE

Preparation time: 15 minutes
Chilling time: 30 minutes
Cooking time: 40 minutes
Serves: 6

Chef: Ruth Deller
Yacht: Pentesilea II

2 cups	Flour
1/4 cup	Butter
1 tsp	Salt
1/4 cup	Sugar
1-1/3 tsp	Cinnamon
1/4 cup	Ground almond
1	Egg
1	Egg white
1	Egg yolk, beaten
10 oz/280 g	Jar raspberry jam
Garnish:	Confectioners' sugar

In a large bowl, mix flour, butter, and salt. Add sugar, cinnamon, almonds, 1 egg and 1 egg white. Mix until ball is formed. On lightly floured surface, knead dough briefly. Wrap in plastic and chill for 30 minutes.

Preheat oven to 350°F/180°C. On lightly floured surface, roll 2/3 dough out to fit an 8 inch (20 cm) tart pan. With a fork prick pastry lightly. Spread raspberry jam over bottom of tart, then fill with remaining jam. Roll out the pastry trimmings and cut into 10 - 12 thin strips. Lay half the strips on the filling then arrange the remaining strips to form a lattice pattern. Brush lattice with beaten egg yolk. Bake in oven for 40 minutes or until golden brown. Sprinkle with confectioners' sugar.

MUSHROOMS STUFFED WITH CRAB MEAT AND GRUYERE

Preparation time: 20 minutes   *Chef: Ruth Deller*
Cooking time: 20 minutes   *Yacht: Pentesilea II*
Serves: 4

1 lb/450 g	Crab meat, flaked
5 Tblsp	Butter
3 Tblsp	Chopped onion
3 Tblsp	Flour
1 cup	Milk
1/8 tsp	Salt
1/8 tsp	Cayenne pepper
2 Tblsp	Grated parmesan cheese
2 Tblsp	Dried bread crumbs
1 Tblsp	Chopped parsley
24	Medium size mushrooms, stems removed
2 Tblsp	Dry sherry
6 Tblsp	Grated gruyère cheese

Preheat oven to 350°F/180°C. Clean crab meat. Melt 3 Tblsp of the butter in a skillet, add the onions and sauté over medium heat until translucent, about 3 minutes. Add the flour and cook an additional 3 minutes, then add the milk and cook 2 to 3 minutes more, stirring until thick and creamy. Remove from heat.

Add the crab meat, salt, cayenne pepper, and parmesan cheese to the pan and combine well. Stir in the bread crumbs and the parsley. At this point the mixture should be as thick as stuffing. Allow it to cool to room temperature.

Heat the remaining 2 Tblsp butter in another pan and sauté the mushroom caps until tender, about 3 minutes. While the pan is still hot, pour in the sherry and carefully light it with a match. Drain the caps and allow them to cool. Mound 1 Tblsp of the stuffing in each mushroom cap and sprinkle with gruyère cheese. Place caps on a greased baking sheet and bake for 10 minutes until bubbling. *Serve hot.*

MARINATED GRILLED SHRIMP

Preparation time: 15 minutes   *Chef: Ruth Deller*
Marinating time: 8 hours or overnight   *Yacht: Pentesilea II*
Grilling time: 4 minutes
Serves: 4

24	**Large shrimp**

Marinade:

1 Tblsp	**Coriander seeds**
2 tsp	**Fennel seeds**
1 Tblsp	**Sesame oil**
2 cloves	**Garlic, crushed**
1 piece	**Lemon grass, 2 inches long, shredded**
1/2 tsp	**Turmeric**
2 tsp	**Sugar**
1/2 tsp	**Salt**
2 Tblsp	**Soy sauce**
1/2	**Lime, juiced**
Garnish:	**Ginger peanut sauce***
	Tomato and cucumber slices

Sauté the coriander and fennel seeds in a fry pan with sesame oil. Grind to smooth. Let cool. Over low heat mix all the other ingredients, then remove from heat and allow to cool. Put 3 raw shrimp on skewers (2 skewers per person) and marinate for 8 hours or overnight in refrigerator.

Grill over low heat 2 minutes each side. *Serve with Ginger Peanut Sauce over a bed of Uncle Ben's Caribbean Rice (Rice and Black Beans).*

* Ginger peanut sauce may be found at *Ample Hamper* in Tortola and other gourmet shops.

Hint: This is equally good with chicken strips.

CHOCOLATE MOUSSE

Preparation time: 15 minutes
Cooking time: 5 minutes
Chilling time: 2 hours
Serves: 4

Chef: Ruth Deller
Yacht: Pentesilea II

4 oz/115 g	**Semi-sweet chocolate**
	(I use Hershey chocolate chips)
2 Tblsp	**Unsalted butter**
1/8 tsp	**Salt**
1/2 tsp	**Vanilla extract**
2	**Large eggs, separated**
1/4 tsp	**Cream of tartar**
1 Tblsp	**Sugar**
1/2 cup	**Heavy cream**
Garnish:	**Whipped cream and mint leaf**

Melt chocolate and butter in microwave oven or melt in a double boiler over low heat. Stir in salt and vanilla and then whisk in yolks, one at a time. Set mixture aside. Beat egg whites with cream of tartar until soft peaks just begin to form. Add sugar and beat until whites are firm but still glossy and smooth. Whisk one quarter of the beaten whites into the chocolate mixture. Fold in remaining whites with a large rubber spatula.

Whip the heavy cream until firm and fold most of it into chocolate mixture. Save a little for garnish. Spoon into individual serving dishes or glasses. Cover and refrigerate for at least 2 hours. *Garnish and serve.*

PSIPSINA SHOPPING LIST

VEGETABLES:
Garlic .... 1 bulb
Scallions 6
Spinach .... 10 oz pkg
Tomato, large 1
Cherry tomatoes .... 2 lbs

FRUITS:
Limes 8
Lemons 3

FRESH HERBS:
Basil .... garnish
Mint, chopped .... 1 Tblsp
Thyme sprigs .... garnish

DRIED SPICES:
Cinnamon .... 2 tsp
Coriander.......................... 1 tsp
Cumin, ground .... 3 tsp
Green peppercorns .... 1-1/2 tsp
Nutmeg .... 1/4 tsp

CONDIMENTS:
Hazelnuts.......................... 1/3 cup
Pecans, chopped .... 1/4 cup
Pine nuts .... 1/3 cup
Tahini .... 1/2 cup
Honey .... 1/3 cup
Oil .... 1 Tblsp
Hot chile oil .... 3 Tblsp
Olive oil............................ 1/3 cup
Butter cooking spray ....

DRY GOODS:
Flour .... 1/4 cup
Orzo, uncooked .... 1-1/2 cups
Sugar, brown .... 1/3 cup
Sugar................................. 1-1/2 cups

CANS AND JARS:
Sundried tomatoes in oil . 17 oz
Garbanzo beans .... 4 cups
Anchovies .... 2 oz
Black olives, pitted .... 6 oz
Capers .... 1-1/2 Tblsp

DAIRY/MILK/CHEESE/BUTTER
Butter................................ 3/4 lb
Eggs 5
Heavy cream .... 2 cups
Sour cream .... 1 cup
Saga blue .... 1/2 cup

MEAT/POULTRY/FISH/SEAFOOD:
Chicken breasts 6
Proscuitto .... 1/3 lb
Mahi mahi filets .... 6-7 oz

MISCELLANEOUS:
Pita bread 6

FROZEN:
White bread dough .... 1 lb

S/Y PSIPSINA

Chef Kathy Corbett
Captain Karl Prosser

MENU
Serves 6

Breakfast

*Honey Pecan Cinnamon Buns

Lunch

*Zorba Chicken Pita Pockets
*Hummus

Hors d'oeuvre

Bleu Cheese Dip
Bugles

Dinner

Wilted Spinach Salad
*Roasted Mahi Mahi with Sun Dried Tomato Tapenade
*Sun Dried and Cherry Tomato Pasta

Chilled White Wine, Frascati or Pinot Grigio

*Lime Mousse and
*Hazelnut Tuiles

PSIPSINA, a 48-foot Privilege catamaran, owned and operated by Captain Karl Prosser and Chef Kathy Corbett. Psipsina takes up to eight guests in four double cabins. Karl is a qualified shipwright and an accomplished sailor, having sailed square-rigged ships, research vessels, tug boats and private and charter yachts. Chef Kathy Corbett also comes from a seafaring background. She helped her father build small wooden boats when her family lived on Africa's West Coast. Her love of international cuisine comes from living in various countries throughout the world.

*Indicates recipe provided

HONEY PECAN CINNAMON BUNS

Preparation time: 15 minutes　　　　　　*Chef: Kathy Corbett*
Rising time: 45 minutes　　　　　　　　　*Yacht: Psipsina*
Cooking time: 20 minutes
Serves: 4

2 tsp	**Ground cinnamon**
2 Tblsp	**Sugar**
1 lb/4540 g	**Frozen white bread dough, thawed**
	Butter flavored cooking spray
1/3 cup	**Honey**
1/3 cup	**Packed brown sugar**
1/4 cup	**Chopped pecans, toasted**

Preheat oven to 350°F/180°C. Combine cinnamon and sugar together. Roll dough into a 16 x 12 inch (40 cm x 30 cm) rectangle onto a floured surface, coat the dough with cooking spray and sprinkle with sugar mixture. Coat dough again with cooking spray and roll tightly starting with the narrow end; eliminate any air pockets. Pinch the end seams. Cut dough crosswise into 1 inch (2.5 cm) slices.

Place the honey in microwave for 5 seconds and pour into a 9 inch (23 cm) pie dish; tilt to cover bottom, then sprinkle with brown sugar and nuts.

Place rolls cut side down in dish and leave 45 minutes or until double in size, see **Tip**. Bake 20 minutes.

Tip: This is my "how to cheat at cinnamon buns recipe". Make these the night before, cover with cling wrap (spray with oil) and pop into the refrigerator to rise overnight. You will find the honey and brown sugar has turned into a toffee topping. *Bring to room temperature and bake.*

Serve with a fresh fruit platter.

ZORBA CHICKEN PITA POCKETS

Preparation time: 20 minutes
Marinating time: 30 minutes
Cooking time: 15 minutes
Serves: 4

Chef: Kathy Corbett
Yacht: Psipsina

Chicken and Marinade:

2	Limes, squeezed
1 tsp	Ground cumin
1 tsp	Ground coriander
1 Tblsp	Fresh chopped mint
6	Chicken breasts, sliced 1/2-inch (1 cm) thick
1/4 cup	Olive oil

HUMMUS:

4 cups	Chick peas (garbanzo beans)
1/2 cup	Tahini
1/3 cup	Boiling water
1 tsp	Olive oil
3	Lemons, squeezed
4 cloves	Garlic, crushed
1-1/2 tsp	Salt
2 tsp	Ground cumin

To serve:

6	Pita breads, cut in half
1/2 cup	Sour cream
1	Large tomato, chopped

Chicken: Blend lime juice, spices and chopped mint. Marinate chicken for at least 30 minutes. Remove chicken from marinade and stir-fry in oil until cooked.

Hummus: Blend all the ingredients in food processor . You might prefer to leave out the water and increase amount of olive oil.

To assemble: Spread hummus on inside of opened pita pocket, fill with chicken and decorate with sour cream and chopped tomatoes.

Serve with Greek salad and a dressing made with fresh oregano leaves.

ROASTED MAHI MAHI
WITH SUNDRIED TOMATO TAPENADE

Preparation time: 20 minutes   Chef: Kathy Corbett
Cooking time: 20 - 25 minutes   Yacht: Psipsina
Serves: 6

6 - 7 oz/200 g	Fillets Mahi Mahi, skinned
1/2 tsp	Black pepper

TAPENADE:

10 oz/280 g	Sundried tomatoes, oil-packed, drained, reserve oil
6 oz/170 g	Tin large pitted black olives
2 - 3/4 oz/42 g	Packets fresh basil
1-1/2 tsp	Green peppercorns in brine, rinsed and drained
2 cloves	Garlic
2 oz/60 g	Tin anchovies, drained, reserve 1/2 the oil
1-1/2 Tblsp	Capers, rinsed and drained
3 Tblsp	Oil from the tomatoes
Garnish:	Basil leaves and olives

Preheat oven to 350°F/180°C. Reserve 6 black olives and 6 basil leaves for decoration. Place all the items, except the fish, into a food processor and blend to a coarse consistency. Wipe down fish and season with a little pepper. Place in a (9 x 13-inch/23 cm x 32.5 cm) baking dish. Top each piece of fish with a portion of tapenade. Decorate with basil leaf dipped in oil, and an olive on top. Bake for 20 - 25 minutes.

SUN DRIED AND CHERRY TOMATO PASTA:

2 Tblsp	Oil from sun dried tomatoes
6	Scallions, sliced
2 cloves	Garlic, crushed
2	Large sprigs of thyme
7 oz/200 g	Sun dried tomatoes, oil-packed
2 lbs/900 g	Cherry tomatoes, halved
1-1/2 cups	Uncooked orzo
1 Tblsp	Oil
8 oz/225 g	Tub of crème fraiche

Heat sun-dried oil in pan, add scallions, garlic and thyme. Sauté gently until opaque. Add sun dried tomatoes and cherry tomatoes. Cook 1-minute, being careful to keep tomatoes intact. Season and discard the thyme. Meanwhile cook orzo with oil to 'al-dente'; drain. Add sun dried tomato mixture to cooked pasta and the crème fraiche; mix together carefully.

LIME MOUSSE
WITH HAZELNUT TUILES

Preparation time: 20 minutes　　　　*Chef: Kathy Corbett*
Cooking time: 16 minutes　　　　　　　*Yacht: Psipsina*
Chilling time: 4 hours
Serves: 6

LIME MOUSSE:

1/2 cup	**Butter**
5	**Eggs**
1 cup	**Sugar**
1 cup	**Lime juice**
1 Tblsp	**Lime zest**
2 cups	**Heavy cream**

Melt butter in pan over simmering water; beat eggs and sugar in a bowl until light and foamy. Add to butter and simmer very gently until custard forms, about 8 minutes. Remove from heat and add lime juice and zest. Cool to room temperature. Whisk cream until very stiff, like butter, stir custard into the cream until just incorporated. Chill for 4 hours.

HAZELNUT TUILES:

1/3 cup	**Butter**
1/3 cup	**Sugar**
1/4 cup	**All purpose flour**
1/3 cup	**Hazelnuts, dry-roasted, finely ground**

Preheat oven to 350°F/180°C. Cream butter and sugar until light and fluffy. Add flour and hazelnuts and mix well. Place a teaspoon of mixture on a prepared baking sheet, wet a fork and flatten out and make into a circle. Bake 6 minutes. *These can be lifted and cooled over a rolling pin to give a curved appearance.*

Hint: Serve in glass dessert bowls.

QWEST SHOPPING LIST

VEGETABLES:
Garlic cloves 2

FRESH HERBS:
Basil, chopped .... 2 tsp
Oregano, chopped .... 2 tsp
Parsley, chopped .... 4 Tblsp
Rosemary, chopped .... 1 Tblsp
Sage, chopped .... 1 Tblsp
Tarragon, chopped .... 1 Tblsp
Thyme, chopped .... 1 Tblsp

DRIED SPICES:
Garlic powder .... 4 tsp
Garlic salt .... 1 Tblsp
Green peppercorns .... 2 Tblsp
Pink peppercorns .... 2 Tblsp
Seasoned salt .... 1/2 tsp

CONDIMENTS:
Cocoa for .... rolling
Chocolate chips white ..... 3/4 cup
Olive oil .... 1/4 cup

DRY GOODS:
Flour .... 6 cups
Sugar .... 1/4 tsp
Yeast, active dry .... 2 pkts

CANS AND JARS:
Pace picante salsa .... 1 cup

DAIRY/MILK/CHEESE/BUTTER

Butter .... 1+ lb
Eggs 9
Whole milk .... 1 cup
Cream .... 1-1/3 cups
Sour cream .... 1/4 cup
Cream cheese .... 8 oz
Cheddar, grated .... 1 cup
Mozzarella, shredded ...... 2 cups
Parmesan, grated .... 3/4 cup

LIQUOR/WINE/SPIRITS:
Cognac .... 2 Tblsp
Irish cream .... 1-1/2 Tblsp

MEAT/POULTRY/FISH/SEAFOOD:
Chicken strips .... 1/2 lb
Sirloin steaks 4

MISCELLANEOUS:
Butter crackers .... 1 box
Vanilla wafers .... 3.5 oz box
Flour tortillas 4

S/Y QWEST

Chef Kim West
Captain Rich West

MENU
Serves 4

Breakfast
*Huevos Rancheros

Lunch

*Chicken Alfredo Pizza
Fresh Tomatoes
with Italian Dressing

Hors d'oeuvre

*Garlic Pepper Cheese Spread with
Butter Crackers

Dinner

*Steak au Poivre
*Garlic-Parmesan Breadsticks
Garden Salad

*White Chocolate Irish Cream Truffles

QWEST, a 46-foot Morgan sailing yacht owned by Captain Rich and Kim West, carries full scuba equipment, an on-board compressor and PADI instructor ready to teach a novice or dive with the experts. After an exhilarating sail, a diving exploration or a leisurely snorkel in tranquil waters, guests can be sure Chef Kim is prepared for ravenous appetites with a big selection of good things to eat. The end of a perfect day brings everyone together for a full-course dinner, served in the cockpit under a tropical sky.

*Indicates recipe provided

HUEVOS RANCHEROS

Preparation time: 5 minutes   *Chef: Kim West*
Cooking time: 10 minutes   *Yacht: Qwest*
Serves: 4

8	Eggs
1/4 cup	Sour cream
1/4 cup	Milk, or water
1 cup	Grated colby or jack cheese
4	Flour tortillas
1 cup	Pace picante sauce, medium

Whisk together eggs, sour cream and milk. In a skillet scramble eggs over medium heat. When thoroughly cooked, add cheese and mix. Put on flour tortillas and top with picante sauce. *Serve immediately.*

Hint: A great cheese to use would be one of the cheese mixes available e.g. taco cheese, cheese with jalapenos, etc. It is also good served with chorizo.

CHICKEN ALFREDO PIZZA

Preparation time: 40 minutes　　　　　　*Chef: Kim West*
Cooking time: 20 minutes　　　　　　　　*Yacht: Qwest*
Serves: 4

PIZZA DOUGH:

1 Tblsp	Dry active yeast
1/2 cup	Tepid water
1/8 tsp	Sugar
3 cups	Flour
1-1/2 tsp	Garlic salt
1 tsp	Garlic powder (optional)
3/4 cup	Milk
2 Tblsp	Olive oil

ALFREDO SAUCE:

1/2 cup	Fresh grated parmesan cheese
1	Egg
1/3 cup	Cream
1/2 lb/225 g	Precooked chicken strips (Italian flavor is best)
2 cups	Shredded mozzarella or pizza blend cheese

Whisk yeast, water and sugar together and let sit for 5 minutes. Blend dry ingredients together. Add milk and oil to the yeast mixture. Slowly add dry ingredients until mixture forms a soft ball. Turn dough out onto a floured surface and knead 60 times. Rest 2 minutes. Knead dough another 30 times. Cover and let rise until doubled. Turn out onto a floured surface. With half of the dough shape a 16 inch (40 cm) pizza.

Preheat oven to 425°F/220°C. **Alfredo Sauce:** Mix parmesan cheese, egg and cream together. On top of dough, add alfredo sauce and chicken strips, then top with mozzarella or pizza blend cheese. Bake for 15 - 20 minutes.

This is great served with side dish of fresh sliced tomatoes and Italian dressing.

Hint: This dough recipe is very versatile and one recipe makes 2 batches of dough. I like to buy the precooked chicken strips, usually found near lunch meat at the grocery store.

GARLIC PEPPER CHEESE SPREAD

Preparation time: 5 minutes
Chilling time: 1 hour
Serves: 4

Chef: Kim West
Yacht: Qwest

8 oz/225 g	Cream cheese
2 Tblsp	Butter
1 Tblsp	Garlic pepper blend
	Butter crackers

Mix cream cheese, butter and garlic pepper together. *Serve with butter crackers.*

Hint: If possible, chill for at least an hour.

STEAK AU POIVRE

Preparation time: 10 minutes
Cooking time: 15 minutes
Serves: 4

Chef: Kim and Rich West
Yacht: Qwest

4	Boneless sirloin steaks
2 Tblsp	Pink peppercorns, crushed
2 Tblsp	Green peppercorns, crushed
1/4 cup	Butter
1 cup	Cream
2 Tblsp	Cognac
1/2 tsp	Seasoned salt

Roll steaks in peppercorns. Melt butter in heavy skillet over medium-high heat. Add steaks and cook 5 minutes on each side for medium-rare. Remove steaks from pan and keep warm. Add cream, cognac and salt to skillet; bring to a boil. Lower heat, simmer for 2 minutes or until thickened. Pour sauce over steaks and *serve immediately. Goes well with garden salad and* **Garlic-Parmesan Bread Sticks.**

Hint: We have a grinder with a coarse setting that we use for the peppercorns, which saves lots of "crushing" time.

GARLIC PARMESAN BREAD STICKS

Preparation time: 10 minutes　　　　　　　*Chef: Kim West*
Cooking time: 15 minutes　　　　　　　　　*Yacht: Qwest*
Serves: 4

1/3 cup	**Butter**
1/3 cup	**Grated fresh parmesan**
1 Tblsp	**Garlic powder**
1/2	**Batch of pizza dough**
	(see *chicken alfredo* recipe)

Preheat oven to 425°F/220°C. Blend butter, parmesan and garlic powder. Shape dough into 12 twists about 1 x 6 inch (2.5 x 15 cm) each. Top with butter mixture. Bake for 15 minutes.

Hint: The butter mixture keeps a long time, so make up large quantities.

WHITE CHOCOLATE IRISH CREAM TRUFFLES

Preparation time: 30 minutes　　　　　　　*Chef: Kim West*
Chilling time: 30 minutes　　　　　　　　　*Yacht: Qwest*
Makes: 18

3-1/2 oz/100 g	**Box vanilla wafers**
3/4 cup	**White chocolate chips**
4 Tblsp	**Butter**
1-1/2 Tblsp	**Irish cream liquor**
	Sweet cocoa

Crush vanilla wafers in a blender or food processor. Melt white chocolate chips. Add butter and blend well. Mix in Irish cream. Add crumbs to chocolate mixture. Form into balls and roll in sweet cocoa. Place in confectionery cups and chill.

Hint: These keep very well in the refrigerator and are handy, just in case.

RENDEZVOUS CAY SHOPPING LIST

VEGETABLES:
Broccoli .... 1 bunch
Carrots 8
Garlic clove 1
Scallions 6
Shallots 3
Yellow onion, grated .... 1 tsp
Red bell peppers 3
Yellow bell peppers 2
Mushrooms, qtrd .... 1-1/2 cups
Tomatoes, plum 6

FRUITS:
Lime 1
Orange 1
Strawberries .... 2 quarts

FRESH HERBS:
Dill .... 1/2 cup
Tarragon, chopped .... 2 Tblsp

DRIED SPICES:
Cinnamon .... 1 tsp
Cloves, ground .... 1/8 tsp
Garlic powder .... pinch
Ginger, ground .... 1/2 tsp
Oregano .... 1 tsp
Red pepper flakes .... 1/2 tsp
Tarragon .... 1 tsp

CONDIMENTS:
Baking powder .... 2-1/2 tsp
Baking soda .... 1/2 tsp
Almonds, sliced .... 1/4 cup
Pine nuts .... 1/4 cup
Accent .... 1/2 tsp
Extra virgin olive oil .... 2/3 cup
Olive oil .... 1 Cup
Peanut oil .... 1/4 cup
Hoisin .... 1/2 cup
Soy sauce .... 1/2 cup
Vinegar, balsamic .... 3/4 cup
Mayonnaise .... 1/2 cup

DRY GOODS:
Flour .... 3 cups
Sugar, light brown .... 1 cup
Sugar .... 3/4 cup
Linguine .... 1 lb
Rice, white cooked .... 6 cups

CANS AND JARS:
Orange marmalade .... 1/2 cup

DAIRY/MILK/CHEESE/BUTTER:
Butter .... 1-1/4 lbs
Heavy cream .... garnish
Buttermilk .... 1 cup
Cheddar, shredded .... 1/4 cup
Mozzarella, shredded ...... 1/4 cup
Parmesan, shaved .... 1/2 cup
Swiss, shredded .... 1/4 cup

MEAT/POULTRY/FISH/SEAFOOD:
Pork tenderloins 3
Shrimp, large .... 2 lbs

MISCELLANEOUS:
Seasoned croutons .... 1-1/2 cups
Dried apricots, chopped .. 1/4 cup
Baguette 1

FROZEN:
Peas .... 1/2 cup
Spinach .... 10 oz pkg

S/Y RENDEZVOUS CAY

Chef Tammy Stonich
Captain Tim Stonich

MENU
Serves 8

Breakfast

Orange Juice
*Spiced Buttermilk Scones

Lunch

*Chilled Shrimp and Vegetable Pasta

Hors d'oeuvre

*Cheese and Tarragon Rounds

Dinner

*Spinach Salad with Mushrooms and Red Peppers
*Pork Tenderloin with Spicy Chinese Sauce
*Glazed Carrots

*Sweet and Tart Fresh Strawberries

Captain Tim Stonich and Chef Tammy Stonich sailed RENDEZVOUS CAY, their 50-foot state-of-the-art catamaran to the Caribbean from South Africa, where she was built, in 1998. Tim and Tammy, from the Midwest, report their dreams came true on Rendezvous Cay. They have fun sharing their sea world and their love of fine food, wine and music with charter guests. Whether tastes run from Pavarotti, Merlot and veal piccata to Jimmy Buffet, margaritas and enchiladas, they're ready to provide.

*Indicates recipe provided

SPICED BUTTERMILK SCONES

Preparation time: 30 minutes
Cooking time: 15 - 25 minutes
Serves: 8

Chef: Tammy Stonich
Yacht: Rendezvous Cay

3 cups	Flour
1/3 cup	Sugar
2-1/2 tsp	Baking powder
3/4 tsp	Salt
1/2 tsp	Baking soda
1/2 tsp	Ground ginger
1/8 tsp	Ground cloves
6 oz/170 g	Cold butter, cut in 1/2 inch (1 cm) cubes
1 cup	Buttermilk
2 Tblsp	Softened butter
1/2 cup	Orange marmalade

Preheat oven to 425°F/220°C. Sift together flour, sugar, baking powder, salt and soda. Mix in ginger and cloves. Cut in butter until mixture resembles small peas. Stir in buttermilk and knead a few times in the bowl until the mix holds together. Divide dough into 4 even pieces and shape into 7 inch (18 cm) rounds on floured surface.

Combine softened butter with 1/4 cup orange marmalade and spread on two of the rounds. Top with remaining two rounds and pinch edges together to seal. Strain remaining marmalade and brush over the top. Cut each round into 6 wedges. Bake 15 - 25 minutes until nicely browned.

CHILLED SHRIMP
AND VEGETABLE PASTA

Preparation time: 45 minutes   *Chef: Tammy Stonich*
Cooking time: 20 minutes   *Yacht: Rendezvous Cay*
Chilling time: 2 hours
Marinating time: 2 hours
Serves: 8

2 lbs/900 g	Large shrimp
2	Yellow peppers, finely, diced
2	Red peppers, finely, diced
6	Ripe plum tomatoes, diced
1/2 cup	Fresh dill
2 Tblsp	Fresh tarragon or 2 tsp dried
2 Tblsp	Chopped shallots
1/2 tsp	Red pepper flakes
1 tsp	Pepper
1 tsp	Salt
1/2 cup	Fresh lime juice
1 cup + 1 Tblsp	Olive oil
1/4 tsp	Hot chili oil
1 lb/450 g	Linguine
1/2 cup	Frozen peas, thawed
1 bunch	Broccoli, broken in florets

Two hours ahead, cook shrimp until tender, about 1 minute in a boil. Rinse, drain and peel. Put in a bowl. Add peppers, tomatoes, dill, tarragon, shallot, pepper flakes, salt and pepper, lime juice, 1 cup olive oil and chili oil. Toss well, cover and refrigerate. Cook linguine per package directions. To serve, cook broccoli one minute, rinse and drain. Mix peas and broccoli with shrimp and toss with linguine.

CHEESE AND TARRAGON ROUNDS

Preparation time: 20 minutes   *Chef: Tammy Stonich*
Cooking time: 7 - 10 minutes   *Yacht: Rendezvous Cay*
Serves: 8

1/4 cup	**Cheddar cheese, shredded**
1/4 cup	**Swiss cheese, shredded**
1/4 cup	**Mozzarella cheese, shredded**
1/2 cup	**Mayonnaise**
1 tsp	**Dried tarragon**
1 tsp	**Oregano**
1/4 tsp	**Salt**
1/4 tsp	**Pepper**
1/2 tsp	**Accent**
1 tsp	**Grated onion**
Pinch	**Garlic powder**
	Bread rounds

Preheat oven to 350°F/180°C. Mix all ingredients together, except bread rounds. Add more mayonnaise if it is not holding together. Sauté or toast bread rounds. Let cool. Spread cheese mixture on rounds. Sprinkle each with additional dried tarragon and oregano. Bake for 5 - 7 minutes, or broil 2 - 3 minutes, until brown and golden. Okay to double, can be frozen.

SPINACH SALAD WITH MUSHROOMS AND RED PEPPERS

Preparation time: 10 minutes   *Chef: Tammy Stonich*
Serves: 8   *Yacht: Rendezvous Cay*

5 Tblsp	Minced shallot
3 Tblsp	Balsamic vinegar
1 clove	Garlic, minced
2/3 cup	Extra virgin olive oil
1-1/2 cups	Mushrooms, quartered
10 oz/284 g	Pkg frozen spinach
1-1/2 cups	Seasoned croutons
1	Large red pepper, diced
1/4 cup	Pine nuts, toasted
4 oz/115 g	Parmesan cheese

Mix shallot, vinegar and garlic in small bowl. Gradually whisk in oil. Season with salt and pepper. Pour 1/4 cup dressing in bowl, add mushrooms and toss to coat. Add all remaining ingredients and enough extra dressing to coat well. Toss gently. Top with shaved parmesan.

Hint: Use a vegetable peeler to shave parmesan.

PORK TENDERLOIN
WITH SPICY CHINESE SAUCE

Preparation time: 15 minutes
Cooking time: 15 minutes
Marinating time: 8 hours
Serves: 8

Chef: Tammy Stonich
Yacht: Rendezvous Cay

Marinade:

1/2 cup	Soy sauce
1/2 cup	Hoisin sauce
4 Tblsp	Vegetable or peanut oil
6 Tblsp	Sugar
3	Pork tenderloins
4 Tblsp	Butter
6 cups	White rice, cooked
6	Scallions, thinly sliced
1/2 cup	Water

Marinate the tenderloins 8 hours—poking and turning occasionally. Drain marinade and reserve. Grill tenderloins over hot coals 12 - 15 minutes. Pour marinade in saucepan, add 1/2 cup water and bring to boil over low heat. Boil several minutes, then add 4 Tblsp butter; bring back to boil. Slice tenderloins thinly across the grain and serve on a bed of white rice with marinade poured over. Garnish with sliced scallions.

GLAZED CARROTS

Preparation time: 10 minutes   *Chef: Tammy Stonich*
Cooking time: 20 minutes   *Yacht: Rendezvous Cay*
Serves: 8

8	**Carrots, peeled and chopped**
1 Tblsp	**Sugar**
1 tsp	**Cinnamon**
6 Tblsp	**Butter**
3 Tblsp	**Orange or tropical juice**
1/4 cup	**Chopped dried apricots**
1/4 cup	**Toasted sliced almonds**

Steam carrots in skillet until just crunchy. Rinse under cold water. Sauté carrots in butter with sugar and cinnamon until glazed, about 5 minutes. Add remaining ingredients and stir until blended.

SWEET TART FRESH STRAWBERRIES

Chilling time: 2 hours   *Chef: Tammy Stonich*
Serves: 8   *Yacht: Rendezvous Cay*

1 cup	**Light brown sugar, packed**
1/4 tsp	**Salt**
1/2 cup	**Balsamic vinegar**
2 qts/2 liters	**Strawberries, hulled and sliced**
Garnish:	**Fresh whipped cream**

Two hours ahead, whisk together brown sugar, salt, vinegar and pour over sliced strawberries. Refrigerate, stirring every 30 minutes.

Serve with dollop of fresh whipped cream.

SHAMOUN SHOPPING LIST

VEGETABLES:
Chives .... garnish
English cucumber 1
Plantains 6
Tomatoes, plum 6

FRUITS:
Bananas, large 6
Limes 2

FRESH HERBS:
Basil .... garnish
Coriander, chopped .... garnish
Parsley .... garnish

DRIED SPICES:
Cardamom, ground .... 1/2 tsp
Coriander, ground .... 1/3 tsp
Cumin, ground .... 1/2 tsp
Peppercorns, green .... 1 Tblsp

CONDIMENTS:
Vanilla extract .... 1/4 tsp
Oil .... 1 Tblsp
Olive oil .... 2 Tblsp

DRY GOODS:
Flour, self rising .... 1 cup
Penne .... 1 lb
Sugar, confectioners' .... garnish
Sugar .... 1/3 cup

CANS AND JARS:
Coconut milk .... 1-1/2 cups
Fish sauce .... 1 Tblsp
Thai green curry paste .... 2 Tblsp
French dressing .... 1 Bottle

DAIRY/MILK/CHEESE/BUTTER
Butter .... 1/4 lb
Eggs 16
Milk, whole .... 1 cup
Yogurt .... 2-1/4 cups
Mozzarella, fresh .... 3 balls
Parmesan, grated .... 1 cup

MEAT/POULTRY/FISH/SEAFOOD:
Salmon, smoked slices 12
Wahoo .... 2 lbs

LIQUOR/WINE/SPIRITS:
Rum, white .... 2 tsp

MISCELLANEOUS:
Baguette 1
English muffins 6

FROZEN:
Vanilla ice cream .... 2 cups

S/Y SHAMOUN

Chef Vanessa van Dinther
Captain Niels van Dinther

MENU
Serves 6

Breakfast

*Scrambled Eggs with Smoked Salmon on
English Muffins

Lunch

*Penne A la Sorrento

Hors d'oeuvre

Crostini

Dinner

*Thai Fish Green Curry
Jasmine or Basmati Rice
*Raitha
*Fried Plantains

*Banana, Pineapple or Mango Fritters
with Vanilla Ice Cream

SHAMOUN, a 108-foot cutter-rigged sloop, was built in Holland in 1999, taking 2-1/2 years to be completed. Captain Niels van Dinther, who is Dutch, and Chef Vanessa van Dinther, who is English, are now on their way around the world, presently spending time in French Polynesia but planning in the next year to head for the Mediterranean. Vanessa's menus reflect a touch of her English heritage but, more exotically, dishes from the many ports they have visited on their sailing travels.

*Indicates recipe provided

SCRAMBLED EGGS WITH SMOKED SALMON ON ENGLISH MUFFINS

Preparation time: 10 minutes   *Chef: Vanessa van Dinther*
Cooking time: 10 minutes   *Yacht: Shamoun*
Serves: 6

2 Tblsp	Butter
12	Large eggs, beaten
	Salt and pepper
6	English muffins
12 slices	Smoked salmon
Garnish:	Chopped chives or parsley

Melt butter in a non stick saucepan. Add eggs, salt and pepper. Stir until eggs are almost cooked. Remove pan from heat (the eggs will continue to cook from heat of pan). Toast the split muffins and butter them if desired. Put 2 halves on each plate, cover with scrambled eggs and 'concertina' of salmon on top. Garnish with chives or parsley.

PENNE A LA SORRENTO

Preparation time: 15 minutes   *Chef: Vanessa van Dinther*
Marinating time: 1 - 2 hours   *Yacht: Shamoun*
Serves: 6

3	Fresh mozzarella balls
6	Plum tomatoes
	French dressing
	Fresh basil
1 lb/450 g	Penne pasta
1 cup	Freshly grated parmesan

Cut mozzarella into 3/4 inch (2 cm) cubes. Cut tomatoes into 6 crescents. Put in a bowl with enough french dressing to cover, add torn basil and marinade. Boil pasta as directed on package, until al dente. Drain and toss in parmesan to coat. Add tomatoes, mozzarella and dressing. *Serve with a green salad and crusty bread.*

THAI FISH GREEN CURRY

Preparation time: 30 minutes   *Chef: Vanessa van Dinther*
Cooking time: 30 minutes   *Yacht: Shamoun*
Serves: 6

2 lb/900 g	**Wahoo or any firm white fish**
	Sunflower oil
2 Tblsp	**Thai green curry paste**
1-1/2 cups	**Coconut milk**
1 Tblsp	**Fish sauce**
1 Tblsp	**Freshly ground green peppercorns**
1 Tblsp	**Sugar**
Garnish:	**Chopped coriander and mango chutney**

Cut the wahoo into 1 inch (2.5 cm) cubes. Heat oil in a wok or saucepan, gently stir in curry paste and cook for 1 - 2 minutes. Slowly stir in coconut milk and then the fish. Bring to a simmer and cook for about 15 minutes. Mix in fish sauce, ground peppercorns and sugar. Sprinkle with coriander. Serve with **Raitha, Fried Plantains**, Mango chutney, and Jasmine or Basmati rice.

Hint: Add 2 stalks of chopped lemon grass, after you add the curry paste and then add 1/2 cup chopped basil when you add the fish sauce.

Hint: This recipe also works well with chicken.

RAITHA

Preparation time: 15 minutes　　　　　*Chef: Vanessa van Dinther*
Draining time: 30 minutes　　　　　　　　*Yacht: Shamoun*
Serves: 6

2	**European cucumbers**
2 tsp	**Salt**
2-1/4 cups	**Greek, bio or plain yogurt**
1/2 tsp	**Ground cumin**
1/2 tsp	**Ground coriander**
1/2 tsp	**Ground cardamom**
	Squeeze lemon or lime
	Pepper and salt to taste

Peel and coarsely grate the cucumbers then put them in a colander and sprinkle with salt. Leave to drain for about 30 minutes (it takes out a lot of the water content). Squeeze out the excess water and add to yogurt with spices and seasoning.

Note: *Serve with* **Thai Fish Green Curry** *or any other spicy Indian or Thai dish.*

FRIED PLANTAINS

Preparation time: 5 minutes　　　　　*Chef: Vanessa van Dinther*
Cooking time: 20 minutes　　　　　　　*Yacht: Shamoun*
Serves: 6

6	**Plantains**
4 Tblsp	**Butter**
2 Tblsp	**Olive oil**

Peel and cut the plantains on an angle into 3/4 inch (2 cm) slices. Heat a large skillet and add butter and oil; when bubbly, add the plantains and fry on each side until golden and soft. *Delicious served with any Indian or Thai dishes.*

BANANA, PINEAPPLE OR MANGO FRITTERS WITH VANILLA ICE CREAM

Preparation time: 15 minutes　　　　　*Chef: Vanessa van Dinther*
Standing time: 15 minutes　　　　　　　　　*Yacht: Shamoun*
Cooking time: 45 minutes
Makes 20 - 24

2	Eggs, lightly beaten
1/8 tsp	Salt
1 cup	Self raising flour, sifted
1/4 cup	Sugar
1 Tblsp	Melted butter
1/4 tsp	Vanilla
1 cup	Milk
2 tsp	White rum
2	Egg whites, beaten to soft peaks
6	Large firm bananas
2 Tblsp	Lime juice
	Oil for cooking
	Confectioners' sugar
	Vanilla ice cream

In a large mixing bowl beat together the eggs, salt, flour, sugar, melted butter and vanilla; gradually add milk and mix to a smooth consistency. Leave to stand for 15 minutes. Just before using add the rum and mix into the batter and fold in egg whites. Cut bananas in half and then in half lengthwise. Brush with lime juice and dip banana slices, one at a time, in batter to coat. Drain off excess batter and drop into hot, but not smoking oil. Fry until golden brown. Lift out with slotted spoon and drain on paper towels. *Serve hot, sprinkled with confectioners' sugar and vanilla ice cream.*

Note: For pineapple or mango fritters. Cut pineapple in large rings and mangoes in large pieces. Brush with lime juice and cook as the bananas.

SHIBUMI SHOPPING LIST

VEGETABLES:
Garlic cloves 4

FRUITS:
Lime 1
Mangos, large 2

FRESH HERBS:
Chives, chopped .... 2 Tblsp

DRIED SPICES:
Cinnamon & sugar .... garnish
Fine herbs .... 1 Tblsp
Oregano .... 1/4 tsp
Thyme .... 1/4 tsp

CONDIMENTS:
Baking powder .... 2-1/2 tsp
Vegetable oil .... 1/2 cup
Olive oil .... 1/4 cup
Vinegar, red wine .... 1 Tblsp
Mayonnaise .... 2 Tblsp
Mustard, Dijon .... 1-1/2 Tblsp
Knorr's vegetable mix ..... 1 pkg

DRY GOODS:
Flour .... 1-1/4 cups
Granola .... 1-1/2 cups
Sugar, confectioners' .... garnish
Sugar .... 1-1/2 cups

CANS AND JARS:
Anchovy filet 1
Black olives, pitted .... 6 oz

DAIRY/MILK/CHEESE/BUTTER
Butter .... 1/4 lb
Eggs 6
Milk, whole .... 1-1/2 cups
Milk, skim .... 1/2 cup
Basil and Feta .... 8 oz
Swiss, shredded .... 1 cup

MEAT/POULTRY/FISH/SEAFOOD:
Salmon filets .... 4 - 7 oz

MISCELLANEOUS:
Baguettes 2
Pita bread .... 1 pkg

FROZEN:
Orange juice concentrate 1/2 cup
Pie crust, 9 inch 1
Spinach .... 9 oz pkg

S/Y SHIBUMI

Chef Cindy Hildreth
Captain Jeff Hildreth

MENU
Serves 4

Breakfast

Orange Juice
*Breakfast Scones

Lunch

*Vegetable Quiche
Crusty French Bread

Hors d'oeuvres

*Whipped Feta
Pita Bread
*Black Olive Tapenade

Dinner

*Grilled Salmon with
*Dijon Sauce
Wild Rice
Steamed Asparagus

*Mango Torte

SHIBUMI, a 51-foot Beneteau, is both a dive boat and a sailing one. As a PADI scuba instructor, Captain Jeff Hildreth can lead divers of all levels. Chef Cindy is a certified diver and Shibumi's snorkel guide. Preparing great food is a major part of Cindy's day and she chooses a varied, international menu designed to suit her guests tastes and preferences. She enjoys offering guests local favorites, often fresh fish which she cooks superbly. Jeff and Cindy are from Cape Cod, famous for its fish dishes.

*Indicates recipe provided

BREAKFAST SCONES

Preparation time: 15 minutes   *Chef: Cindy Hildreth*
Cooking time: 20 minutes   *Yacht: Shibumi*
Serves: 6

1-1/4 cups	**Flour**
1-1/2 cups	**Granola**
1/2 cup	**Dried fruit bits**
1/2 cup	**Sugar**
1-1/2 tsp	**Baking powder**
1/2 tsp	**Salt**
1/2 cup	**Skim milk**
1/2 cup	**Frozen orange juice, thawed**
1/2 cup	**Vegetable oil**
Garnish:	**Powdered sugar**

Preheat oven to 400°F/200°C. Mix all dry ingredients together and then add milk, orange juice, and vegetable oil. Mix until just blended. Shape dough into 8 inch (20 cm) circles and place on a lightly greased baking sheet. Bake 20 minutes or until a pick inserted in center comes out clean. Sprinkle top with powdered sugar.

Note: Good way to use up bits of left-over granola.

VEGETABLE QUICHE

Preparation time: 15 minutes　　　　　　*Chef: Cindy Hildreth*
Cooking time: 50 - 55 minutes　　　　　　　　　*Yacht: Shibumi*
Serves: 6

4	**Eggs, beaten**
1-1/2 cups	**Milk**
1 cup	**Shredded swiss cheese**
1 pkg	**Knorr spring vegetable or vegetable soup mix**
9 oz/255 g pkg	**Frozen chopped spinach thawed, squeezed dry**
1	**9 inch (23 cm) frozen pie crust**

Preheat oven to 375°F/190°C. Heat cookie sheet. Combine all ingredients and pour into crust. Bake about 50 minutes or until knife inserted halfway between center and edge, comes out clean.

Note: You can use egg substitute.

Hint: I also use onion soup mix. Capt. Jeff likes this best!

WHIPPED FETA

Preparation time: 10 minutes   *Chef: Cindy Hildreth*
Serves: 4 - 6   *Yacht: Shibumi*

8 oz/225 g	**Block basil and tomato feta cheese**
3 cloves	**Garlic**
2 Tblsp	**Olive oil**
1 pkg	**Pita bread**

In a food processor crumble feta and add peeled cloves of garlic. Pulse several times to break up feta. Drizzle oil slowly, 1 Tblsp at a time while blending, until you get consistency of lumpy cream cheese. *Serve with pita bread or torn bread chunks.*

Note: Also great with black pepper feta cheese.

BLACK OLIVE TAPENADE

Preparation time: 15 minutes   *Chef: Cindy Hildreth*
Chilling time: 1 hour   *Yacht: Shibumi*
Serves: 4 - 6

6 oz/170 g	**Black olives, pitted**
1 clove	**Garlic, peeled**
1	**Anchovy**
1/2 tsp	**Black pepper**
1/4 tsp	**Thyme**
1/4 tsp	**Oregano**
4 Tblsp	**Olive oil**
1 Tblsp	**Wine vinegar**
1	**Baguette**

Combine all ingredients in a food processor or blender. Mix until blended. Chill or let stand 1 hour to blend flavors. *Serve with Baguette.*

Hint: Prepare the tapenade and the **Whipped Feta** and serve with warm herbed focaccia bread.

GRILLED SALMON
WITH DIJON SAUCE

Preparation time: 5 minutes   *Chef: Cindy Hildreth*
Cooking time: 12 - 14 minutes   *Yacht: Shibumi*
Serves: 4

4 - 7 oz/195 g	Salmon fillets, or steaks
1 Tblsp	Fresh lemon juice
1 Tblsp	Fine herbs

DIJON SAUCE:

2 tsp	Fresh lemon juice
2 Tblsp	Chopped chives, or green onion
2 Tblsp	Mayonnaise
1-1/2 Tblsp	Dijon mustard

Preheat grill. Sprinkle salmon lightly with lemon juice and fine herbs. Grill 6 to 7 minutes on each side. DO NOT OVERCOOK. Mix together all sauce ingredients. Spread on salmon last three minutes on grill (Do not turn after you put sauce on). *Serve with wild rice and steamed asparagus or green beans.*

MANGO TORTE

Preparation time: 30 minutes   *Chef: Cindy Hildreth*
Cooking time: 50 minutes   *Yacht: Shibumi*
Serves: 8

1/2 cup	Butter
1 cup	Sugar
1 cup	Flour
1 tsp	Baking powder
Pinch	Salt
2	Eggs
2	Mangoes, canned or frozen
	Sugar and cinnamon

Preheat oven to 350°F/180°C. Cream together sugar and butter. Add flour, baking powder, and salt. Mix until blended. Add eggs and mix. Grease a 9 inch (23 cm) spring form pan. Add mixture. Top with slices of mango in a pinwheel. Sprinkle lightly with sugar and cinnamon. Bake for about 50 minutes.

SILENT PARTNER II SHOPPING LIST

VEGETABLES:
Garlic cloves 4
Romaine leaves 6
Red onion 1
Yellow onion 1
Green peppers 2
Red bell pepper 1
Yellow bell pepper 1
Tomatoes 3
Cherry tomatoes .... 1 lb

FRUITS:
Bananas 2
Lime 1
Orange 1

FRESH HERBS:
Parsley, chopped .... 3/4 cup
Rosemary, chopped .... 3 Tblsp

DRIED SPICES:
Garlic powder .... 1/2 tsp
Onion powder .... 1/2 tsp

CONDIMENTS:
Baking soda .... 1 tsp
Pecans, chopped .... 1/2 cup
Pecan pieces .... 1/4 cup
Mustard, Dijon .... 3 Tblsp
Olive oil .... 1/8 cup
Vegetable oil .... 1/4 cup
Tabasco .... to taste
Worchestershire .... to taste
Mayonnaise .... 7 Tblsp
Catsup .... to taste

DRY GOODS:
Flour .... 2-1/4 cups
Rolled oats .... 1/2 cup
Wild rice, uncooked .... 1 cup
Sugar .... 1-1/2 cups

CANS AND JARS:
Crab meat .... 6 oz can
Chicken broth .... 1 cup

DAIRY/MILK/CHEESE/BUTTER
Butter .... 1/2 lb
Eggs 2
Milk, whole .... 1/3 cup
Cheese whip .... 6 oz

MEAT/POULTRY/FISH/SEAFOOD:
Chicken breasts, boneless 6
Grouper filets .... 2-1/2 lbs

MISCELLANEOUS:
Orange juice .... 1 cup
Tapioca, minute .... 1 Tblsp
English muffins 6
Tortillas, flour 6

FROZEN:
Fruit mix .... 1 lg bag

S/Y SILENT PARTNER II

Chef Laurie Rainthorpe
Captain Gary Rainthorpe

MENU
Serves 6

Breakfast

*Banana Nut Bread

Lunch

*California Chicken Wrap

Hors d'oeuvre

*Crab Wedges

Dinner

*Garlic Parsley Grouper
*Wild Nutted Rice
*Piperade

*Mixed Fruit Crisp

A performance yacht redesigned for the charter market, SILENT PARTNER II is a new sprightly C&C 52-foot sloop owned by two Canadians – Captain Gary Rainthorpe and his wife, Laurie, who acts as crew and chef. Silent Partner, a classy sailing ship in one of the world's best sailing areas, is bound to have world-class cuisine. When at anchor her guests enjoy just that. Among many letters of praise thanking them for a great holiday is one that Laurie treasures with a smile: "And the meals.............ooh, la, la!"

*Indicates recipe provided

BANANA NUT BREAD

Preparation time: 10 minutes
Cooking time: 1 hour
Serves: 6

Chef: Laurie Rainthorpe
Yacht: Silent Partner II

2	**Ripe bananas**
1 Tblsp	**Fresh lemon juice**
1/2 cup	**Pecans, chopped**
1-3/4 cups	**Flour**
2/3 cup	**Sugar**
1/2 cup	**Butter**
1/3 cup	**Milk**
2	**Eggs**
1 tsp	**Baking soda**
1/2 tsp	**Salt**

Preheat oven to 350° F/180°C. In a food processor (with a steel blade) process bananas with lemon juice. Add 1/4 cup of nuts and all the remaining ingredients. Pulse until flour is moistened. Batter should be lumpy. Pour into a greased loaf pan 8-1/2 x 4-1/2 x 4-1/2 inch (21 x 11 x 11 cm). Sprinkle remaining 1/4 cup of nuts over batter. Bake until a pick inserted in the center comes out clean, about 1 hour. *Serve warm with butter.*

CALIFORNIA CHICKEN WRAP

Preparation time: 10 minutes
Marinating time: 30 minutes
Cooking time: 10 minutes
Serves: 6

Chef: Laurie Rainthorpe
Yacht: Silent Partner II

6	**Chicken breasts, boneless and skinless**
	Marinade of your choice
6	**Tortillas**
6 Tblsp	**Mayonnaise**
3 Tblsp	**Dijon mustard**
6	**Romaine lettuce leaves**
1	**Green pepper, finely chopped**
3	**Tomatoes, sliced**
1	**Red onion, peeled and thinly sliced**
	Black pepper

Slice chicken breasts in long strips about 1 inch (2.5 cm) wide. Marinate for 30 minutes or longer. Pan fry. Spread mayonnaise and Dijon mustard on wraps. Add lettuce leaves, cooked chicken strips, green pepper, tomatoes, and onion. Season to taste with freshly ground pepper. Roll up wraps and secure with toothpicks.

Note: *Marinade of your choice; lemon pepper, teriyaki or Jamaican jerk works well.*

CRAB WEDGES

Preparation time: 10 minutes   *Chef: Laurie Rainthorpe*
Cooking time: 15 minutes   *Yacht: Silent Partner II*
Serves: 6

1/4 lb	**Butter**
1/2 tsp	**Garlic powder**
1/2 tsp	**Onion powder**
6 oz/168 g	**Cheese whiz**
1 Tblsp	**Mayonnaise**
	Worcestershire sauce, tabasco sauce and ketchup to taste
6 oz/180 g	**Can crab meat**
6	**English muffins**

Preheat oven to 350°F/180°C. Mix together first five ingredients; add enough worcestershire sauce, tabasco and ketchup to 'mask' the cheese whiz flavour. Add crab meat, spread on English muffins. Cut muffins in quarters and bake for 15 minutes. *Serve hot.*

GARLIC PARSLEY GROUPER

Preparation time: 10 minutes *Chef: Laurie Rainthorpe*
Cooking time: 20 minutes *Yacht: Silent Partner II*
Serves: 6

2-1/2 lbs/1.1 kg	**Grouper, fillet**
1/2 tsp	**Salt**
1/3 cup	**Butter**
1/4 cup	**Vegetable oil**
3/4 cup	**Freshly chopped parsley**
2 Tblsp	**Freshly chopped Rosemary**
4 cloves	**Garlic, minced**

Heat oven to 350°F/180°C. Slice grouper fillet into 4 equal pieces and place in oven proof pan. Sprinkle a little salt evenly over fish. Mix all other ingredients together and spread over fish. Bake uncovered for 20 minutes or until fish flakes easily.

Serve with **Wild Nutted Rice** *and* **Piperade.**

WILD NUTTED RICE

Preparation time: 10 minutes　　　　　*Chef: Laurie Rainthorpe*
Cooking time: 45 minutes　　　　　　*Yacht: Silent Partner II*
Serves: 6

1-1/2 cups	**Uncooked wild rice**
1 cup	**Orange juice**
1 cup	**Chicken broth**
2 cups	**Water**
1/2 tsp	**Salt**
1/3 cup	**Pecan pieces**
2 Tblsp	**Orange rind, grated**
2 tsp	**Olive oil**

In a saucepan bring first 5 ingredients to a hard boil. Reduce heat, cover tightly and simmer for 45 minutes. Drain, add remaining ingredients. *Serve at room temperature.*

Hint: This rice goes well with chicken or fish.

PIPERADE

Preparation time: 10 minutes　　　　　*Chef: Laurie Rainthorpe*
Cooking time: 10 minutes　　　　　　*Yacht: Silent Partner II*
Serves: 6

1	**Green pepper, sliced long and thin**
1	**Red pepper, sliced long and thin**
1	**Yellow pepper, sliced long and thin**
1	**Medium onion, sliced thin**
2 Tblsp	**Olive oil**
1 lb/450 g	**Cherry tomatoes**
	Worcestershire sauce
	Tabasco sauce

Sauté peppers and onions in oil until slightly soft. Add the cherry tomatoes and warm through. Season with worcestershire sauce and tabasco, to taste.

A very colorful presentation. Goes well with fish and chicken dishes.

MIXED FRUIT CRISP

Preparation time: 15 minutes   *Chef: Laurie Rainthorpe*
Cooking time: 40 minutes   *Yacht: Silent Partner II*
Serves: 6

1 large pkg	**Frozen fruit mixture, no juice – strawberries, blueberries etc.**
3/4 cup	**Sugar**
1 Tblsp	**Minute tapioca**

Topping:

1/2 cup	**Flour**
1/2 cup	**Rolled oats**
1/2 cup	**Butter**
1 cup	**Brown sugar**

Preheat oven to 375°F/190°C. Thaw fruits in an oven proof dish; drain any juice. Top the fruits with sugar and tapioca. Mix **Topping** ingredients together until crumbly and spread over fruits. Bake for about 40 minutes, until topping is golden. *Refreshingly rich!*

SOJOURN SHOPPING LIST

VEGETABLES:
Avocados 2
Carrots 1
Celery stalk 1
Cucumber 1
Garlic cloves 4
Leeks 2
Mesclun bouquets 6
Scallions, chopped .... garnish
Yellow onions 2
Tomatoes 2
Tomatoes, vine ripened ... 2

FRUITS:
Bananas 2
Lemons 3
Anjou pears 6

FRESH HERBS:
Basil sprigs .... garnish
Coriander leaves .... garnish
Ginger .... 1 inch pc
Mint sprigs .... garnish

DRIED SPICES:
Bay leaves 2
Cinnamon sticks 3
Cloves, whole 3
Curry .... 1 Tblsp
Nutmeg .... 3/4 tsp

CONDIMENTS:
Cornstarch .... 3 Tblsp
Basil oil .... 1/2 cup
Olive oil .... 2 Tblsp
Vinaigrette .... 1/4 cup

DRY GOODS:
Flour .... 1-1/2 Tblsp
Sugar .... 1 cup

CANS AND JARS:
Unsweetened coconut milk
.... 1 cup
Beef broth .... 4 cups
Chicken broth .... 1 cup
Mango chutney .... 2 Tblsp
Red current jelly .... 1/4 cup
Tomato juice cocktail ...... 1 cup
Hot sauce .... to taste

DAIRY/MILK/CHEESE/BUTTER
Butter .... 1-1/4 lbs
Eggs 10
Whipping cream .... garnish
Milk, whole .... 1 cup
Yogurt .... 1/2 cup
Cheddar, shredded .... 1-1/2 cups
Emmenthaler, grated ...... 1-1/2 cups
Mascarpone .... 1 cup

MEAT/POULTRY/FISH/SEAFOOD:
Bacon .... 1/2 lb
Chicken breast .... 2 lbs
Filet mignon .... 1-1/2 lbs
Shrimp, large .... 1 lb
Smoked fish .... 2-1/2 lb

FROZEN:
Phyllo pastry sheets 12
Puff pastry sheets 6

S/Y SOJOURN

Chef Gerda Dehrmann
Captain Jerome Blair

MENU
Serves 6

Breakfast

*Breakfast Underway
Crisp Bacon Slices
Coffee and Tea

Lunch

*Macedonian Phyllo Pie
Tossed Greek Salad
Fougasse Bread

Dinner

*Tian of Smoked Fish with *Cocktail Sauce
*Chicken and Shrimp Braised in
Coconut Curry

*Poached Pears with Spiced Mascarpone

Captain Jerry Blair and Chef Gerda Dehrmann are the crew on board the 50-foot Morgan SOJOURN, a beamy sailing yacht which carries two to six passengers — and often families. Jerry is a PADI dive master and teaches U.S. sailing certification school. No wonder, he's been sailing since he was two years old. Gerda has a wide ethnic background to draw on for recipes but she learned her major culinary skills training with international hotels and restaurants, specializing in taste, eye appeal and wines.

*Indicates recipe provided

BREAKFAST UNDERWAY

Preparation time: 30 minutes   *Chef: Gerda Dehrmann*
Cooking time: 30 - 35 minutes   *Yacht: Sojourn*
Serves: 6

1-1/2 cups	**Shredded cheddar cheese**
6 sheets	**Puff pastry (6 inch/15 cm) square**
6	**Eggs**
1 cup	**Cooked bacon bits**
	Salt and pepper

Preheat oven to 400°F/200°C. Lightly grease baking sheet. Dust working surface with flour and place shredded cheese in the center of each thawed pastry square, making a well in the center of the cheese. Carefully crack an egg in the center of each and sprinkle with bacon bits; season with salt and pepper. Bring one corner of the square to meet the opposite corner. Brush a little water on and seal. Bake 30 to 35 minutes or until golden.

Note: Easy for guests to eat, especially if it is an early morning start and breakfast is 'underway'. Always a great hit.

MACEDONIAN PHYLLO PIE

Preparation time: 20 minutes   *Chef: Gerda Dehrmann*
Cooking time: 1 hour   *Yacht: Sojourn*
Serves: 6

1-1/2 lbs/680 g	Fillet of beef tenderloin, diced
5	Onions, chopped
2	Leeks, white parts diced
4 cups	Beef stock or water
3 Tblsp	Cornstarch
1 cup	Milk
4	Eggs
1-1/2 cups	Grated emmenthaler, parmesan or other hard cheese
	Salt and pepper
1/2 tsp	Grated nutmeg
4 cups	Melted butter
12 sheets	Phyllo pastry

Preheat oven to 350°F/180°C. Bring meat, onion, leeks and stock to boil; reduce heat and allow to simmer until cooked. Mix cornstarch with milk and add to saucepan, stirring constantly until gravy thickens. Remove from heat and allow to cool slightly. Gradually beat in eggs, cheese, salt, pepper and nutmeg. Butter a large baking dish and layer half the sheets of phyllo; butter each one. The pastry should come up the sides of the dish. Put the filling on top and fold the side flaps in. Cover with the remaining phyllo sheets, buttering each one. Score the pie with a sharp knife and brush over any remaining butter. Bake for about 1 hour or until golden. Serve warm with tossed salad and fresh bread.

TIAN OF SMOKED FISH

Preparation time: 40 minutes
Serves: 6

Chef: Gerda Dehrmann
Yacht: Sojourn

2 cloves	**Garlic, roasted**
1 cup	**Tomato cocktail juice**
1/2	**Lemon, juiced**
2	**Vine-ripened tomatoes, thinly sliced**
18	**Thin slices cucumber**
2	**Avocado, cut in 4, lengthwise**
2-1/2 lbs/1.1 kg	**Sliced smoked fish, bream, salmon, trout, mackerel, etc**
6	**Small bouquets mesclun leaves**
	Sprigs fresh basil
1/4 cup	**Vinaigrette**
	Salt and pepper
1/2 cup	**Basil oil**

Cocktail Sauce: Mix garlic, tomato cocktail juice and lemon juice in a blender. Season and chill until ready to serve.

To assemble tian: In a 2-1/2 inch (6 cm) diameter cookie cutter, place tomato, cucumber, avocado and fish slices in neat layers to form a stack approximately 2-1/2 inches (6 cm) high. Place tian (with cutter still around it) onto an individual serving plate. Carefully remove cutter. Repeat with remaining ingredients. You will now have 6 individual tians. Garnish the top of each with mesclun bouquet and fresh basil; drizzle with vinaigrette. Pour cocktail sauce over the back of a spoon around the tian then drizzle with basil oil.

CHICKEN AND SHRIMP BRAISED IN COCONUT CURRY

Preparation time: 40 minutes
Cooking time: 1 hour 30 minutes
Serves: 6

Chef: Gerda Dehrmann
Yacht: Sojourn

2 Tblsp	Olive oil
2	Cinnamon sticks
2 lbs/900 g	Boneless chicken breasts, sliced
2	Onions, chopped
2 cloves	Garlic, crushed
2	Bay leaves
1 inch/2.5 cm	Piece of ginger, grated
1 Tblsp	Curry powder
1/2 tsp	Cumin
1/2 cup	Chopped carrots
1/2 cup	Chopped celery
1 cup	Chicken stock
1 cup	Unsweetened coconut milk
1-1/2 Tblsp each	Flour and butter, make into paste
2	Tomatoes, chopped
2 Tblsp	Chutney
1 Tblsp	Lemon juice
	Salt and ground pepper
	Hot sauce
1 lb/450 g	Large shrimp, shelled and deveined
1/2 cup	Buttermilk or yogurt
Garnish:	Coriander (cilantro) leaves and chopped scallions

Heat oven to 350°F/180°C. Heat oil in saucepan; add cinnamon sticks and brown chicken pieces. Transfer both to a baking dish. Add onion, garlic, bay leaves, ginger, curry powder, cumin, carrots, and celery. Stir in stock and coconut milk. Bring to a boil and simmer 10 minutes. Remove from heat and whisk in flour and butter paste; stir until smooth. Add tomatoes, chutney, lemon juice, salt, pepper and hot sauce to taste. Bring to a boil and pour over chicken. Bake covered for 45 minutes. Stir in shrimp and bake covered another 15 minutes. Remove cinnamon sticks and bay leaves. Stir in buttermilk or yogurt. Garnish. *Serve over rice.*

Note: *Makes a fun Indian evening with a table full of accompanying condiments - rice, cucumber raita, fresh salsa, kuchela, mango chutney, coconut dahl, poppadums or Nan bread and extra hot sauce.*

POACHED PEARS WITH SPICED MASCARPONE

Preparation time: 20 minutes　　　　　　　　*Chef: Gerda Dehrmann*
Cooking time: 15-20 minutes　　　　　　　　　　*Yacht: Sojourn*
Chilling time: 2 hours
Serves: 6

1 cup	Sugar
1/4 cup	Red currant jelly
3	Whole cloves
1	Cinnamon stick
1/4 tsp	Grated nutmeg
5 cups	Water
2 Tblsp	Lemon juice
6	Fresh ripe Anjou pears
1 cup	Mascapone flavoured to taste with cinnamon, cloves and nutmeg
Garnish:	Whipped cream and sprigs mint

Place first seven ingredients in a large saucepan; bring to a boil. Peel and core pears leaving stems intact. Add pears to liquid, reduce heat and simmer until fork-tender. Chill pears in cooking liquid. Just before serving, pipe mascarpone mixture into cored pears. Arrange pears on individual serving plates in a pool of chilled poaching liquid and garnish.

NOTES:

SPITFIRE SHOPPING LIST

VEGETABLES:
Garlic .... 2 bulbs
Vidalia onion 1
Potato, large 1
Tomato, large 1

FRUITS:
Mixed fruits .... 3 cups
Lemon 1

FRESH HERBS:
Basil .... 1 bunch
Chives, chopped .... 1/2 cup
Ginger, large 1
Parsley .... 1 bunch
Thyme, chopped .... 1/4 cup

DRIED SPICES:
Cinnamon .... 1/2 tsp

CONDIMENTS:
Macadamia, chopped ...... 1/4 cup
Pecan, crushed .... 1/2 cup
Honey .... 7 Tblsp
Maple syrup .... 1 bottle
Olive oil .... 2 Tblsp
Sesame oil .... 1/2 tsp
Szechuan sauce .... 5 oz
Teriyaki .... 5 oz

CANS AND JARS:
Crab meat backfin .... 14 oz
Pineapple slices 4

DAIRY/MILK/CHEESE/BUTTER
Butter .... 1/4 lb
Eggs 13
Cheddar, shredded .... 1/2 cup
Cream cheese .... 8 oz
Goat/chèvre .... 5 oz
Ricotta .... 2/3 cup

MEAT/POULTRY/FISH/SEAFOOD:
Chicken breasts 6
Proscuitto .... 1/3 lb

LIQUOR/WINE/SPIRITS:
Grand Marnier .... 1/2 cup
White wine .... 1-1/2 cups

MISCELLANEOUS:
Pound cake slices 4
Egg roll wrappers 24
Baguette 1
Monkey bread slices 4

S/Y SPITFIRE

Chef Barbara Emerson
Captain Greg Freitas

MENU
Serves 4

Breakfast

Orange Juice
*Upside Down Pecan-Grand Marnier French Toast
Warmed Maple Syrup

Lunch

*Broiled Crab Omelette
Tossed Green Salad
*Boursin Spread with Warm Sliced Baguette
Chilled Bottle of Fumé Blanc

Hors d'oeuvre

*Goat Cheese Crab Ravioli with Basil

Dinner

*Chicken Wat Gai
Grilled Pineapple Slices
Boiled Long Grain White Rice
Medley of Stir Fry Vegetables

Chilled Spicy Gerwurstrameiner

*Tropical Fruits with Kiwi Sauce

Captain Greg Freitas on SPITFIRE, a 51-foot Skye sailing yacht, is a Cape Codder and former engineer in oceanography (designing deep sea sensors). Captain/Chef Barbara Emerson was an avid equestrian before discovering sailing. Though from highly different interests, they have worked together as a team for the last 10 yeas, chartering in Caribbean and New England waters. One of Barbara's pleasures — entertaining and exhibiting her culinary skills. One of Greg's — teaching sailing.

*Indicates recipe provided

UPSIDE DOWN PECAN GRAND MARNIER FRENCH TOAST

Preparation time: 15 minutes   *Chef: Barbara Emerson*
Cooking time: 20 minutes   *Yacht: Spitfire*
 Serves: 4

4 Tblsp	**Butter**
4 Tblsp	**Honey**
1/2 cup	**Crushed pecans, or walnuts**
4	**Eggs**
1/2 cup	**Grand Marnier***
1/4 tsp	**Salt**
1/2 tsp	**Cinnamon**
4 slices	**Bread 1/4 inch (5 mm) thick, monkey bread or your favorite**
	Maple syrup

Preheat oven to 350°F/180°C. Melt butter and honey in glass casserole dish, large enough to fit 4 large slices of bread. Sprinkle nuts evenly over melted butter and honey. In a separate bowl, mix eggs, Grand Marnier, salt and cinnamon. Soak bread slices 30 seconds on each side. Place in casserole. Bake 12-14 minutes. Flip onto warmed plates and serve with maple syrup.

*Orange juice may be substituted for the Grand Marnier.

BROILED CRAB OMELETTE

Preparation time: 20 minutes   *Chef: Barbara Emerson*
Cooking time: 10 minutes   *Yacht: Spitfire*
Serves: 4

2 Tblsp	**Extra virgin olive oil**
1	**Medium size vidalia onion**
1	**Sliced large tomato**
1	**Large cooked potato, sliced**
6	**Eggs**
1/2 cup	**Chopped chives**
1/2 cup	**Shredded cheese, your favorite**
8 oz/225 g	**Fresh backfin crab, or canned**
1/4 tsp	**Salt**
1/2 tsp	**Ground black pepper**
1 tsp	**Fresh chopped parsley**
1 tsp	**Fresh chopped basil**
1 tsp	**Fresh chopped thyme**

Heat 1 Tblsp olive oil in a 10 inch/25 cm nonstick frying pan. Peel, chop and sauté onion, until just softened. Add tomato slices, then potato slices. Beat eggs and chives together and add to pan. Run spatula around edge of pan, tilting to absorb uncooked portion of egg. After 2-3 minutes, drizzle remaining olive oil around edge of skillet. Add cheese, crab, salt, pepper and herbs. Cook 1 more minute. Remove from heat and put under broiler until brown and puffy — yummy! *Serve immediately.*

Note: Great lunch served with a tossed green salad, warm crunchy bread and a nice bottle of chilled wine—Fumé Blanc.

BOURSIN SPREAD WITH WARM
SLICED BAGUETTE

Preparation time: 15 minutes   *Chef: Barbara Emerson*
Chilling time: 2 hours   *Yacht: Spitfire*
Serves: 4

8 oz/225 g	Pkg cream cheese, softened
4 Tblsp	Butter, softened
2 cloves	Garlic, crushed
1/4 cup	Fresh basil
1/4 cup	Thyme
1/4 cup	Parsley
	Salt and pepper, to taste
1	Baguette

Put all ingredients except baguette in a blender and process until smooth. When ready to serve, warm baguette and slice. *Serve with spread.*

Note: Spread is best prepared a couple of hours ahead. *May be prepared a day or two ahead.*

GOAT CHEESE CRAB RAVIOLI
WITH BASIL

Preparation time: 30 minutes   *Chef: Barbara Emerson*
Cooking time: 3 minutes   *Yacht: Spitfire*
Serves: 4

2 cloves	**Garlic, finely chopped**
5 oz/140 g	**Soft goat cheese**
2/3 cup	**Ricotta cheese**
1/2 cup	**Chopped fresh basil**
2	**Large egg yolks**
6 oz/225 g	**Can crabmeat**
24	**Egg roll wrappers**
1	**Egg beaten**
	Extra virgin olive oil
	Chopped basil

In a processor blend garlic, goat cheese, ricotta cheese and basil. With a spoon blend in egg yolks and crabmeat. Cut 4 inch (10 cm) circles out of egg roll wrappers. Put 1 scant Tblsp of blended mixture in center of each circle and brush edges with beaten egg. Fold in half and seal.

Boil water and add raviolis. Cook until tender about 2-3 minutes. Remove with slotted spoon. Serve in shallow bowls. Drizzle with oil and sprinkle with basil.

Hint: The raviolis can be made ahead and then cooked.

CHICKEN WAT GAI

Preparation time: 15 minutes
Marinating time: overnight
Cooking time: 45 minutes
Serves: 4

Chef: Barbara Emerson
Yacht: Spifire

5 oz/148 ml	**Bottle teriyaki sauce**
12 cloves	**Garlic**
1 large	**Ginger root, peeled and grated**
1-1/2 cups	**White wine**
1 Tblsp	**Honey**
1/2 tsp	**Sesame oil**
1/2 cup	**Szechuan sauce**
2 lbs/950 g	**Chicken thighs and wings**
Garnish:	
4	**Pineapple slices, grilled**
4 sprigs	**Fresh parsley**

In a large glass dish mix together first seven ingredients . Add chicken and marinate overnight.

Preheat grill. Remove garlic cloves and wrap them in tin foil and bake them in oven while the chicken is grilling. Cooking time for chicken varies between white and dark meat. Grill about 30 minutes, turning often, or until cooked to your taste.

Should you decide to bake this dish, preheat oven to 400°F/200°C. Cover, leaving garlic in with chicken. Cook 30 minutes then drain off marinade and remove cover. Cook another 15 minutes to brown chicken.

Garnish with grilled pineapple slices and sprigs of parsley.

Serve over boiled long grain white rice with a medley of stir fry vegetables. A nice bottle of spicy Gerwurstrameiner goes well.

Hint: *Also delicious with halved chicken breasts.*

TROPICAL FRUIT
WITH KIWI SAUCE

Preparation time: 15 minutes　　　　*Chef: Barbara Emerson*
Serves: 4　　　　　　　　　　　　　　　　　*Yacht: Spitfire*

4 slices	**Pound cake**
3 cups	**Chopped tropical fruits of your choice**
1/4 cup	**Chopped macadamia nuts, or almonds**

KIWI SAUCE:

2	**Kiwi fruits, peeled**
2 Tblsp	**Honey**
1 tsp	**Lemon juice**

In a processor blend sauce ingredients. Put a slice of cake on individual plates. Spoon fruits on top and pour sauce over all. Sprinkle with macadamia nuts or almonds.

TAZA MAS SHOPPING LIST

VEGETABLES:
Garlic .... 1 bulb
Romaine leaves 6
Red onion 1
White onion 1
Idaho potatoes, large 6
Potatoes .... 1-1/2 lbs
Tomatoes, large 3

FRUITS:
Lemons 2

FRESH HERBS:
Ginger .... 8 oz
Mint leaves 4
Parsley, chopped .... 3/4 cup
Sage leaves 10
Rosemary sprig................ 1

CONDIMENTS:
Baking powder .... 3 tsp
Dark chocolate................. 7 oz
Extra virgin olive oil .... 1-1/4 cups
Olive oil............................ 1/2 cup
Vinegar, red wine .... 1/8 cup

CANS AND JARS:
Strawberry jam .... 6 Tblsp
Vegetable broth .... 5 cups
Kalamata olives, pitted 6

DRY GOODS:
Flour .... 3 cups
Sugar................................ 1-1/8 tsp
Sugar, raw........................ 4 Tblsp

DAIRY/MILK/CHEESE/BUTTER
Butter............................... 1-1/4 lbs
Eggs 6
Whipping cream .... 6 Tblsp
Milk, whole .... 5 cups
Milk, skim .... 1-1/2 cups
Feta .... 1/4 lb

MEAT/POULTRY/FISH/SEAFOOD:
Pork Tenderloin .... 5 lbs

MISCELLANEOUS:
Baguette........................... 1

FROZEN:
Peas.................................. 2 cups

S/Y TAZA MAS

Chef Liam Flynn
Captain David Schafer

AFTERNOON TEA AND
FIVE COURSE DINNER MENU
Serves 6

Afternoon Tea

*Scones with Strawberry Jam
and Whipped Cream
*Chinese Ginger Tea

5 Course Dinner Menu

*Warm Bath of Olive Oil,
Feta Cheese and Rosemary Spread on
a Sliced Baguette
*Pea and Mint Purée Soup
*Tomato and Red Onion Salad
*Loin of Pork Braised in Milk
*Sautéed Potatoes

*Chocolate Mousse

The 93-foot ketch-rigged motor sailer, TAZA MAS, elegant and stylish, has a crew of 4 to care for 8 guests. Built in Greece in 1993, a remodeling was completed in early 2,000. Captain David Schafer is in charge of this spacious and fully air conditioned ship. Chef Liam Flynn, a New Zealander, runs the galley with considerable flair. He is known for his creative recipes, many of which have won awards. He is also known for his sense of humor and love of telling a story or two to amuse not only guests but crew.

*Indicates recipe provided

SCONES WITH STRAWBERRY JAM AND WHIPPED CREAM

Preparation time: 20 minutes
Cooking time: 20 minutes
Makes: 9 scones

Chef: Liam Flynn
Yacht: Taza Mas

3 cups	**Flour**
3 tsp	**Baking powder**
1 Tblsp	**Butter**
1 tsp	**Sugar**
1-1/2 cups	**Skim milk**
	Butter
	Strawberry jam (preserves)
	Whipped cream

Preheat oven to 400°F/200°C. Butter a baking tray. Sift flour and baking powder into a bowl, add butter and sugar and cut them into the mixture with a knife. Add enough milk to make a wet dough and mix roughly*. Place the dough on baking tray and shape into a square approximately 9 x 9 inches (23 x 23 cm) and 1-1/2 inches (3.5 cm) thick. Cut into 9 equal squares and separate. Bake for 20 minutes. Remove and cool 5 minutes, then gently slice each of the scones in half. Spread with butter, strawberry jam and a dollop of whipped cream.

It is important that the dough is mixed briefly and roughly.

CHINESE GINGER TEA

Preparation time: 10 minutes　　　　　　　*Chef: Liam Flynn*
Cooking time: 35 minutes　　　　　　　　*Yacht: Taza Mas*
Serves: 6

8 oz/225 g　　　　**Fresh ginger root**
7 cups　　　　　　**Cold water**
4 Tblsp　　　　　　**Raw sugar**

Thoroughly clean the ginger root. Slice it finely, diagonally across the grain into slivers to reveal plenty of internal surface. Place in saucepan with water and bring to a boil. Reduce heat and simmer uncovered for 35 minutes or until tea becomes a golden colour. Add sugar to taste and serve hot.

Chef Liam Flynn's philosophy on food....

Cook and live by the maxim "K.I.S.S. - Keep it Simple Stupid": Cook with the ingredients you can find at the local market. It's all about being versatile and adaptable, much like a good character actor. A good cook or chef will find as much about the local culture and it's origins as he will about the local cuisine; after all, cuisines are built on cultures and vice-versa.

Five Course Dinner Menu for six

The meal is extravagant and may look complicated, but by preparing the foods in the correct order, it will be a straight forward, stress-free process and a delight for your guests. Remember to enjoy your time in the galley or kitchen and keep cooking simple.

Method and Recipes:
First prepare the **Chocolate Mousse** as this needs time to chill and set in the refrigerator; preparing this dessert one day in advance is prudent; it can be prepared, chilled and served in 4 hours.

QUICK CHOCOLATE MOUSSE

Preparation time: 15 minutes　　　　　　　　　*Chef: Liam Flynn*
Chilling time: 4 - 24 hours　　　　　　　　　　*Yacht: Taza Mas*
Serves: 6

7 oz/200 g	**Dark chocolate**
1/4 cup	**Butter**
6	**Fresh eggs, separated**
1/8 tsp	**Sugar**

Place chocolate and butter in a bain-marie and melt on medium heat, then remove from the heat and let cool slightly. Whisk in the egg yolks, one at a time. Using a clean whisk add the sugar to the egg whites and whisk them until they form stiff peaks. Fold the egg whites with a spoon into the egg mixture and spoon the mousse into 6 ramekins. Cover and refrigerate for a minimum of 4 hours up to 24 hours.

*Now prepare and cook the **Loin of Braised Pork in Milk.***

LOIN OF PORK BRAISED IN MILK

Preparation time: 15 minutes
Cooking time: 1-1/2 - 2 hours
Serves: 6

Chef: Liam Flynn
Yacht: Taza Mas

3 lb/1.4 kg	**Boned loin of pork, fat and rind removed**
	Salt and freshly milled black pepper
3 Tblsp	**Olive oil**
4 Tblsp	**Butter**
5 cloves	**Garlic, peeled and halved**
10 leaves	**Fresh sage**
5 cups	**Milk, heated**
2	**Lemons, rind only**

Generously season the pork with salt and pepper. Heat olive oil in a heavy bottomed saucepan, with a lid, just large enough to hold the pork. Brown the meat on all sides, remove pork and pour away any excess fat and oil. Melt the butter in the saucepan. Add enough hot milk to come 3/4 the way up the pork in the pan. Bring to boil, add the lemon rind and reduce the heat to a low simmer. Place the lid on the saucepan, slightly askew, and simmer for about 1-1/2 to 2 hours. Resist the temptation to disturb the meat.

*The **Pea and Mint Soup** can now be made and the **Sautéed Potatoes** be prepared.*

When the pork is cooked, the milk will have curdled into brown nuggets. Carefully remove the meat, slice quickly, spoon over the sauce and serve.

WARM BATH OF OLIVE OIL, FETA CHEESE AND ROSEMARY

Preparation time: 5 minutes   *Chef: Liam Flynn*
Cooking time: 45 seconds (microwave)   *Yacht: Taza Mas*
Serves: 6

1 cup	**Virgin olive oil**
1/4 lb/115 g	**Feta cheese, broken into large chunks**
1 sprig	**Rosemary, chopped in half**
6	**Pitted black kalamata olives, optional**
1	**Warm baguette, sliced**

Put all ingredients into a microwave safe bowl and heat for 45 seconds on high power. If you do not have a microwave gently heat the oil, olives and rosemary in a small saucepan, then add the feta cheese and serve in an appropriate bowl or individual ramekins. *Serve with warmed baguette.*

*Now you may serve the **Pea and Mint Soup**.*

PEA AND MINT SOUP

Preparation time: 20 minutes   *Chef: Liam Flynn*
Cooking time: 30 minutes   *Yacht: Taza Mas*
Serves: 6

4 Tblsp	**Butter**
1 Tblsp	**Olive oil**
1	**Large white onion, finely diced**
5 cups	**Vegetable stock**
1-1/2 lbs/680 g	**Potatoes, peeled and diced**
2 cups	**Frozen peas**
4	**Fresh mint leaves**

Heat butter and olive oil in a large saucepan, add onion. Cover pan with a lid to 'sweat' the onion until transparent, about 6 minutes. Add vegetable stock and potatoes, bring to a boil and then simmer until the potatoes are properly cooked, about 12 minutes. Add peas and simmer 3 minutes. Remove saucepan from heat and let sit 5 minutes. Add mint leaves and purée in a blender to a smooth consistency. To serve: reheat and ladle portions into warmed soup tureens.

Note: *This soup may be served warm or hot.*

SAUTEED POTATOES

Preparation time: 15 minutes   *Chef: Liam Flynn*
Cooking time: 1-1/2 - 2 hours   *Yacht: Taza Mas*
Serves: 6

6	Large Idaho potatoes, scrubbed and unpeeled
4 Tblsp	Olive oil
4 Tblsp	Butter
3/4 cup	Freshly chopped parsley
	Salt and white pepper

Pierce the potatoes with a fork and place in the microwave on medium-high power for 20 to 25 minutes. Slice potatoes and set aside with oil, butter, parsley, salt and pepper. Sauté the potatoes after the **Tomato and Red Onion Salad** has been served. Simply heat a skillet on high, add the oil, potatoes, butter and toss to brown them evenly. Finally add the parsley, salt and pepper.

TOMATO AND RED ONION SALAD

Preparation time: 20 minutes   *Chef: Liam Flynn*
Serves: 6   *Yacht: Taza Mas*

6	Medium size lettuce leaves
3	Large ripe tomatoes
1/2	Medium red onion, finely chopped
2 Tblsp	Red wine vinegar
3 Tblsp	Virgin olive oil
	Salt and freshly milled black pepper

Wash and dry lettuce. Break into bite size pieces or slice chiffonade. Core and slice tomatoes into 1/4-inch slices. Lay out 6 small plates. Place even amounts of lettuce on the centre of each plate. Layer the sliced tomatoes over the lettuce fashioned in a fan and sprinkle with salt and pepper. Drizzle the vinegar and the oil over the salad. *Serve immediately.*

*The **potatoes** may now be sautéed.*

THREE MOONS SHOPPING LIST

VEGETABLES:
Broccoli .... 1 cup
Garlic .... 2 bulbs
Green onions 3
Red onions 2
Yellow onions 3
Green bell peppers 1-1/2
Red bell peppers 1-1/2
Yellow bell pepper 1
Potatoes, large 2
Red potatoes, medium 8
Yellow squash 1
Cherry tomatoes .... 1 cup
Zucchini 1

FRUITS:
Lemons 4

FRESH HERBS:
Chives, chopped .... garnish
Dill sprigs .... garnish

DRIED SPICES:
All spice .... 1/4 tsp
Bay leaves 8
Cayenne .... 1/4 tsp
Celery seed .... 1-1/2 tsp
Cinnamon .... 1/4 tsp
Garlic powder .... 1 tsp
Mustard seeds .... 2-1/2 tsp
Mrs Dash .... 2 Tblsp

CONDIMENTS:
Tabasco .... dash
Coconut, toasted, shredded
.... 1/2 cup
Pecans, chopped .... 2 cups
Currants .... 1/2 cup
Horseradish .... 1 tsp
Worchestershire .... 2 tsp
Capers .... 2-1/2 Tblsp
Oil .... 1 Tblsp

Olive oil .... 1-1/8 cups
Vegetable oil .... 3/4 cup
Vinegar .... 3/4 cup
Vinegar, cider .... 1/2 cup
Italian dressing .... 1-1/4 cups

DRY GOODS:
Brownie mix .... 22.5 oz
Sugar, light brown .... 1/4 cup
Sugar .... 1/2 cup

CANS AND JARS:
Teriyaki sauce .... 10 oz
Caramel sauce .... 1/2 cup
Cherry pie filling .... 21 oz can
Dried beef .... 2.25 oz
Peanut butter, crunchy ..... 1/2 cup
Artichoke hearts .... 14 oz can
Black olives, pitted .... 6 oz can
Tomatoes, diced .... 32 oz can

DAIRY/MILK/CHEESE/BUTTER
Butter .... 6 oz
Eggs 8
Sour cream .... 2 cups
Cheddar, medium, grated 3-1/2 cups
Cream cheese .... 16 oz
Parmesan, grated .... 1/2 cup

MEAT/POULTRY/FISH/SEAFOOD:
Salmon filets .... 3 lbs
Shrimp, large .... 2-1/2 lbs
Bacon .... 1/2 lb
Canadian bacon, diced ..... 1/2 cup

LIQUOR/WINE/SPIRITS:
Amaretto .... 1/2 cup
White wine .... 1/4 cup

FROZEN:
Cool Whip .... 8 oz

MISCELLANEOUS:
Cheese tortellini .... 16 oz

S/Y THREE MOONS

Chef Shelly Tucker
Captain Randy Tucker

MENU
Serves 8

Breakfast

Assorted Juices
*Hearty O'Brien Frittata

Lunch

*Shrimp Athena and
*Cocktail Sauce
*Tortellini Salad
Crusty French Bread

Hors d'oeuvre

*Cheese Ball and Tomato Chutney
Assorted Crackers

Dinner

*Teriyaki Pecan-Crusted Salmon
Sautéed Medley of Veggies
*Twice Baked Pommes de Terre

*Cherry Chocolate Lunacy

On THREE MOONS, a comfortable 72-foot Irwin ketch owned by Captain Randy Tucker and his wife Shelly, there are all the usual busy amenities and something more — a spa! It's called Sea Spa Pampering and massages, facials, aromatherapy pedicures and other indulgences are always available except at mealtime when Shelly produces sensational dishes. Born into a family of culinary artists, she has had many recipes published and won, in 1998 and 1999, 5 culinary contest awards.

*Indicates recipe provided

HEARTY O'BRIEN FRITTATA

Preparation time: 20 minutes
Cooking time: 25 minutes
Serves: 8

Chef: Shelly Tucker
Yacht: Three Moons

1-1/2 cups	**Peeled and diced baking potatoes**
3 Tblsp	**Butter**
1 Tblsp	**Oil**
1	**Small red onion, peeled and diced**
1/2	**Red bell pepper, seeded and diced**
1/2	**Green bell pepper, seeded and diced**
1/2 cup	**Canadian bacon, diced**
8 cloves	**Garlic, minced**
8	**Eggs lightly beaten**
2 cups	**Shredded cheddar cheese**
1 cup	**Sour cream**

Preheat oven to 450°F/230°C. Heat a 10 inch (25 cm) nonstick skillet over medium heat. Grease skillet with cooking spray and sauté potatoes until almost tender. Add butter and oil then onion, bell peppers, bacon, and garlic; sauté 10 minutes or until vegetables are soft. Stir in eggs and spread evenly. Cook over medium-low heat 5 minutes or until almost set. Wrap handle of skillet with foil, place skillet in oven, and bake for 5 minutes or until egg is set. Sprinkle cheese on top and bake until cheese melts. *Remove from oven, cut in wedges and serve with a dollop of sour cream on each.*

Great garnish idea: Take a big fresh strawberry and place it tip side up in an egg slicer. Cut strawberry up to, but no further than, the cap. Fan the cut strawberry and use as a garnish, like on top of each slice of frittata.

My favorite breakfast! And YES, the chef loves ketchup on her frittata.

SHRIMP ATHENA AND TORTELLINI

Preparation time: 20 minutes   *Chef: Shelly Tucker*
Marinating time: 2 hours   *Yacht: Three Moons*
Serves: 8

2-1/2 lbs/1.2 kg	Large shrimp, peeled and steamed
14 oz/390 g	Can artichoke hearts, drained
6 oz/170 g	Pitted black olives 1 Medium sweet onion, peeled and thinly sliced
8	Bay leaves
3/4 cup	Vegetable oil
3/4 cup	Olive oil
3/4 cup	Vinegar
2-1/2 Tblsp	Capers, with juice
2-1/2 tsp	Celery seeds
1-1/2 tsp	Salt
1 tsp	Mustard seeds
1/2 tsp	Mrs. Dash, salt-free seasoning
1 dash	Tabasco sauce
	Cocktail sauce (see recipe)

Combine shrimp, olives, and artichoke hearts in a bowl. In a separate bowl mix all the other ingredients. Pour over shrimp mixture, tossing to coat. Marinate, covered, in refrigerator for 24 hours, stirring occasionally. Before serving, drain and discard the marinade. Arrange on a serving platter with the cocktail sauce.

TORTELLINI SALAD:

16 oz/450 g	Cheese tortellini, cooked
1 cup	Italian dressing
1 cup	Cherry tomatoes, halved
1 cup	Broccoli, steamed
1/2 cup	Grated parmesan cheese

Mix tortellini with Italian dressing, add tomatoes, broccoli and toss. Top with parmesan cheese. *Serve.*

COCKTAIL SAUCE: Mix together 1 cup ketchup, 2 tsp Worcestershire sauce, 1 tsp Mrs. Dash, 1/2 tsp garlic powder, 1 tsp lemon juice and 1 tsp horseradish.

CHEESE BALL AND CHUTNEY**

Preparation time: 15 minutes   *Chef: Shelly Tucker*
Chilling time: 30 minutes   *Yacht: Three Moons*
Cooking time: 60 minutes
Serves: 12

CHEESE BALL:

2 - 8 oz/225 g	Pkgs cream cheese, softened
2.25 oz/65 g	Jar Armour dried beef, rinsed and dried
3	Green onions, chopped
1/2 tsp	Garlic powder
1/4 tsp	Mrs. Dash – salt free seasoning
1/4 tsp	Black pepper
1/2 cup	Finely chopped pecans

Beat cream cheese in a mixing bowl until light. Add dried beef, onions, garlic powder, Mrs. Dash and pepper. Shape into a ball and cover with chopped pecans. Chill until serving time. *Serve with tomato chutney and assorted crackers.*

TOMATO CHUTNEY:

1 - 32 oz/900 g	Can diced tomatoes
1	Onion, peeled and chopped
1	Lemon, zested
1/2 cup	Sugar
1/2 cup	Cider vinegar
1/2 cup	Currants
1 1/2 tsp	Mustard seeds
1/2 tsp	Salt
1/4 tsp	Cayenne
1/4 tsp	Allspice
1/4 tsp	Cinnamon

Mix all ingredients in a saucepan and cook at medium heat for 30 minutes, then at a low heat for another 30 minutes until reduced. Put in jars. Serve with cheese ball and assorted crackers.

Note: Store chutney in jars. Will keep in the refrigerator for up to 3 months.

***3rd place winner in the VICL May 1998 culinary competition.*

TERIYAKI PECAN CRUSTED SALMON

Preparation time:
Cooking time: 10 minutes
Marinatng time: 2 hours
Serves: 8

Chef: Shelly Tucker
Yacht: Three Moons

10 fl oz/300 ml	**Bottle teriyaki sauce**
1/4 cup	**Light brown sugar, packed**
2 Tblsp	**Olive oil**
1/2 cup	**Butter**
1 cup	**Chopped pecans**
2	**Lemons, juiced**
3 lbs/1.4 kg	**Salmon filets**

Mix teriyaki, sugar and oil in a large flat container. Place salmon in and marinate for 2 hours. In a skillet, add butter and sauté pecans until lightly browned; add lemon juice and simmer until slightly colored. Remove from heat and keep warm.

Cut salmon into 8 pieces and pat dry. Heat large skillet over medium heat. Add a little butter and oil. Arrange fish in skillet without crowding pan. For pieces less than 1/2 inch (1 cm) thick, cook until tops look milky white, about 2 to 4 minutes. Turn pieces then immediately begin transferring them to a warm platter. For pieces 1/2 to 3/4 inch (1 cm to 2 cm) thick, cook on both sides and brown until slightly translucent or wet inside when cut in thickest part, about 6 minutes. Repeat with any remaining pieces, adding more butter and oil if needed. *Top with pecan mixture and serve.*

TWICE BAKED POMMES DE TERRE

Preparation time: 15 minutes
Cooking time: 25 minutes
Cooling time: 30 minutes
Chilling time: 2 hours
Serves: 8

Chef: Shelly Tucker
Yacht: Three Moons

6	**Medium red potatoes**
1 Tblsp	**Olive oil**
1 cup	**Finely chopped bacon**
4 Tblsp	**Sour cream**
1/2 cup	**Shredded cheddar cheese**
2 Tblsp	**Finely chopped red onion**
1/2 tsp	**Garlic powder**
1/2 tsp	**Mrs. Dash original salt free seasoning**
	Ground black pepper, to taste
Garnish:	**Chopped fresh chives**

Preheat oven to 400°F/200°C. Scrub potatoes, cut in half crosswise, pat dry and place in a large bowl. Add the olive oil and stir until the potatoes are well coated. Place the potatoes cut side down on a large heavy baking sheet and bake for 25 minutes, or until just tender. Remove from baking sheet and let stand until completely cooled. Sauté bacon, drain on paper towels.

Combine the bacon, sour cream, cheese, and onion in a bowl. Add seasonings to taste. Cut a small slice from the rounded side of each potato to form a base; place potatoes, base side down on a serving platter. Scoop out about a teaspoon of pulp from the center of each potato with a melon baller or a small spoon. Add the potato pulp to the bacon mixture and beat with an electric mixer until smooth. Fill the cavity of each potato. Place stuffed potatoes on a baking sheet, bake at 425°F/220°C for 10 to 15 minutes until lightly brown on top.

Note: The potatoes and bacon mixture may be prepared a day ahead. Chill separately and assemble before serving. Garnish.

Hint: For a variation use 1/2 cup chopped smoked salmon, 2 Tblsp drained capers and 1 Tblsp horseradish, in place of the bacon and cheese. Stuff the potatoes and then return them to the oven to bake until golden brown and bubbly.

CHERRY CHOCOLATE LUNACY**

Preparation time: 30 minutes   *Chef: Shelly Tucker*
Cooking time: 45   *Yacht: Three Moons*
Serves: 8 - 10

22.5 oz/670 g	Pkg brownie mix, baked, cooled, and crumbled
1/2 cup	Amaretto
3.9 oz/110 g	Pkg chocolate pudding mix, prepared
1/2 cup	Caramel sauce, warmed
1/2 cup	Crunchy peanut butter, warmed
21 oz/595 g	Can cherry pie filling
8 oz/225 g	Cool whip

Garnish:
1/2 cup	Chopped pecans
1/2 cup	Shredded toasted coconut

In a trifle bowl place 1/2 crumbled brownie mix. Drizzle 1/2 amaretto over mixture. Layer 1/2 prepared chocolate pudding mix. Combine the caramel sauce with the peanut butter, mix well. Layer over the pudding mix. Layer 1/2 of cherry pie filling and top with 1/2 the cool whip. Repeat layers (except the caramel/peanut butter layer.) Garnish.

**2nd* *place winner in the VICL May 1998 culinary competition.*

TRI WORLD SHOPPING LIST

VEGETABLES:
White onion, small 1
Yellow onions 2
Tomato, large 1
Romaine leaves 6
Mushrooms 12

FRESH HERBS:
Chives, chopped .... garnish
Dill sprigs .... garnish

DRIED SPICES:
Jamaican jerk seasoning .. coating
Basil .... 1 tsp
Curry .... 1 tsp
Garlic salt .... 1/2 tsp

CONDIMENTS:
Baking powder .... 1 tsp
Baking soda .... 2-1/2 tsp
Paul Prudhomme blackened
seasoning .... 4 Tblsp
Cocoa .... 3/4 cup
Almond extract .... 1-1/2 tsp
Vanilla extract .... 2-1/4 tsp
Vegetable oil .... 1/2 cup
Soy sauce .... 2 Tblsp
Walnuts, chopped .... 3/4 cup
Mayonnaise .... 6 Tblsp

DRY GOODS:
Flour .... 3-3/4 cups
Sugar, confectioners' .... 1-1/3 cups
Sugar .... 4 cups
Italian bread crumbs .... 1 cup
Bread crumbs .... 1-2 Tblsp

CANS AND JARS:
Raspberry preserves .... 10 oz
Evaporated milk .... 3 cans
Cream of mushroom .... 1 can
Tomato soup .... 2 cans

DAIRY/MILK/CHEESE/BUTTER
Butter .... 2-1/4 lbs
Eggs 5
Sour cream .... 1 cup
Swiss slices 9

MEAT/POULTRY/FISH/SEAFOOD:
Bacon .... 1-1/2 lbs
Chicken breasts, boneless 6
Catfish filets 6

LIQUOR/WINE/SPIRITS:
Amaretto for frosting
White wine .... 1/4 cup

MISCELLANEOUS:
Hoagie rolls 6

S/Y TRI WORLD

Chef Katie Eldridge
Captain Jim Eldridge

MENU
Serves 6

Breakfast

Fruit juice
*Walnut Raspberry Coffee Cake

Lunch

*Baked Jamaican Jerk Chicken

Hors d'oeuvre

*Stuffed Mushrooms

Dinner

*Crab Bisque
*Blackened Catfish
Rice Pilaf and Carrots

*Deep Dark Chocolate Cake with Amaretto Frosting

"Come dive off our back porch" smiles Captain Jim Eldridge as he and his wife, Chef Katie Eldridge, prepare to take off on TRI WORLD, their 58-foot trimaran. It's all here — sailing, water-skiing, tubing, kayaking, windsurfing, fishing, snorkeling, swimming, beachcombing, even relaxing. But the big pluses are 2 to 3 dives a day with night dives and lobster hunts a specialty. When lobster is triumphantly brought aboard, there's a feast. But there will be a feast anyway. Katie has been a chef for 12 years.

*Indicates recipe provided

WALNUT RASPBERRY COFFEE CAKE

Preparation time: 10 minutes   *Chef: Katie Eldridge*
Cooking time: 60 minutes   *Yacht: Tri World*
Cooling time: 15 minutes
Serves: 6

1 cup	Butter, softened
2 cups	Sugar
3	Eggs
1 cup	Sour cream
1 tsp	Almond extract
2 cups	Flour
1 tsp	Baking soda
1 tsp	Baking powder
1/4 tsp	Salt
3/4 cup	Walnuts, chopped
10 oz/280 g	Jar raspberry preserves

Glaze: (optional)

1/3 cup	Confectioners' sugar
5 tsp	Warm water
1/2 tsp	Almond extract

Preheat oven to 350°F/180°C. In a mixing bowl, cream butter and sugar. Add eggs, sour cream, almond extract, flour, baking soda, baking powder and salt. Mix well. Spread 1/2 the batter in a greased and floured bundt pan. Sprinkle with 1/2 of walnuts. Spread 1/2 of the preserves to within 1/2 inch of the edges. Cover with remaining batter. Spoon remaining raspberry preserves over the batter. Sprinkle with rest of walnuts. Bake for 55 to 60 minutes or until a toothpick inserted near the center comes out clean. Cool 15 minutes, invert onto a serving platter and glaze.

Glaze: *Combine all ingredients and spread over coffee cake.*

BAKED JAMAICAN JERK CHICKEN

Preparation time: 15 minutes   *Chef: Katie Eldridge*
Cooking time: 20 -30 minutes   *Yacht:Tri World*
Serves: 6

6	**Boneless skinless chicken breasts**
	Jamaican jerk seasoning
1 cup	**Italian bread crumbs**
1/2 lb/225 g	**Bacon**
1	**Large tomato, sliced**
2	**Onions, chopped**
9 slices	**Provolone or swiss cheese**
6	**Hoagie rolls**
6	**Lettuce leaves**
	Mayonnaise
	Garlic salt
	Pepper

Heat oven to 350°F/180°C. Pound each chicken breast then sprinkle both sides with garlic salt, pepper and Jamaican jerk seasoning. Sprinkle with Italian bread crumbs. Bake 25 to 30 minutes. You can add a little water to the pan, this will help keep the chicken moist. Do not turn chicken while cooking. Sauté bacon and onions. When the chicken is cooked, remove from oven and place the bacon, onions, tomato and cheese on top. Return to oven until the cheese melts. Place on roll with lettuce and mayonnaise. *Serve with chips, pickles or potato salad.*

STUFFED MUSHROOMS

Preparation time: 10 minutes   *Chef: Katie Eldridge*
Cooking time: 25 minutes   *Yacht: Tri World*
Serves: 6

12	**Mushrooms**
8 Tblsp	**Butter, melted**
1	**Small onion**
1/2 tsp	**Garlic salt**
1/2 tsp	**Black pepper**
1 tsp	**Basil**
2 Tblsp	**Soy sauce**
	Seasoned bread crumbs

Preheat oven to 350°F/180°C. Remove stems from mushrooms. Wash and drain both caps and stems, then dip caps in melted butter and place in baking dish. Finely chop the stems and sauté with onion, garlic salt, pepper, basil and soy sauce. Add enough seasoned bread crumbs to make a good mixture (not too dry). Stuff mushroom caps and bake for 20 minutes.

CRAB BISQUE

Preparation time: 10 minutes   *Chef: Katie Eldridge*
Cooking time: 15 minutes   *Yacht: Tri World*
Serves: 6

12 oz/340 g	**Fresh crabmeat or 2 cans, with juice**
2 - 11 oz/305 g	**Cans tomato soup**
11 oz/300 g	**Can cream of mushroom soup**
3 - 13 oz/380 ml	**Cans of evaporated milk**
1/4 cup	**White wine**
1 tsp	**Curry powder**
	Salt and pepper

In a large saucepan mix all ingredients together and keep stirring on low heat until heated through. *Serve with crumbled crackers on top.*

Note: *This is one soup the guests just love.*

BLACKENED CATFISH

Preparation time: 10 minutes   *Chef: Katie Eldridge*
Chilling time: 30 minutes   *Yacht: Tri World*
Cooking time: 10 minutes
Serves: 6

12 oz/340 g	**Butter**
6	**Fillets of catfish**
	Paul Prudomme's blackened seasoning

Melt butter in a pan with about 2 Tblsp of seasoning. Lay out the fish fillets in an oblong pan and season on both sides. Pour the butter over them and refrigerate until ready to cook. You want the butter to coagulate. Preheat the grill to very hot. Place the fish on the open grill (no aluminum foil on grate). Immediately put the spiced butter on top of the fish (this will cause the grill to flame up which will singe and blacken the fish quickly) After 5 minutes turn fillets and cover with remaining spice butter. Grill for only 5 more minutes. Remove from grill. *Serve with rice pilaf and carrots with honey glaze.*

Hint: *Other fish like grouper are also good blackened.*

DEEP DARK CHOCOLATE CAKE
WITH AMARETTO FROSTING

Preparation time: 10 minutes
Cooking time: 45 minutes
Serves: 6

Chef: Katie Eldridge
Yacht: Tri World

1-3/4 cups	Flour
2 cups	Sugar
3/4 cup	Hershey's cocoa
1-1/2 tsp	Baking soda
1 tsp	Salt
1 cup	Milk
2	Eggs
1/2 cup	Vegetable oil
2 tsp	Vanilla extract
1 cup	Boiling water

Preheat oven to 350°F/180°C. Combine all dry ingredients in a bowl. Add milk, eggs, oil and vanilla, Beat at medium speed until well blended. Stir in boiling water; batter will be thin. Pour batter into a greased and floured bundt pan. Bake for 45 minutes or until the cake springs back up when you press it with your finger.

AMARETTO FROSTING:

1 cup	Confectioners' sugar
2 tsp	Butter, softened
1/4 tsp	Vanilla
	Amaretto

Mix sugar, butter and vanilla. Add enough amaretto to make it easy to spread, then frost the top of the cake.

URSA MINOR SHOPPING LIST

VEGETABLES:
Cabbage, small .... 1 head
Cucumber 1/2
Garlic cloves 3
Green onions 3
Red onions 2
Vidalia onion 1
Green bell peppers 2
Red bell pepper 1
Plantains, very ripe 2
Tomatoes 2
Romaine .... 1 head
Mixed greens .... 4 cups
Portabello mushroom 1

FRUITS:
Bananas 2
Lemons 3
Mango 1
Strawberries 6

FRESH HERBS:
Basil, chopped .... 1 Tblsp
Oregano .... 1 Tblsp

DRIED SPICES:
Cinnamon .... 1/8 tsp
Ponape green peppercorns 1/4 cup

CONDIMENTS:
Chocolate chips .... 6 oz
Horseradish .... 2 tsp
Mustard, brown .... 1 tsp
Maple syrup .... 1 bottle
Olive oil .... 1-1/4 cups
Chili sauce .... 1/3 cup
Worchestershire .... 1/8 tsp
Vinegar, red wine .... 5 Tblsp

DRY GOODS:
Bisquick .... 2 cups
Brownie mix .... 1 box
Sugar .... 3-4 Tblsp

CANS AND JARS:
Anchovy paste .... 1 Tblsp
Raspberry sauce .... 1 jar
Beef broth .... 2 cups
Greek black olives, diced .. 1/4 cup

DAIRY/MILK/CHEESE/BUTTER
Eggs 3
Whipping cream .... 1/2 cup
Milk, whole .... 1 cup
Yogurt .... 1 cup
Feta, crumbled .... 1/4 cup
Parmesan, grated .... 1/4 cup
Rondelé .... 4 oz

MEAT/POULTRY/FISH/SEAFOOD:
Filet mignons 4
Fake crab meat .... 1/2 lb
Shrimp, cooked .... 1 lb

LIQUOR/WINE/SPIRITS:
Madeira wine .... 1 cup

MISCELLANEOUS:
Croutons .... 1 cup

S/Y URSA MINOR

Chef Judy Knape
Captains Bryan Lane and Judy Knape

MENU
Serves 4

Breakfast

*Banana Pancakes with Mangoes and Strawberries
Sausage or Bacon
Maple Syrup

Lunch

*Seafood Salad "Louis"
Beer Bread or Rolls

Hors d'oeuvres

*Greek Salsa
Warm Pita Triangles
*Plantains with Cheese

Dinner

*Ponape Pepper Steak with
*Portabello-Vidalia Bordelaise
Garlic Potatoes
*Caesar Salad

*Double Chocolate Bundt Cake with
Melba Sauce and Whipped Cream

URSA MINOR, a beautiful new 46-foot Saga cruiser, ideal for 2 couples, a family (If children are over 5) and a happy ship for honeymooners, was designed for speed and comfortable passage in the tropics. Her 2 captains, Captain Bryan Lane and Captain Judy Knape plan their days around sailing, guided snorkeling, touring, picturesque hiking and leisurely relaxation. Judy supervises the galley, emphasizing healthy meals with a tropical flair and, on occasion, producing a sinfully delicious dessert.

*Indicates recipe provided

BANANA PANCAKES WITH MANGO AND STRAWBERRIES

Preparation time: 30 minutes   *Chef: Judy Knape*
Cooking time: 10 minutes   *Yacht: Ursa Minor*
Serves: 4

2 cups	**Bisquick**
1 cup	**Milk**
2	**Eggs**
2	**Ripe bananas, mashed**
1 Tblsp	**Sugar**
1/8 tsp	**Cinnamon**
1	**Mango**
	Several strawberries, sliced and sugared
	Maple syrup

Stir together bisquick, milk and eggs. Add mashed bananas, sugar and cinnamon and mix. Pour by 1/4 cupful onto hot griddle and cook until edges are dry. Turn, cook until golden. Serve each guest 2 or 3 pancakes with sausage or bacon. Let guests top pancakes with any or all of mango, strawberries, butter, and maple syrup.

Hint: I usually make this the first morning of charter, after including fresh strawberries on a cheese and pate hors d'oeuvres platter the night before, using any remaining strawberries with this breakfast.

SEAFOOD SALAD "LOUIS"

Preparation time: 20 minutes　　　　　　　*Chef: Judy Knape*
Cooking time: 5 minutes　　　　　　　　*Yacht: Ursa Minor*
Standing time: 2 hours
Serves: 4

Dressing:

1 cup	Non-fat plain yogurt, strained
1/3 cup	Chili sauce
4	Scallions, minced
1/2	Lemon, juiced
2 tsp	Horseradish sauce
2 Tblsp	Sugar
	Salt and pepper, to taste

Salad:

4 cups	Mixed greens
1 cup	Finely sliced red cabbage
1	Red pepper, sliced in rings
1	Green pepper, sliced in rings
1	Small red onion, sliced in rings
1/2 lb/225 g	Imitation crab meat, flaked
1 lb	Cooked shrimp, peeled

Garnish:

1	Tomato, cut in wedges
1	Lemon, cut in wedges

Dressing: Strain yogurt for two hours or more in yogurt strainer or sieve lined with paper towel. This removes excess moisture, and give a mayonnaise consistency with no fat. Add remaining dressing ingredients and mix.

Salad: Mound greens mixed with red cabbage on plate. Top with pepper rings, onion, "crab" and shrimp. Garnish plate with tomato and lemon wedges. Serve with *Dressing* and freshly baked beer bread.

Hint: I also often add black or green olives, cucumber slices, wedges of hard-boiled egg, or other fresh vegetables around the side of the plate for additional color and flavor.

Note: *This is a very colorful, healthy meal.*

GREEK SALSA

Preparation time: 15 minutes   *Chef: Judy Knape*
Serves: 4   *Yacht: Ursa Minor*

1	**Large tomato, diced**
1/2	**Green bell pepper, diced**
1/2	**Small red onion, diced**
1/4 cup	**Black Greek olives, diced**
1/2	**Cucumber, seeded and diced**
1/4 cup	**Feta cheese, finely crumbled**
2 Tblsp	**Lemon juice or wine vinegar**
1 Tblsp	**Olive oil**
	Oregano or basil, to taste
	Salt and pepper, to taste

Mix all ingredients together and *serve with warm pita bread triangles.*

PLANTAINS WITH CHEESE

Preparation time: 5 minutes   *Chef: Judy Knape*
Cooking time: 20-25 minutes   *Yacht: Ursa Minor*
Serves: 4

2	**Very ripe plantains**
4 oz/112 g	**Garlic and herb soft cheese, rondele, alouette or homemade**

Preheat oven to 350°F/180°C. Plantains should have lots of black on skins, but not be totally soft. Peel plantains, halve lengthwise and scoop a trough down the middle. Bake in a greased dish for about 15-20 minutes or until soft, then spread cheese in trough and bake another 5 minutes until slightly melted. *Cut in 2 inch/5 cm slices and serve.*

PONAPE PEPPER STEAK WITH PORTABELLO-VIDALIA BORDELAISE

Preparation time: 10 minutes   *Chef: Judy Knape*
Cooking time: 30 minutes   *Yacht: Ursa Minor*
Serves: 4

4 - 7 oz/730 g	**Fillet mignon, NY strip, or steak of your choice**
1/4 cup	**Ponape, or other good quality peppercorns**

Sauce:

2 cups	**Beef broth**
1 cup	**Madeira wine**
1	**Vidalia or other sweet onion, diced**
1	**Portabello mushroom, cut 1/8 x 1 inch (3 mm x 2.5 cm)**
	Salt and pepper, to taste

Portabello-Vidalia Bordelaise: Reduce beef broth and wine to about 1-1/2 cups and season to taste. Sauté onions and mushrooms in olive oil until soft, add reduced broth/wine mix, and simmer for 5 minutes. Serve over steak.

Heat grill. Finely crush peppercorns (I use my coffee bean grinder) and coat both sides of steaks.Place the meat on the grill and cook on both sides according to taste. Cooking time will depend on the thickness of the meat, the exact temperature of the grill and on individual tastes. *Serve with* **Portabello-Vidalia Bordelaise,** *Caesar Salad, and garlic roasted potato wedges.*

Note: Ponape (also spelled Pohnpei) is an island in Micronesia known for its exotic peppercorns. I discovered them while living there and can now order them on the internet.

CAESAR SALAD

Preparation time: 15 minutes
Chilling time: 30 minutes
Serves: 4

Chef: Judy Knape
Yacht: Ursa Minor

1 head	**Romaine lettuce**
	Grated parmesan cheese
	Croutons (see recipe below)
Dressing:	
1	**Egg white, coddled**
3 cloves	**Garlic, minced**
1 Tblsp	**Anchovy paste**
1/8 tsp	**Worcestershire sauce**
1 tsp	**Brown mustard**
1	**Lemon, squeezed**
5 Tblsp	**Wine vinegar**
8 Tblsp	**Olive oil**
	Salt and pepper

Mix all dressing ingredients together and shake. (To coddle egg white, place boiling water in coffee cup, add unbroken egg for one minute, remove, cool slightly, and crack and separate egg white.) Wash romaine lettuce and tear into bite size pieces. Chill. Just before serving, toss chilled lettuce with freshly grated parmesan, add croutons and dressing to taste.

Hint: When I have time, I make the *Croutons* myself, using sourdough, whole wheat or French bread (cut in small cubes), dried basil, minced garlic and olive oil. Heat the oil in a small frying pan. Add garlic, bread cubes, and dried basil, fry until bread cubes are golden all over. Drain the croutons on paper towels. Or, toss the bread cubes, garlic, oil and basil together, then bake at 375°F/190°C on a preheated cookie sheet until golden and crisp; stir occasionally.

DOUBLE CHOCOLATE BUNDT CAKE

Preparation time: 5 minutes   *Chef: Judy Knape*
Cooking time: 30 minutes   *Yacht: Ursa Minor*
Serves: 4

1 pkg	**Brownie mix**
	Eggs
	Water ⎤ Check package for quantities
	Oil
6 oz/170 g	**Chocolate chips**
Garnish:	**Bottled raspberry sauce**
	Whipped cream

Preheat oven to 350°F/180°C. Grease bundt pan with cooking spray. Prepare brownie mix according to package directions for cake-like brownies, then add about 2/3 cup of chocolate chips. (Reserve remaining chips for garnish.) Bake in bundt pan until top starts to crack. Cool and invert on plate. Decorate individual serving plates with streaks of raspberry sauce, add slice of cake which should be hot and gooey in center, top with whipped cream and sprinkle with chocolate chips.

WAI-O-TIRA SHOPPING LIST

VEGETABLES:
Cabbage, small .... 1 head
Carrots, large 2
Celery, stalks 2
Garlic cloves 6
Yellow onions, large 2
Green bell pepper 1
Red bell pepper 1
Potato, large 1
Tomato 1
Kumara sweet potatoes,
large 2

FRUITS:
Granny Smith 2
Bananas 3

DRIED SPICES:
Curry .... 1 tsp

CONDIMENTS:
Baking powder .... 3 Tblsp
Baking soda .... 3-1/4 tsp
Baking bran .... 1-1/2 cups
Coconut, flaked .... 1 cup
Cocoa .... 3 Tblsp
Dates, chopped .... 1/2 cup
Vanilla extract .... 2 tsp
Mustard .... 3/4 cup
Oil .... 1 Tblsp
Olive oil............................ 2 Tblsp
Vinegar .... 3 Tblsp
Golden syrup .... 1 bottle

DRY GOODS:
Flour .... 15-17 cups
Sugar .... 4 cups

CANS AND JARS:
Corn kernels .... 16 oz can

DAIRY/MILK/CHEESE/BUTTER
Butter .... 3/4 lb
Eggs 4
Milk, whole .... 2-1/3 cups
Parmesan, grated .... 1 cup

MISCELLANEOUS:
Active dry yeast .... 2 Tblsp
Mushroom soup, dry .... 1 pkt

S/Y WAI O TIRA

Chef Glenys Robertson
Captain Laurie Robertson

MENU FROM CRUISING
AROUND THE WORLD
Serves 6

Breakfast

*Sweet Scones with Dates
*Bran Muffins

Lunch

*Savoury Rice Salad
*Basic Bread
*Fudge Cake

Hors d'oeuvres

*Pikelets
*Kumara Dip

Dinner

*Vegetable Pie
Mashed Potatoes

*Wacky Cake

The sailing yacht WAI O TIRA, a 55-foot ketch, lives up to her sailing designation. Those sails have been put to good use as Captain Laurie Robertson and his wife, Glenys, spent the last 10 years cruising the world, stopping off at places like the British Isles, the Canaries, the Mediterranean, Africa, and Australia. Glenys, in charge of the galley, says "All my recipes are used while sailing. For ocean crossings I buy in bulk, but at anchorage we always use the fresh fruit and vegetables of the area".

*Indicates recipe provided

SWEET SCONES WITH DATES

Preparation time: 20 minutes
Cooking time: 10 minutes
Makes: 12 scones

Chef: Glenys Robertson
Yacht: Wai O Tira

2 cups	Flour
4 tsp	Baking powder
1/2 tsp	Salt
2 Tblsp	Butter
2 Tblsp	Sugar
2/3 cup	Milk
1/2 cup	Chopped dates

Preheat oven to 425°F/220°C. Sift flour, baking powder and salt into bowl. Rub in butter and sugar. Add milk, mix to a soft dough. Roll out on floured board to rectangle 1/2 inch (1 cm) thick. Spread chopped dates on 1 half, then fold the other half over and press gently. Cut into squares and place on cold lightly floured oven tray. Bake about 10 minutes.

BRAN MUFFINS

Preparation time: 20 minutes
Cooking time: 12 - 15 minutes
Makes: 16 - 20 muffins

Chef: Glenys Robertson
Yacht: Wai O Tira

1 cup	Flour
1 tsp	Baking powder
1/2 tsp	Salt
1-1/2 cups	Baking bran*
1/4 cup	Sugar
1 Tblsp	Butter
1 tsp	Golden syrup
1 cup	Milk
1 tsp	Baking soda
1	Egg

Preheat oven to 425°F/220°C. Sift flour, baking powder and salt. Mix in bran and sugar. Warm butter and golden syrup together; dissolve soda in milk and add to dry ingredients with egg. Mix with milk mixture, should be moist but still retain shape. Spoon into greased patty pans.

* Have also used breakfast bran successfully.

SAVOURY RICE SALAD

Preparation time: 20 minutes   *Chef: Glenys Robertson*
Cooking time: 30 minutes   *Yacht: Wai O Tira*
Chilling time: 2 hours
Serves: 6

1 cup	Rice
1	Large onion, finely diced
1 cup	Diced celery
1 cup	Diced apple
1/2 cup	Vinaigrette dressing (see below)

Vinaigrette:
1 Tblsp	Vinegar
2 Tblsp	Oil
1 tsp	Mustard

Boil rice for 30 minutes and drain. Add chopped onion, celery and apple. Stir in vinaigrette; mix well. Chill.

FUDGE CAKE

Preparation time: 10 minutes   *Chef: Glenys Robertson*
Cooking time: 10 minutes   *Yacht: Wai O Tira*
Makes: 20 slices

4 oz/115 g	Butter
1/2 cup	Sugar
1 cup	Flour
1 cup	Desiccated coconut (flaked)
1 Tblsp	Cocoa

Preheat oven to 350°F/180°C. In a saucepan melt together butter and sugar, then mix in flour, coconut and cocoa. Press into a greased shallow cake tin and bake about 10 minutes.

BASIC BREAD

Preparation time: 20 minutes   *Chef: Glenys Robertson*
Standing time: 1 hour   *Yacht: Wai O Tira*
Cooking time: 30 minutes
Makes: 2 loaves

5 - 7 cups	**Plain white flour or**
	2 - 3 cups may be wholemeal
1 Tblsp	**Sugar**
1 tsp	**Salt**
2 Tblsp	**Dried yeast**
1 cup	**Cold water or milk**
1 cup	**Boiling water**
1 Tblsp	**Butter or oil**

Put 2 cups white flour, sugar, salt and yeast in a bowl. Add cold water followed immediately by the boiling water, stir to paste and let stand 2 to 3 minutes. Add butter and wholemeal flour if used, then enough plain flour to make a soft but not sticky dough. Knead until dough is soft and elastic (6-8 minutes) adding more flour if dough becomes sticky. Place in a greased bowl and cover with a damp cloth; stand in a warm place for 30 minutes. Knead again briefly and make into desired cooking shapes, i.e. loaves or rolls. Put in greased tins, cover and let stand again in a warm place for 30 minutes, or until dough doubles in size. Loaves bake at 450°F/220°C for 10 minutes then 350°F/180°C for 30 - 40 minutes. Rolls bake at 425°F/210°C for 20 - 30 minutes.

Hint: Half the quantity of bread lasts us a couple of days for breakfast and lunch.

Note: *If you give the dough a thorough kneading (smooth and shiny in appearance) you only have to let it rise once.*

PIKELETS

Preparation time: 10 minutes
Cooking time: 20 minutes
Makes: 12 - 14

Chef: Glenys Robertson
Yacht: Wai O Tira

2 Tblsp	**Sugar**
1/2 cup	**Milk**
1	**Egg**
1 cup	**Flour**
1 tsp	**Baking powder**
Pinch	**Salt**
2 Tblsp	**Butter**

Whisk sugar, milk and egg together. Add flour, baking powder and salt. Heat butter in a heavy based pan until it sizzles. Pour dessert spoon size lots of batter into pan. Cook until bubbles appear or mixture looks set; flip and cook other side. *Serve with butter, jam or preserves and whipped cream.*

KUMARA DIP

Preparation time: 35 minutes
Cooking time: 5 - 10 minutes
Chilling time: 2 hours
Serves: 6

Chef: Glenys Robertson
Yacht: Wai O Tira

2	**Large kumaras or sweet potatoes**
1 tsp	**Curry powder**
Pinch	**Cumin**
2 cloves	**Garlic, finely chopped**
	Salt and pepper to taste

Peel and cube kumaras, place in saucepan and just cover with water. Add cumin and curry powder; boil until tender. Drain and mash well. Add garlic. If a stronger curry flavour is required add more at this stage. If mix is too dry add a small amount of butter. Chill. *Serve with crackers or potato chips.*

VEGETABLE PIE

Preparation time: 30 minutes
Cooking time: 20 minutes
Steaming time: 10 minutes
Serves: 6 - 8

Chef: Glenys Robertson
Yacht: Wai O Tira

1	**Large potato, peeled and sliced**
2	**Large carrots, peeled and sliced**
2 cups	**Shredded cabbage**
4 cloves	**Garlic, finely chopped**
16 oz/450 g	**Can sweet corn**
1	**Large onion, finely chopped**
1	**Red bell pepper, chopped**
1	**Green bell pepper, chopped**
1 pkt	**Mushroom soup**
1 cup	**Grated parmesan cheese**
1	**Tomato, sliced**

Preheat oven to 350°F/180°C. Place potatoes and carrots in steamer and steam until just cooked; add cabbage last 3 minutes of steaming time. Layer potato, carrots, cabbage, garlic, corn, onion and bell peppers. Mix mushroom soup with 1 cup cold water until smooth. Pour onto layered vegetables. Add cheese and tomato. Bake in oven for 20 minutes or in microwave for 5 - 8 minutes at full power.

Variations are endless: Instead of potato, use rice or pasta. This is a basic recipe and an excellent way for using up all that is left in the vegetable bin: celery, mushrooms, sweet potato, pumpkin, squash courgettes, leeks, beans, spinach etc. Be creative. Use your favourite herbs. Add meat, or fish. We are chilli and garlic addicts and always add these to everything.

WACKY CAKE

Preparation time: 15 minutes
Cooking time: 1 hour
Makes: 1 large cake

Chef: Glenys Robertson
Yacht: Wai O Tira

3 cups	Flour
2 cups	Sugar
3 Tblsp	Cocoa
1 tsp	Salt
2 tsp	Baking soda
3/4 cup	Salad oil
2 Tblsp	Vinegar
2 tsp	Vanilla
2 cups	Cold water

Preheat oven to 350°F/180°C. Place flour, sugar, cocoa, salt, and baking soda in a large baking tin, no grease needed. Make 3 holes in mix, into 1st add oil, 2nd vinegar and 3rd vanilla. Pour the water over all and mix until smooth. Bake for 1 hour.

Hint: If using a square baking tin, it may be easier to mix cake in a mixing bowl and then pour into baking tin.

Note: I halve these quantities and microwave at full power (mine is 800 watts) in a medium sized plastic bowl for 9 minutes. If the centre is still soft, cook for another 1 - 2 minutes. Makes a lovely rich chocolate cake. Ice with butter chocolate icing. The full quantity makes a large cake more suitable for hungry teenagers.

WALL STREET SHOPPING LIST

VEGETABLES:
Avocados 2
Carrot, large 1
Garlic cloves 3
Yellow onion, medium 1
Yellow onions, large 2
Alfalfa sprouts .... 1 pkg
Romaine leaves 6

FRUITS:
Bananas 2
Lemon 1
Orange 1

FRESH HERBS:
Cilantro, chopped .... 1/2 cup
Ginger, grated .... 1 tsp

DRIED SPICES:
Bay leaves 6
Cinnamon .... 1/8 tsp
Chili powder .... 1 Tblsp
Curry .... 1 tsp
Fine herbs .... 1/4 tsp
Nutmeg .... 1/8 tsp
Red pepper flakes .... 1 tsp
Turmeric .... 1/4 tsp

CONDIMENTS:
Vanilla extract .... 1 tsp
Maple syrup .... 1 bottle
Raisins .... 1/2 cup
Dark chocolate .... 8 oz
Coconut .... 1/2 cup
Instant coffee .... 1 Tblsp
Oil .... 2-3 Tblsp
Mayonnaise .... to taste

DRY GOODS:
Yellow rice .... 1 box
Sugar .... 1/2 cup

CANS AND JARS:
Salsa .... 1/2 cup
Mint relish .... 1 jar
Evaporated milk .... 1/2 cup
Devilled ham .... 15 oz
Apricot jam .... 4 tsp
Pineapple, crushed .... 1 cup
Mandarin oranges .... 11 oz can
Beef broth .... 1/2 cup

DAIRY/MILK/CHEESE/BUTTER
Eggs 12
Cream .... 1 cup
Milk, whole .... 3/4 cup
Cream cheese .... 8 oz
Monterey jack slices 6

MEAT/POULTRY/FISH/SEAFOOD:
Bacon bits .... 1/3 cup
Chicken breasts, boneless 6
Ground beef .... 1-1/2 lbs

LIQUOR/WINE/SPIRITS:
Grand Marnier .... 5 Tblsp

MISCELLANEOUS:
Baguettes 2
Poppodums .... 1 box
Bread, white slices 7

S/Y WALL STREET

Chef Debbie Campbell
Captain Sean Campbell

MENU
Serves 6

Breakfast

Orange Juice
*Grand Marnier French Toast

Lunch

*Open-Faced Chicken Salad Sandwich

Hors d'oeuvre

*Surprise Spread
Assorted Crackers

Dinner

*Poppadums with Mint Relish
*Bobotie
(A Cape-Dutch South African Meal)
Salsa, Coconut and Banana
Yellow Rice

*Easy Chocolate Mousse

Captain Sean and Debbie Campbell sailed WALL STREET, a 43-foot catamaran, from Cape Town, South Africa to their chosen piece of paradise — the Caribbean — to enter the charter business. It is all they had hoped for, and more. Guests rave about their easy South African style and about the offerings from Chef Debbie's galley which sometimes include one of her unique Cape Dutch African dishes. Dining is always al fresco and with it a million-dollar view from the cockpit at anchorage.

*Indicates recipe provided

GRAND MARNIER FRENCH TOAST

Preparation time: 15 minutes
Cooking time: 10 minutes
Serves: 6

Chef: Debbie Campbell
Yacht: Wall Street

1/2 cup	**Evaporated milk**
1/8 tsp	**Cinnamon**
1/8 tsp	**Nutmeg**
1 tsp	**Vanilla essence**
3 Tblsp	**Grand Marnier**
6	**Eggs**
	Water to dilute, if needed
2 loaves	**French bread**
Garnish:	**Orange slices**
1 tsp	**Grated orange rind**
1/2 cup	**Sugar**
	Maple syrup

Combine all ingredients (except bread) with a whisk. Cut french loaf in slices and soak in mix until wet through. Fry on griddle or sauté in hot skillet over medium heat until golden brown and puffy. Garnish with orange slices; sprinkle grated orange and sugar over top. *Serve with maple syrup.*

OPEN FACED CHICKEN SALAD SANDWICH

Preparation time: 20 minutes　　　　　　*Chef: Debbie Campbell*
Chilling time: 2 hours　　　　　　　　　　*Yacht: Wall Street*
Cooking time: 20 minutes
Serves: 6

6	**Cooked boneless chicken breasts**
	Mayonnaise, to taste
1	**Medium onion, chopped**
1 Tblsp	**Chili powder**
1 tsp	**Crushed red pepper**
1/2 cup	**Chopped cilantro**

Cut chicken into cubes. Mix all ingredients together and refrigerate for 2 hours.

Sandwich ingredients:

11 oz/310 g	**Can mandarin oranges**
6 slices	**Bread, of choice**
	Mayonnaise, to taste
6	**Lettuce leaves**
	Chicken salad (above)
6 slices	**Monterey jack cheese**
2	**Avocados, peeled and sliced**
	Alfalfa sprouts

To make sandwiches: place about 5 mandarins around border of each plate. Layer bread with above ingredients. *Serve immediately.*

SURPRISE SPREAD

Preparation time: 20 minutes　　　　　　*Chef: Debbie Campbell*
Freezing time: 2 hours　　　　　　　　　　*Yacht: Wall Street*
Serves: 6

3 - 5 oz/140 g	**Tins devilled ham**
8 oz/225 g	**Cream cheese, softened**
1 cup	**Crushed pineapple, drained**
1/3 cup	**Bacon bits**

Shape ham into a loaf and freeze. Spread cream cheese over ham; cover with pineapple and bacon bits. *Serve with crackers.*

POPPADUMS WITH MINT RELISH

Preparation time: 5 minutes   Chef: Debbie Campbell
Cooking time: 5 minutes   Yacht: Wall Street
Serves: 6

1	**Box Poppadums**
1/4 cup	**Oil for frying**
1 bottle	**Mint relish**
1 cup	**Mango chutney**

Heat a little oil in a skillet. Fry poppadums for a few seconds on each side until crisp and puffy. Serve with mint relish and chutney. *Serve as a starter before* **Bobotie.**

Tip: For a low-fat version, try microwaving the poppadums. Each one will take about 30 seconds to become crisp and fluffy. Two or three can be cooked at the same time. Place in a single layer on a paper towel and microwave on high.

EASY CHOCOLATE MOUSSE

Preparation time: 20 minutes   Chef: Debbie Campbell
Chilling time: 30 minutes   Yacht: Wall Street
Serves: 4-6

4	**Eggs, separated**
8 oz	**Dark cooking chocolate**
2 Tblsp	**VD Hum Liquor* or Grand Marnier**
1 Tblsp	**Instant coffee granules**
1 cup	**Cream**

Separate eggs. Beat yolks until light and creamy. Melt chocolate in microwave on defrost setting for 3 minutes. (watch it carefully!) Add chocolate, VD Hum and coffee to egg yolks; stir until well combined. Whip cream and gently fold into chocolate mixture with metal spoon. Whisk egg whites to soft peak stage and fold into mixture. Chill at least 30 minutes.

*VD Hum Liquor is from South Africa.

BOBOTIE
(A Cape—Dutch South African Meal)

Preparation time: 30 minutes	*Chef: Debbie Campbell*
Cooking time: 45 minutes	*Yacht: Wall Street*
Serves: 6	

1 slice	**Bread**
1/2 cup	**Beef stock**
1 Tblsp	**Oil**
1-1/2 lbs	**Ground beef**
2	**Large onions, peeled and chopped**
3 cloves	**Garlic, crushed**
1 tsp	**Fresh grated ginger**
4 tsp	**Apricot jam**
1	**Large carrot, grated**
1 tsp	**Medium curry powder**
1/4 tsp	**Dried mixed herbs**
1/4 tsp	**Turmeric**
	Salt and pepper to taste
1 tsp	**Lemon juice**
1/2 cup	**Raisins**

Topping:

3/4 cup	**Milk**
	Salt and freshly ground black pepper
2	**Extra large eggs**
6	**Bay leaves**

Garnishes: **Yellow rice**
Small bowl of salsa, shredded coconut and banana

Preheat oven to 350°F/180°C. Soak bread in beef stock, then break into small pieces. Heat oil in a large skillet over high heat and sauté half of the ground beef until meat changes colour. Stir to break up lumps. Transfer to a bowl. Sauté other half and cook until it changes colour, then transfer to a bowl. In the skillet sauté onion, garlic and ginger until soft, then return the meat to the skillet. Add remaining ingredients, including bread. Transfer to a casserole dish.

Topping: Whisk milk, pepper, and eggs together and pour over meat. Place bay leaves upright in mixture. Bake about 20 to 30 minutes or until topping sets. Serve with garnishes and a large bowl of yellow rice.

WHISPER THE WIND SHOPPING LIST

VEGETABLES:
Red cabbage, small 1
Garlic .... 2 bulbs

Yellow onions 3
Red bell pepper 1

FRUITS:
Granny Smith apples 2
Limes 2
Lemon wedges .... garnish
Peaches 2-3
Strawberries .... garnish

FRESH HERBS:
Ginger .... 2 inch pc
Lemon grass 1
Mint .... garnish
Parsley .... 1 bunch
Fresh herbs, chopped ...... 1/2 cup

DRIED SPICES:
Cinnamon .... 1/4 tsp
Chili powder .... 1 tsp
Coriander, ground .... 1 Tblsp
Cumin, ground .... 2 tsp
Oregano .... 1 tsp
Turmeric .... 1/2 tsp

CONDIMENTS:
Vanilla extract .... 1 tsp
Dark chocolate .... 5 oz
Peanuts .... 2 Tblsp
Raisins .... 1/4 cup
Oil .... 2 Tblsp
Olive oil .... 1/4 cup
Worchestershire .... 2 Tblsp
Vinegar, red wine .... 1 Tblsp

DRY GOODS:
Bran .... 1 tsp
Instant mashed potatoes . 6-1/2 oz
Flour .... 2-1/2 cups
Flour, self rising .... 3 cups
Rolled oats .... 6 oz
Sugar, brown .... 1 Tblsp
Sugar, confectioners' .... 1/2 cup
Sugar, confectioners' .... garnish
Sugar .... 3-1/2 Tblsp

CANS AND JARS:
Mustard Piccalilli .... 8 oz
Orange marmalade .... 8 oz
Peanut butter .... 18 oz
Red hot pepper .... 1 jar
Cream of coconut .... 15 oz can

DAIRY/MILK/CHEESE/BUTTER
Butter .... 1-1/4 lbs
Eggs 7
2 % milk .... 1/4 cup
Cream cheese .... 8 oz

MEAT/POULTRY/FISH/SEAFOOD:
Chicken breasts, boneless 6
Squid .... 2 lbs

LIQUOR/WINE/SPIRITS:
Beer .... 1 can
Red wine .... 1 cup
White wine .... 1 cup

FROZEN:
Raspberries .... 16 oz

S/Y WHISPER THE WIND

Chef Mollie Foster
Captain John Simmons

MENU
Serves 6

Breakfast

*Potato Oat Cakes with *Pear Chutney

Lunch

*Squid with Ginger and White Wine Sauce
*Herb Beer Bread

Hors d'oeuvre

*Red Pepper Dip and Crudités

Dinner

*Chicken with Satay Sauce
*Super Red Cabbage
*Rice and Parsley Timbales

*Brownies Cockaigne with
*Raspberry Coulis

WHISPER THE WIND, a 42-foot catamaran, is captained by John Simmons with Mollie Foster as chef. This English couple are a talented pair. John, a former engineer, boat designer, builder, fisherman, inventor, artist and poet, claims if he can't weld or plate it, Mollie can paint or sew it, to say nothing of her cooking abilities. She, in turn, has designed a big aquarium, been a jazz club owner, Harrod's buyer, milliner, artist, writer and conducted a radio recipe program. Those recipes are on her menus.

*Indicates recipe provided

POTATO OAT CAKES WITH PEAR CHUTNEY

Preparation time: 5 minutes
Cooking time: 20 minutes
Serves: 6

Chef: Mollie Foster
Yacht: Whisper the Wind

1-1/2 cups	**Plain flour**
1/2 pkg	**Instant mash potatoes**
6 oz/170 g	**Porridge oats (rolled oats)**
1/2 tsp	**Salt**
2	**Eggs**
1/4 cup	**2% milk**
2 Tblsp	**Oil**

Put flour, instant mash potatoes, oats and salt in a bowl. Beat eggs and add a little milk. Whisk eggs and milk into flour mixture. Add milk to the flour mixture until the desired consistancy (batter should be thick). Heat oil in a large skillet and put tablespoonfuls of batter mix into the skillet and cook until brown. Add more oil if necessary. *Serve with* **Pear Chutney** *or a good strong fruit jam.*

PEAR CHUTNEY:

Preparation time: 5 minutes
Serves: 6

Chef: Mollie Foster
Yacht: Whisper the Wind

8 oz/225 g	**Sweet mustard piccalilli**
8 oz/225 g	**Thick orange marmalade**
2 tsp	**Sugar**
2	**Pears, diced or more as required**

Mix all ingredients together and serve with potato oat cakes.

SQUID WITH GINGER AND WHITE WINE SAUCE

Preparation time: 15 minutes
Cooking time: 15 minutes
Serves: 6

Chef: Mollie Foster
Yacht: Whisper the Wind

2 Tblsp	Olive oil
1	Onion, sliced
4 cloves	Garlic, thinly sliced
2	Red bell pepper, chopped
2 Tblsp	Grated fresh ginger
2 lb/900 g	Squid (calamari), cleaned and cut into rings
1 cup	White wine
	Olive oil
	Salt and Pepper
Garnish:	Chopped parsley
	Lemon wedges

Heat oil in a large skillet and sauté onions and garlic until translucent. Add red pepper and ginger, then add squid. Cook until just done, add white wine. Simmer to reduce liquid for a few moments. Sprinkle with parsley and serve with lemon wedges. Eat hot or cold. *Serve with crusty homemade bread.*

HERB BEER BREAD

Preparation time: 10 minutes   *Chef: Mollie Foster*
Cooking time: 45 minutes   *Yacht: Whisper The Wind*
Makes: 1 loaf

1 Tblsp	**Sugar**
3 cups	**Self rising flour**
1/2 cup	**Finely chopped fresh herbs, or**
	3 Tblsp dried
1 tsp	**Bran**
1can	**Beer, room temperature**
1	**Egg for wash**

Preheat oven to 350°F/180° C. Mix sugar and flour together, add herbs and bran. Pour in beer and mix to a smooth texture. Grease a bread tin, pour mixture in and brush with egg. Sprinkle with more chopped fresh herbs. Cook until golden brown, about 45 minutes. *Serve warm.*

Hint: It is also good toasted.

RED PEPPER DIP AND CRUDITES

Preparation time: 5 minutes   *Chef: Mollie Foster*
Serves: 6   *Yacht: Whisper The Wind*

8 oz/225 g	**Jar red peppers drained and chopped**
8 oz/225 g	**Cream cheese, softened**
5 cloves	**Garlic crushed**
2 Tblsp	**Worcestershire**

Blend all ingredients and serve with selection of crudités.

CHICKEN WITH SATAY SAUCE

Preparation time: 15 minutes   *Chef: Mollie Foster*
Marinating time: overnight   *Yacht: Whisper the Wind*
Cooking time: 12 minutes
Serves: 6

6	**Boneless, skinless, chicken breasts**
1	**Lemon grass stalk (white only)**
1	**Large onion, finely chopped**
2 Tblsp	**Finely chopped roasted peanuts**
1 Tblsp	**Ground coriander**
2 tsp	**Ground cumin**
1/2 tsp	**Turmeric**
1/4 tsp	**Ground cinnamon**
1 tsp	**Salt**
2 tsp	**Sugar**
	Olive oil to cook
Garnish:	**Lemon wedges**

Chop lemon grass. Mix with onion, peanuts, coriander, cumin, turmeric, cinnamon, salt and sugar. Rub into chicken and marinate overnight. Heat oil in large skillet, cook over high heat as whole pieces. *Serve with **Satay Sauce** and lemon wedges.*

Hint: Chicken can be cut into pieces and threaded on wet skewers and barbecued.

SATAY SAUCE:

Preparation time: 5 minutes   *Chef: Mollie Foster*
Cooking time: 5 minutes   *Yacht: Whisper the Wind*
Serves: 6

18 oz/510 g	**Jar peanut butter**
4 cloves	**Garlic crushed, or to taste**
1 Tblsp	**Sugar**
1 Tblsp	**Soy sauce**
1/4 cup	**Lime or lemon juice, or to taste**
15 oz/420 g	**Can cream of coconut**
1 tsp	**Chili powder**

Mix peanut butter with garlic, add remaining ingredients. Heat slowly in a saucepan. Do not overcook or fat will separate.

Hint: *You may mix ingredients the day before then heat gently when ready to use.*

SUPER RED CABBAGE

Preparation time: 5 minutes   *Chef: Mollie Foster*
Cooking time: 30 minutes   *Yacht: Whisper the Wind*
Serves: 6

4 Tblsp	**Butter**
1	**Medium onion, chopped finely**
1/2	**Small red cabbage, thinly shredded**
2	**Apples, peeled and diced**
1/4 cup	**Raisins**
2 Tblsp	**Fresh grated ginger**
1 Tblsp	**Red wine vinegar**
1 cup	**Red wine**
1 Tblsp	**Brown sugar**

In a large saucepan melt butter and cook onion until translucent. Add cabbage, apples, raisins, ginger, red wine vinegar, red wine and sugar. Cook over low heat until most of liquid has reduced and cabbage is glossy. *Serve with **Chicken Satay**, **Rice and Parsley Timbales**.*

Hint: May be made ahead and reheated.

RICE AND PARSLEY TIMBALES

Preparation time: 15 minutes   *Chef: Mollie Foster*
Cooking time: 20 minutes   *Yacht: Whisper the Wind*
Serves: 6

3 cups	**Basmati rice**
6 cups	**Water**
1/2 tsp	**Salt**
1/2 cup	**Butter, divided**
1/2 cup	**Finely chopped parsley**
Garnish:	**Sprigs of parsley**

In a saucepan, put rice in water with salt and 1 Tblsp butter, bring to a boil, cover, reduce heat and simmer about 10-15 minutes, or until water is absorbed and rice is cooked. Let stand 10 minutes. Mix in parsley with a fork. Add the remaining butter. Butter a ramekin dish. Press spoonfuls of rice into dish and invert onto a plate. *Place sprig of parsley on top.*

BROWNIES COCKAIGNE WITH RASPBERRY COULIS

Preparation time: 15 minutes　　　　　　　　*Chef: Mollie Foster*
Cooking time: 20-30 minutes　　　　　　*Yacht: Whisper The Wind*
Serves: 6-12

1/2 cup	Butter
5 oz/140 g	Unsweetened chocolate
4	Eggs, room temperature
1/4 tsp	Salt
1 cup	Sugar
1 tsp	Vanilla essence
1 cup	Sifted flour
Garnish:	Confectioners' sugar
	Mint leaves, slices of strawberry or kiwi fruit

Preheat oven to 325°F/160°C. Grease and flour 9 inch (23 cm) round cake tin. Melt butter and chocolate in pan over hot water. Do not boil water as chocolate will separate. Cool. Beat eggs with salt until light and creamy. Add sugar and vanilla. Combine cooled chocolate mix, eggs and sugar. Do not use a beater. Fold in sifted flour and bake. Leave center of cake gooey. Cut into wedges when cool. Place wedge, cut side down, on individual serving plates. Pour **Raspberry Coulis** over one corner of wedge and around. Dust top side with icing (confectioners') sugar and garnish.

Note: Use only unsweetened chocolate.

RASPBERRY COULIS:

Preparation time: 3 minutes　　　　　　　　*Chef: Mollie Foster*
Cooking time: 3 minutes　　　　　　　*Yacht: Whisper the Wind*
Serves: 6

16 oz/450 g	Frozen raspberries
1/2 cup	Confectioners' sugar

Blend raspberries and sugar until coulis is like a thickish syrup. Pour over one side of brownie wedge. Decorate corner of wedge with mint leaves and 1/2 of a strawberry or pieces of kiwi fruit.

WILD SALMON SHOPPING LIST

VEGETABLES:
Garlic .... 2 bulbs
Yellow onions, medium 5
Red bell peppers 2
Potatoes .... 1 lb
Pumpkin .... 1 lb
Portabello mushrooms ..... 2 lbs

FRUITS:
Mangos 6

FRESH HERBS:
Ginger, grated .... 1 Tblsp
Parsley, chopped .... garnish

DRIED SPICES:
Cinnamon .... garnish
Chili powder .... 1 tsp
Cumin .... 1 tsp
Garam masala .... 1 tsp

CONDIMENTS:
Olive oil .... 3 Tblsp
Soy sauce .... dash
Capers .... 1/2 cup

DRY GOODS:
Spaghetti .... 1 lb
Sugar .... 1+ cup

CANS AND JARS:
Coconut milk .... 1/2 cup
Peanut butter, crunchy ..... 1/2 cup
Black olives, chopped .... 1 cup
Tomato paste .... 2 Tblsp
Tomatoes, plum .... 32 oz can

DAIRY/MILK/CHEESE/BUTTER
Butter .... 5 oz
Ghee* .... 2 Tblsp
Eggs 12
Cream .... 1 cup
Milk, whole .... 1 cup
Yogurt .... 2 cups
Swiss, grated .... 1 cup

MEAT/POULTRY/FISH/SEAFOOD:
Chicken breasts, boneless 6 - 8 oz
Shrimp, extra large 36

*Clarified butter

S/Y WILD SALMON

Chef Marilyn Jones
Captain Steve Johnson

MENU
Serves 6

Breakfast

*Kiwi Omelette

Lunch

*Pasta Puttanesca
Hot Crusty Bread

Hors d'oeuvre

*Peanut Prawns

Dinner

*Portabello Chicken with
Mashed Potato Pumpkin
Baby Carrots and Peas

*Mango Delight

Sailing yacht WILD SALMON, a 62-foot Bruce Farr, circumnavigates the world though she's especially fond of the waters of New Zealand, Fiji, Thailand, the Mediterranean and Caribbean. Captain Steve Johnson and Chef Marilyn Jones are always along for the ride. When they charter in the Virgin Islands, the exotic isles of the Pacific, or somewhere else in this world, Marilyn's outstanding menus often bring 'compliments to the chef'. As is her habit, she sometimes slips in a New Zealand "surprise" dish.

*Indicates recipe provided

KIWI OMELETTE

Preparation time: 10 minutes　　　　　　*Chef: Marilyn Jones*
Cooking time: 30 minutes　　　　　　　*Yacht: Wild Salmon*
Serves: 6

4 Tblsp	Butter
2	Medium onions, diced
1	Red bell pepper, sliced
2 cups	Sliced mushrooms
12	Eggs
1 cup	Milk
1 cup	Grated swiss cheese
Garnish:	Chopped parsley

In a nonstick pan, melt butter and sauté onions and bell pepper; add mushrooms. Beat together eggs and milk and add to pan. Cook until eggs become firm. Remove from heat; add cheese, place under griller/broiler until brown. Serve immediately in pan. Garnish. *Serve with some good hot sauce.*

MANGO DELIGHT

Preparation time: 10 minutes　　　　　　*Chef: Marilyn Jones*
Chilling time: 1 hour　　　　　　　　*Yacht: Wild Salmon*
Serves: 6

6	Mangoes
2 cups	Plain yoghurt
1 cup	Sugar
Garnish:	Cinnamon

Prepare mangoes. In a blender purée mangoes, add yoghurt and sugar; mix well. Pour into decorative glasses and chill. Sprinkle with cinnamon before serving.

PASTA PUTTANESCA

Preparation time: 10 minutes
Cooking time: 45 minutes
Serves: 6

Chef: Marilyn Jones
Yacht: Wild Salmon

1 lb/450 g	Spaghetti
2 Tblsp	Olive oil
2	Medium onions, diced
8 cloves	Garlic, crushed
2	Medium red bell peppers, chopped
2 Tblsp	Tomato paste
2 - 16 oz/450	Cans peeled plum tomatoes
1 tsp	Sugar
Dash	Soy sauce
	Salt and pepper
1 cup	Chopped black olives
1/2 cup	Capers

Cook pasta according to directions. In a large saucepan put olive oil, onions, garlic and peppers. Cook until tender. Stir in tomato paste, tomatoes and sugar, mix together. Bring to a medium boil for 10 minutes. Add soy sauce, a little salt and lots of pepper; boil down. Add olives and capers and leave to sit. Fold half the sauce through pasta. *Serve in bowls with extra sauce on top and hot crusty bread.*

PEANUT PRAWNS

Preparation time: 10 minutes   *Chef: Marilyn Jones*
Cooking time: 5 minutes   *Yacht: Wild Salmon*
Serves: 6

2 oz/60 g	Ghee*
1	Onion, chopped
1 tsp	Garam masala**
1 tsp	Cumin
1 tsp	Chilli powder
2 cloves	Garlic, crushed
1 Tblsp	Grated fresh ginger
1/2 cup	Crunchy peanut butter
3/4 cup	Water
1/2 cup	Coconut milk
36	Large cooked prawns, tails on

Melt ghee, add onion and cook until golden. Add garam masala, cumin, chilli powder and garlic; cook for 2 minutes. Stir in ginger, crunchy peanut butter, water and milk; bring to a boil, then reduce heat and simmer for 5 minutes. *Serve shrimp on a bed of torn lettuce with bowl of sauce in the middle.*

*similar to clarified butter.

** **GARAM MASALA:** This aromatic spice blend usually contains cardamoms, cumin and pepper but recipes vary. Store-bought versions are available, but it is worth making your own for better flavour. Only make small quantities as the flavour does not stay fresh. Grind together........

4	Black cardamoms
10	Green cardamoms
1 Tblsp	Black peppercorns
2 tsp	Cumin seeds

The amounts may be adjusted according to taste and spices such as whole coriander seeds and dried red chillies may be added.

PORTABELLO CHICKEN

Preparation time: 30 minutes　　　　　*Chef: Marilyn Jones*
Cooking time: 20 minutes　　　　　　　*Yacht: Wild Salmon*
Serves: 6

4 Tblsp	Butter
2 lbs/900 g	Portabello mushrooms, sliced
6 - 8 oz/250 g	Boneless chicken breasts
1 cup	Cream
1 lb/450 g	Potatoes
1 lb/350 g	Pumpkin
	Salt and freshly ground pepper
1 Tblsp	Olive oil
2 Tblsp	Butter

Melt butter in a nonstick pan; add mushrooms, 'sweat down', add more butter as needed. Add cream and let sit. Boil together potatoes and pumpkin, drain and mash with salt and pepper; stir in onion. Heat another nonstick pan and sauté the chicken until cooked. Place potato mixture in centre of plate with chicken on top and pour portabello sauce over. *Serve with steamed baby carrots and peas.*

NOTES:

EQUIVALENT CHART

WHEN THE RECIPE CALLS FOR: **USE:**

WHEN THE RECIPE CALLS FOR:	USE:
1/2 cup butter	1 stick/8 Tblsp
	4 ounces
2 cups butter	1 pound
4 cups all purpose flour	1 pound
4-1/2 – 5 cups sifted cake flour	1 pound
1 square chocolate	1 ounce
1 cup semi-sweet chocolate pieces	1 - 6 ounce package
2 - 1/4 cups packed brown sugar	1 pound
4 cups confectioners' sugar	1 pound
2 cups granulated sugar	1 pound
18 graham cracker squares	1-1/4 cups crumbs
12 chocolate sandwich cookies	1 cup crumbs
20 chocolate wafer cookies	1 cup crumbs
24 vanilla wafers	1 cup crumbs
18 ginger snaps	1 cup crumbs
1 large egg	3 Tblsp egg
1 large egg white	2 Tblsp white
1 large egg yolk	1 Tblsp yolk
1 cup whipped cream	1/2 cup heavy cream
2/3 cup evaporated milk	1 small can
1-2/3 cups evaporated milk	1 13 ounce can
4 cups sliced or chopped apples	4 medium
1 cup mashed banana	3 medium
2 cups pitted cherries	4 cups unpitted
3 cups shredded coconut	1/2 pound
4 cups cranberries	1 pound
1 cup pitted dates	1 - 8 ounce package
1 cup candied fruit	1 - 8 ounce package
3-4 Tblsp lemon juice plus 1 tsp grated rind	1 lemon
1/3 cup orange juice plus 2 tsp grated rind	1 orange
4 cups sliced peaches	8 medium
2 cups pitted prunes	1 - 12 ounce package
3 cups raisins	1 - 15 oz package
1 cup chopped nuts	4 ounces shelled *or* 1 pound unshelled

SUBSTITUTIONS

IF YOU DON'T HAVE:	SUBSTITUTE:
1 cup cake flour	1 cup minus 2 Tblsp all purpose flour
1 Tablespoon cornstarch	2 Tblsp all purpose flour or 1 Tblsp tapioca
1 teaspoon baking powder	1/4 tsp baking soda plus 1/2 tsp cream of tarter
1 cup granulated sugar	1 cup packed brown sugar or 2 cups sifted powdered sugar
1 cup honey	1-1/4 cups granulated sugar plus 1/4 cup liquid or 1 cup corn syrup
1 cup corn syrup	1 cup granulated sugar plus 1/4 cup liquid
1 square unsweetened chocolate, 1 ounce	3 Tblsp unsweetened cocoa powder plus 1 Tblsp butter
1 cup sour milk or buttermilk	1 Tblsp lemon juice or vinegar plus whole milk to make 1 cup (let stand 5 minutes before using) or 1 cup whole milk plus 1-3/4 tsp cream of tarter or 1 cup plain yogurt
1 cup sour cream	7/8 cup sour milk plus 3 Tblsp butter
1 cup whole milk	1/2 cup evaporated milk plus 1/2 cup water or 1 cup reconstituted non-fat dry milk plus 2 tsp butter
1 cup light cream	2 Tblsp butter plus 1 cup minus 2 Tblsp milk
1 tsp lemon peel, finely grated	1/2 tsp lemon extract
1 whole egg	2 egg yolks (for most uses)

PROVISIONING, HINTS AND TIPS

When you are a guest on a charter yacht, your only concern is to have a good time — and your crew will make that possible. One will wonder how your chef can concoct such marvelous meals in a galley smaller than most people's closet.

Over the years the chefs have developed some "tricks of the trade" to make their life easier in the galley. Many have been gracious enough to share some of their hints and tips about provisioning, storing, and cooking.

When provisioning buy all you can at local supermarkets and get the "hard to find" items from the provisioning companies (purveyors). Buy non perishable items and store them first.

If you have the freezer space, stock up on boneless chicken breasts, quality beef, salmon and tuna before you go 'down island'. Any slightly unusual ingredient is either hard to find or ridiculously expensive —$8 for a can of hearts of palm in Grenada.

Good provisioning in St. Maarten (St. Martin) and Martinique but very sketchy from Martinique to Grenada. Do not get caught without the essentials. One stop in Carriacou found all 3 grocery stores out of eggs, (despite the usual number of chickens running on the streets). Chicken breasts are hard to find; West Indians prefer leg quarters.

Martinique offers frozen herbs in handy boxes. It is also good to buy a French/English dictionary before shopping in the French islands.

Provisioning for a cruise often turns into a last minute panic. With some planning it is not a tough task and it will save you some hassles later.

From the menus you have selected start your list with the non perishable, then fresh and finally the frozen. Purchase the perishables at the last moment to insure freshness and longer life. Salad ingredients do not last longer than a few days so do not buy too much. Green and red cabbage will last for a couple of weeks if kept in an airy space. Pumpkin, squash, under ripe melons, apples (Granny smith last the longest), oranges, onions and potatoes will keep 2 to 3 weeks. (Do not store the onions and potatoes next to each other). Buy bananas with green tips, hard pears and avocados; tomatoes with some yellow and green will ripen but not the pink ones. Use the purveyors as much as you can. It will save you time and most of them deliver. If you don't see what you need in the store, ask the manager. He will often be able to find it for you, either on another shelf or in the back.

On your computer, keep a shopping list with every possible ingredient needed for two weeks. Then plan your menu with reference to the preference sheet, the number of guests and the number of days you will be out. A good idea is to color code your index cards (yellow for breakfast, purple for lunch and so forth). On the back of the card, write all the ingredients necessary for that meal and any tricky preparation instructions, then get your master shopping list and tick off what you need. This system makes a weekly job fairly easy, especially with a 24 hour turn around. Keep a log of every meal and keep an up to date provisioning sheet for inventory and shopping.

Keep on hand canned fruits, condensed milk, dried herbs etc. to replace fresh that may go bad during charter. Buy fruit purées and freeze in labelled squeeze bottles. Take out what you need and thaw before the charter.

When you buy fresh coconuts, look for the ones without mold; check the eyes or cracks. Choose coconuts that are heavy for their size, a sign they have plenty of liquid and the flesh will not be dry. Coconut water is awesome to drink; it is also good to cook rice, or add to soups.

COOKING TIPS...

Make large quantities of salad dressings. Make bread dough ahead of time and freeze. When you freeze dough, remember to allow for rising time after the dough has thawed.

Make bread pudding with not so fresh bread. Before a charter prepare sugar syrup and squeeze enough lemons and limes for a week. This way you can make a sorbet quickly, and still have fresh citrus juice on hand; the juice takes less room than two dozen lemons and limes needed for a week. Also make a crème anglaise, a pastry cream and a tulip paste for a quick decoration and garnish.

Pre-mix all dry ingredients for homemade cakes, muffins, and bread. Write a list of the wet ingredients outside the package.

Have several meals easy and quick to prepare for times when things do not go as planned. Stock ingredients for a vegetarian meal, just in case. If you run out of fresh milk or have a guest who is lactose intolerant, use coconut milk as a substitute. It makes great chocolate mousse and can be used in almost any baking that calls for yogurt, milk or cream. When cooking a vegetarian meal, use agar instead of gelatin to set mousse. Agar is seaweed base and gelatin is from animal marrow; you can find agar in most health food stores.

For a more exotic dessert, substitute an equal amount of passion fruit juice for lemon juice.

For best salads, place greens in an ice water bath, lifting gently a number of times.

Marinate meat, poultry and fish at least an hour before cooking. To make sure fish is cooked, pull the grain of the meat gently with two forks. If it separates easily, it is ready.

Use fresh cabbage. You can store it for a month in the refrigerator. Serve it as a vegetable, stuff it with ground meat, or use it in salad and coleslaw, top with crispy warm bacon instead of a dressing. Stir fry red cabbage and onions over high heat for 4 - 5 minutes and mound a small amount on dinner plates. Great way to add color quickly.

Do not throw out your overripe papaya. Use your favorite zucchini bread recipe, substituting papaya for shredded zucchini. Toss you leftover vegetables in vinaigrette and serve as an antipasti with olives and nuts.

Soups sauces and casserole improve with time. Make them in the morning to let the flavor develop.
When preparing dough for bread or pizza, let it rise in the engine room; perfect temperature.

You want to make bread more attractive? Before baking mix 1 egg white and 1 Tblsp of water, brush the dough quickly, spread fresh herbs and brush again with egg mixture. Flat leaves work best.
When you cannot find graham cookies to make a crust, use crushed cornflakes, they work well.

Flavor olive oil by sautéing minced garlic for 8 - 10 minutes over medium heat, stirring constantly, then serve with bread for dipping.

To microwave regular popcorn, place in a paper bag with 1/2 cup oil and cook for 2 minutes on high.

Fresh brown coconut: Preheat oven to 400°F/200°C. Pierce softest eye of coconut with a metal skewer or small screwdriver and drain liquid into a bowl to sample. If the milk tastes oily, it's rancid; if it's sweet, then it is fresh. Bake coconut in oven for 15 minutes reduce oven temperature to 375°F/190°C. With a hammer or back of heavy cleaver, break shell of coconut and with point of a strong knife remove flesh, levering it out carefully. With a vegetable peeler shave roughly 1-1/2 inch (3.5 cm) long pieces. Working in batches, in a shallow baking pan, evenly spread coconut shavings and toast in middle of oven until golden, 8 - 10 minutes. Cool coconut. It will keep in an airtight container at room temperature for 3 days.

STORAGE AND PACKING...

Ziplock (reclosable) bags are a must to go to sea. Yacht chefs use them for various reasons.
- Remove meats from original packaging and repack in portions—mark well.
- Trim vegetables before the charter and place in bags; get rid of the parts that will end up in the trash anyway.
- Double bag dry goods to keep bugs away and protect from dampness.
- To stop celery from going limp place in bag with a splash of water.
- Excellent to keep dough (cookie, bread, pizza) in the freezer.
- Bougainvillea washed and drip dried will keep for a week. Put it in a ziplock bag with paper towels. Colors up your dishes or table naturally.

Canning jars and empty wine bottles are great for storing marinades and dressings.

Keep bread fresh by keeping it in plastic grocery bags.
Freeze fruit purées in squeeze bottles; pull them out to thaw before charter.

Tightly wrap and freeze ginger to keep it longer. Peel and grate while still frozen. It works only if the ginger is frozen solid.

When it is lime season, buy a lot of them; juice and store in ice cube bags. Or freeze the juice in ice cube trays and then store in reclosable bags. Thaw as you need fresh lime juice. Keep jug of water in refrigerator to make up frozen concentrate juices.

Store the ingredients you use most in accessible see through containers. Store pasta and flour in original packages in refrigerator or put bay leaves inside the pasta and flour bags.

Use square stackable containers, especially in refrigerator and freezer; they save space, are easier to pull out, and you will not have to keep the door open so long.

When you can buy fresh farm eggs—leave them unwashed and unrefrigerated. Keep them in their cartons and stow them in a safe, cool and airy locker. Simply turn them upside down once a week and they will last for weeks.

TOOLS OF THE TRADE AND GENERAL TIPS...

A good investment is a set of T-fal Ingento cookware. The set of 5 pans have removable handles. They are easy to stack and take up less space. You can cook, bake, microwave and serve with these pans. Propane stoves can be hard to bake on, but these pans do it beautifully. They are quite reasonable: $80 - $100 a set.

The new gladware square shaped disposable containers are great space savers.

The vaculock bag sealer is another great investment for resealing bags of chips, crackers, cereal, etc.

A pressure cooker is important—it reduces your cooking time by half and keeps your dish more than 24 hours. (It is under pressure-airtight without putting it in the refrigerator). Also good to store other things in when not in use.

Always label with an indelible marker.
Use a small appetizer cutter to cut shapes out of thick cheese slices, slices of beets, vegetables, anything to decorate plates.

Have a stationery locker for all those letters, postcards, office supplies, boat's filing work and customs papers. A game locker is also a good idea.

Have a galley gadget party. This is a great way to get together, exchange gadgets, get rid of extras you have and receive ones that are needed. Good organization is the key to a great galley!

PROVISIONS FOR A 3 MONTH PERIOD*

Following is a list of provisions for 4 people for a three month voyage, allowing for an extra month in case the trip takes longer than anticipated.

Canned goods:	Size:	Quantity:
Red Peppers	500 g	24
Olives (black)	395 g	12
Corn (whole)	340 g	48
Whole tomatoes	500 g	48
Baked beans	425 g	24
Spaghetti	425 g	24
Green beans	500 g	24
Green peas	340 g	30
Mixed vegetables	500 g	48
Tuna	1 kg	6
Anchovies	150 g	12
Sardines (oil)	115 g	10
Sardines (tomato sauce)	115 g	10
Ham	900 g	12
Corned beef	340 g	24
Peaches	1 kg	12
Pears	1 kg	12
Pineapple	500 g	12
Jam	450 g	12
Honey	500 g	12
Dry Goods:	**Size:**	**Quantity:**
Spaghetti	500 g	15 packets
Macaroni	250 g	20 packets
Penne	500 g	30 packets
Haricot beans	500 g	5 packets
Red kidney beans	500 g	5 packets
Mixed beans	500 g	5 packets
Chick peas	500 g	2 packets
Brown lentils	500 g	2 packets
Milk:		
Dried milk	1 kg	10 packets
UHT milk	1 Lt	20 packets
Nesquick (chocolate)	800 g	2 packets
Instant coffee	800 g	2 packets
Tea Bags	500 g	200 bags
Cereals:		
Alpen museli	750 g	6 boxes
Rolled oats	510 g	8 boxes
Soft drinks:		
Coca Cola	24 cans	
Sprite	24 cans	

*From S/Y Wai O Tira

"WHERE-TO-SHOP" SUGGESTIONS...

St Thomas
Marina Market .... Red Hook 340-774-2411
The Fruit Bowl .... Wheatley Center 340-774-8565
Gourmet Gallery .... Crown Bay 340-776-8555
.... Havensight Mall 340-774-4948
Plaza Extra .... Tutu Park 340-775-5646
Cost-U-Less .... Dunoe 340-777-3588
K-Mart .... Tutu Park 340-777-3036
Pueblo Supermarkets .... Four locations
S & P Seafood .... Crown Bay 340-774-5280
The Market Place .... Market Square, end of Main Street

St John
Tropicale 340-693-7474/Fax 340-693-7699

Tortola
K-Marks Yacht Provisioning 284-494-6999
Ample Hamper .... Road Town 284-494-2494
.... Soper's Hole 284-494-4684
Rite Way 284-494-2262
Port Purcell Market 284-494-2424; 494-2727
La Baguette 284-494-5068

Anegada
Sailor's Ketch 284-495-1100

St. Maarten/St Martin ......
Market Marigot Bay .... Open Wed and Sun/Fresh produce
Guichard International .... Fresh fruits
Epicerie de Marie .... Caviar, meat, seafood
Cappucino .... Real homemade Gelato

Deshaies, Guadeloupe
La Bonne Entrecôte .... Meat
Ti Prix .... Supermarket
2 Outdoor Markets .... Fruits and vegetables
L'Almondine .... Bakery

Antigua
Local Market .... On the way to St John
Sister Grant .... Fruits and vegetable
Gary at TCM .... Seafood

St Lucia, Rodney Bay
LeMarché de France
The Bread Basket
JQ's Shopping Center

St Lucia, Gablewoods
Wintrade Supermarket

St Lucia, Castries
Fruit and Vegetables Market
J & Charles Supermarket
Caribbean Chateaux .... Wine, they deliver to your boat

St Vincent
Greaves Supermarket .... Will deliver to Bequia through the ferry
Kingstown, St Vincent
Fish Market
Fruit and Vegetable Market
Bequia
Doris .... Call ahead 784-458-3625
Grenada
Foodfair .... St Georges and Grand Anse
Food Land .... St Georges
Fruit and Vegetable Market ..... St Georges
Fish Market .... St Georges

Additional provisioning information can be found in the Cruising Guide to the Windward Islands and Cruising Guide to the Leeward Islands.

Auckland, New Zealand
Stevy D's, Total Provisioning ... 64-9-373-3853/Fax 64-9-377-8467
Ft Lauderdale
Int'l Market & Wine Depot .... Most gourmet items that can't
.... be found elsewhere
Barnacle Seafood company ...... Seafood
Liberty Pride – DGP Foods ...... Meats, they can get anything
Captain Ed's Seafood .... Provisions for Deltique

I would like to thank the following chefs for sharing their information: Debbie Campbell, *Wall Street;* Tammy Stonich, *Rendezvous Cay;* Pam Costa, *Jayed;* Jan Netherland, *Orphee III;* Pamela Pandella; Connie Harclerode, *Desirade II;* Gerda Dehrmann, *Sojourn;* Shelly Tucker, *Three Moons;* Ann E. Brown-McHorney, *Of Course;* Dominique Feix, *La Dolce Vita;* Betsy Millson, *Gale Winds;* Julie Bennett, *Blu Moon;* Laurie Rainthorpe, *Silent Partner II;* Kathy Corbett, *Psipsina;* Teresa Dancy, *Flamboyance;* Bronwyn Carrick, *Equity;* Helen Hoyt, *Christmas Winds,* Jennifer Solomon, *Catbalu;* Andrea Logie, *Bonjez;* Cindy Hildreth, *Shibumi;* Marilyn Jones, *Wild Salmon;* Vicky Shilder, *Mungl;* Glenys Robertson, *Wai O Tira.*

INDEX

www.SHIPTOSHOREINC.com
1-800-338-6072
CapJan@aol.com

ORDER ADDITIONAL COPIES

Qty	Title	Price	Total
	STORE TO SHORE	$19.95	
	SHIP TO SHORE I	$16.95	
	SHIP TO SHORE II	$15.95	
	SWEET TO SHORE	$15.95	
	SEA TO SHORE	$16.95	
	SLIM TO SHORE	$15.95	
	BAHAMA MAMA'S COOKING	$12.95	
	SIP TO SHORE	$12.95	
	CARIBBEAN ADVENTURES	$12.95	
	6.5% Tax (NC only)		
	Freight $3.00 per book		
	TOTAL		

Autograph to: _____

Ship to: _____

_____

_____

_____

Autograph to: _____

Ship to: _____

_____

_____

_____

SHIP TO SHORE, INC.

Please charge my:
MasterCard ☐ Visa ☐ Check ☐ Money order ☐
Payable to: Ship to Shore, Inc.
My credit card number is:

☐☐☐☐☐☐☐☐☐☐☐☐☐☐☐☐

Exp. date ☐☐☐☐

For orders
call toll free
1-800-338-6072
or use our website
www.shiptoshoreinc.com
CapJan@aol.com

Signature_____ Date_____

✂ –

THE PERFECT GIFT
FOR ANY OCCASION

FREE

Share the Ship to Shore Cookbook Collection with your friends. We will send your friends a beautiful color brochure. Simply fill out and mail this form, call **1-800-338-6072**, email CapJan@aol.com or visit our website **www.shiptoshoreinc.com**

Name _____
Address _____
City _____
State _____ Zip _____

Name _____
Address _____
City _____
State _____ Zip _____

www.shiptoshoreinc.com   To order toll free 1-800-338-6072—Visa/Mc

ORDER ADDITIONAL COPIES

Qty	Title	Price	Total
	STORE TO SHORE	$19.95	
	SHIP TO SHORE I	$16.95	
	SHIP TO SHORE II	$15.95	
	SWEET TO SHORE	$15.95	
	SEA TO SHORE	$16.95	
	SLIM TO SHORE	$15.95	
	BAHAMA MAMA'S COOKING	$12.95	
	SIP TO SHORE	$12.95	
	CARIBBEAN ADVENTURES	$12.95	

Autograph to: _____

Ship to: _____

_____

_____

_____

_____

Autograph to: _____

Ship to: _____

_____

_____

_____

6.5% Tax (NC only)		
Freight $3.00 per book		
TOTAL		

SHIP TO SHORE, INC.

Please charge my:
MasterCard ☐ Visa ☐ Check ☐ Money order ☐
Payable to: Ship to Shore, Inc.
My credit card number is:

☐☐☐☐☐☐☐☐☐☐☐☐☐☐☐☐

Exp. date ☐☐ ☐☐

For orders
call toll free
1-800-338-6072
or use our website
www.shiptoshoreinc.com
CapJan@aol.com

Signature_____ Date_____

✂ —

FREE

THE PERFECT GIFT
FOR ANY OCCASION

Share the Ship to Shore Cookbook Collection with your friends. We will send your friends a beautiful color brochure. Simply fill out and mail this form, call **1-800-338-6072**, email CapJan@aol.com or visit our website **www.shiptoshoreinc.com**

Name _____

Address _____

City _____

State _____ Zip _____

Name _____

Address _____

City _____

State _____ Zip _____

www.shiptoshoreinc.com   To order toll free 1-800-338-6072—Visa/Mc